Grace *for* *Shame*

Grace for Shame

The Forgotten Gospel

John A. Forrester

Pastor's Attic Press

Toronto

www.pastorsatticpress.com

This book is dedicated to

my wife Betty

who has all these good years

so generously provided for me a place

of love, encouragement, hope, and grace,

without which I could have accomplished little,

and certainly not this work.

Thank you my love.

Contents

Introduction

We Western pastors have a blind spot. In a word, that blind spot is shame. We don't learn about shame in seminary. We don't find it in our theological reading. We don't recognize it on the pages of Scripture. We don't see it in our people. Shame is just not part of our pastoral perspective. And yet, as the helping professionals around us are discovering, large numbers of people are deeply and negatively affected by shame.

Do pastors have anything to say to shame? Does the Christian Gospel offer anything for shame? Well, it turns out that once we begin to ask the right questions, we discover the Bible has a lot to say about shame. We discover that Jesus ministered (and still ministers) grace for shame as well as grace for guilt. And we, as pastors, are invited to participate with God in this broader ministry of grace.

A taboo subject

If we are serious about understanding shame, we will have to travel far. This is not a three-day cruise. We need to undertake a major exploration into long forgotten territory. Why has shame been such a neglected field? This book addresses this question from a number of angles. But to begin with here, we quickly discover that shame is simply not easy to talk about. We resist bringing up the subject. The very idea of shame is shameful. Even writing about shame is unsettling. Try telling people you are reading a book about shame and wait for the awkward silence! Shame has a contagious feel to it. This strangeness is reflected in the poverty of English shame vocabulary. Other languages have a range of words for shame, English has one. Other cultures speak much more readily about shame, for us shame is a taboo subject.

Even the theologians and exegetes have difficulty addressing this subject. For example, the 1988 edition of *The New Dictionary of Theology* has no entry for shame. Thomas Oden's otherwise comprehensive *Pastoral Theology* does not have shame in the subject index. James Fowler finds Bonhoeffer to be "almost alone among twentieth century theologians in giving importance to shame."[1] Shame is almost totally absent from modern theological writing.

Remarkably, shame, even in psychology, has only recently emerged as a subject for investigation. Sigmund Freud and Carl Jung rarely speak of shame. Jill McNish reports "only thirty-six indexed uses of the word *shame* in *The Standard Edition of the Complete Psychological Works of Sigmund Freud"* (twenty-four volumes), and only five indexed references in Carl Jung's *Collected Works* (eighteen volumes).[2] Alfred Adler only begins to address the subject. Shame was a neglected orphan in the psychological world until other fields of study brought shame out into the open. It was the anthropologists, in their cultural

---

[1] James Fowler, "Shame: Towards a Practical Theological Under-standing," *Christian Century,* 110 (1993): 819; *The New Dictionary of Theology,* Sinclair B. Ferguson, D. G. Wright, and J. I. Packer, eds. (Downers Grove, IL: IVP, 1988); Thomas C. Oden, *Pastoral Theology* (San Francisco, CA: Harper Collins, 1983).

[2] Jill L. McNish, *Transforming Shame: A Pastoral Response* (Bing-hamton, NY: The Haworth Press, 2004), 86 & 112.

inquiries, who first recognized the importance of shame.[3] Then, beginning with a trickle in the 1970s, a growing stream of material has been published from different quarters.

A new call to pastors

It was not until the 1990s that much was written about shame from a faith perspective, but now there is a growing chorus of voices urging pastors to catch up in this field. In 1993 James Fowler reviewed some of the recent literature on shame and urged pastors (and theologians) to become more acquainted with this field. "Becoming more aware of the dynamics of shame that permeate our society allows one to approach theology and ministry in new ways."[4] Even in the year 2000 Stephen Pattison could write: "Pastoral theology is still ignorant and uninformed about the nature and complexities of shame. . . . Above all pastoral theology has little to offer in the way of proven effective methods for helping integrate shame individually and socially."[5] Robert Albers, writing in the same year, added one more voice: "It appears to me that we in the Christian community have focused so exclusively on grace as forgiveness for our sins of commission or omission, that our message of acceptance to those who are shame-based is muffled, muted or non-existent."[6] The time has come to heed these voices.

---

[3] P. Hultberg, "Shame—A Hidden Emotion," *Journal of Analytical Psychology,* 33 (1988): 111f.

[4] Fowler, "Shame," 816.

[5] Stephen Pattison, *Shame: Theory, Therapy, Theology* (New York: Cambridge University Press, 2000), 223.

[6] Robert H. Albers, "Shame and the Conspiracy of Silence," *Journal of Ministry in Addiction & Recovery,* 7 (1) (2000): 66.

- 11 -

The more we learn about shame the more we recognize how pervasive this issue is not only for individuals but also for communities. Yet shame remains hidden at the corporate level also. Pastors can learn from the teaching concept of the "hidden curriculum." This is the "cultural agenda for learning that surrounds schooling."[7] What is the church's hidden shame curriculum? First it must be recognized, then evaluated; then, where necessary, adjustment must begin. Failing such intentional inquiry, we may wake up one morning to discover that Friday night Bingo is doing more to mitigate shame than Wednesday night Bible study!

Thus the evidence accumulates from various fields, anthropology, sociology, psychology, and lately biblical studies, that shame, long neglected, is now crying for attention. It is time for the church to begin to understand the often submerged but nonetheless powerful cross currents of shame. Is this easy territory?—certainly not. Yet it is important to pursue this trail, and to do so in hope, recognizing that shame is no surprise to God. We are only just becoming aware of the rich resources of grace for shame which God has already made available in Christ.

The need for a conservative, evangelical contribution

For some people the question at this point will be: Is all this "shame talk" just another way to distract people from "guilt talk"? Or perhaps: Is this just another author diluting the Gospel message of deliverance from sin? In defense I ask first for patience. I write as an evangelical. I also write as a pastor

---

[7] Judith E. Lingenfelter and Sherwood G. Lingenfelter, *Teaching Cross-Culturally: An Incarnational Model for Learning and Teaching* (Grand Rapids, MI: Baker, 2003), 28.

dealing with real people needing real deliverance from real sin. What I am arguing is that our practice of restricting the conversation to guilt both underestimates the full extent of God's grace and short-circuits the full effectiveness of God's grace. Shame, too, is a consequence of sin. What I am arguing is that "shame talk" needs to be *added* to "guilt talk" in order to manifest more fully the glory of God in the Gospel of Jesus Christ. We fallen human beings need grace for shame as much as we need grace for guilt. The church is hungering for it. Surely the Spirit of God is urging us to get on with it.

If we in the evangelical churches do not learn to minister grace for shame, people will look elsewhere. For example, Buddhist authors are thoughtfully addressing the subject and many are finding help there. And some recent Christian studies suggest the only way to move forward is to leave behind traditional biblical ethical standards and orthodox theology. But what a loss. Because firstly, the Christian Gospel heard clearly does, in fact, offer great hope for shame, and because secondly, the help found outside the work of Christ is insufficient to deal adequately with the real roots of shame. I believe the church is hungry for thoughtful contributions from evangelical practitioners and theorists. I trust this book makes such a contribution.

A reader's map
Stated simply, this book is organized around three inquiries. Part one: What are the shame questions? Part two: What are the Bible answers to the shame questions? Part three: How do we apply these answers in pastoral ministry? Three parts, each with two chapters.

For those who want a little more detail, the heart of this study is the center section, part two, where I explore the theme of shame in Scripture. What does the Bible have to say about shame? I believe that a humble dependence on "God's Word written" is foundational for those of us claiming to follow the pilgrim way of Christian orthodoxy. For me it is the only source of confidence. In chapter three I look at vocabulary and general themes in both Old and New Testaments. In chapter four I focus on the life and ministry of Christ, and what the Gospel of Christ has to say to shame.

But before setting out on this fresh exploration of Scripture I believe it is important to discover what the new questions are that we need to ask. We miss much because we ask little. So part one, chapter one, introduces the subject of shame from psychological and cultural perspectives. Chapter two focuses on the church in the West and how the role of shame is surfacing as a major ministry issue today. I have been deeply blessed and encouraged as I have come back to Scripture with these new questions and found new answers. Praise God, there *is* grace for shame!

For some people the "how to" section, part three, will be most appealing. But I encourage you to do at least some reading in parts one and two. We need to wrestle with the questions, then bring those questions to the Scriptures, before we can minister with depth and authority in this difficult area. What ties the material in chapter five together is the cognitive, word-based emphasis. I explore the question: What kind of words are healing for shame? In contrast, in the final chapter I attempt to unpack the concept of shame as a relational problem. Grace for shame will have to be mediated, not only through words but also through human interaction, both one-on-one and in the life of the congregation. This is the incarnational response to shame.

Disclaimers

There are, of course, limits to this study. This is not a counseling manual. This is an attempt to become better acquainted with the range of guilt and shame dynamics that are present in twenty-first-century congregations. What can we expect? Why is it like this? How can pastors and other church leaders minister more adequately in this context? We do expect, however, that with this deeper understanding of shame, pastors will know better when shame-troubled people need to be referred for professional psychological care.

There are other limits to this study. It is helpful to consider *anxiety* along with shame and guilt as primary negative emotions. Anxiety results when existence is challenged; shame results when worth is challenged; guilt results when behavior is challenged. While all three emotions are present in every culture, some have suggested, broadly speaking, a guilt orientation in the West, a shame orientation in the East, and an anxiety orientation on the African continent. But such a trinitarian formulation takes us beyond the focus of this book. Here it is simply stated that all three find resolution in God's amazing grace.[8]

And there is another limit that is inherent in this kind of presentation. Paradoxically, the very nature of an academic study such as this, with its rational, distanced, ink-on-paper

---

[8] For more on this, see David W. Augsburger, *Pastoral Counseling Across Cultures* (Philadelphia, PA: Westminster Press, 1986), esp. 113f.; and Bruce J. Malina, *The New Testament World: Insights from Cultural Anthropology* (Atlanta, GA: John Knox, 1993), 54.

stance, may actually contribute another brick to the enclosure which is shame. This book began its life as an academic study. Though I have done extensive rewriting it may still at times feel like an academic project. If your immediate objective is to find healing for shame it would be better to talk face-to-face, over a hot mug of coffee and a fresh muffin! Nevertheless, it seems helpful to put these thoughts into print, with the hope that, indirectly, this impersonal project may prompt the kind of real personal engagement that is the cornerstone of shame recovery.

Part One

The (Re)Discovery of Shame

1. An Introduction to Shame

The Reality and Necessity of Shame

Shame is complex and paradoxical. To begin with, as we have already seen, shame is difficult to express. This is partly because we have limited language for shame, especially in English. In addition the theory that shame often originates in prelinguistic infancy seems to support this experience that shame is not easy to express. Then again, who *wants* to talk about shame? The very topic is uncomfortable, if not itself shaming. So perhaps it comes as no surprise that shame has been largely ignored until recently. What is surprising is that so many of the people who do write about shame have suffered from the burden of shame in their own lives. It seems counter-intuitive, but the way of release seems to be to walk into the face of shame: to expose the exposure.

Getting shame on the table

So how did shame become a topic of academic discourse? The modern roots appear to go back to Ruth Benedict and her 1946 description and analysis of Japanese culture in a book entitled *The Chrysanthemum and the Sword.*[1] Benedict, a disciplined,

---

[1] Ruth Benedict, *The Chrysanthemum and the Sword* (New York: Meridian Books, 1946).

methodical anthropologist, simply described what she found. It turned out she was describing a culture profoundly shaped by the concept of shame. It was the exigencies of war that called on her to study Japanese culture: she was assigned the task by the U.S. government. Nevertheless Benedict's remarkably evenhanded inquiry (given war time sentiments) had, so to speak, let the cat out of the bag. Shame was on the academic table.

Cross-cultural studies continued to play a strong role in the development of the field. Shame was seen in a new light through the lens of other cultures. In 1966 Jean Peristiany edited an important collection of essays on honor and shame in Mediterranean cultures.[2] This included the classic study by Julian Pitt-Rivers that eventually led to a deeper appreciation of shame in biblical cultures. Bruce Malina, in his study *The New Testament World: Insights from Cultural Anthropology* (first published in 1981), was a key player in popularizing this aspect of biblical studies. There were other contributions in the biblical field. A notable early example is Krister Stendahl, *Paul Among Jews and Gentiles, 1976.*[3]

Changes, however, came slowly. It took even more time for the implications of this new shame awareness to immerge in applied theology. Tom Goodhue wrote a helpful article in 1984,[4] but not much was published from the perspective of faith until the 1990s. The outstanding exception was Lowell Noble's 1975 book, *Naked and Not Ashamed: An Anthropological, Biblical and Psychological Study of Shame.* The fact

---

[2] Jean G. Peristiany, ed., *Honor and Shame: The Values of Mediterranean Society* (Chicago, IL: University of Chicago Press, 1966).

[3] Krister Stendahl, *Paul Among Jews and Gentiles* (Philadelphia, PA: Fortress Press, 1976).

[4] Tom Goodhue, "Shame," *Quarterly Review,* 4 (2) (1984): 57-65.

that it was self-published may be one indication of how much ahead of his time he was. Noble, like others, was nudged into this area by missiological concerns.

Meanwhile secular psychology had entered the fray. In 1953 Gerhart Piers and Milton Singer published *Shame and Guilt: A Psychoanalytical and Cultural Study* (note the word "cultural" in the title.) Five years later, Helen Lynd wrote *On Shame and the Search for Identity*. Among subsequent publications Gershen Kaufman's *Shame: The Power of Caring* (1980) is highly regarded. Then John Bradshaw brought the field out into the public arena in the late 1980s. We will explore the cultural and biblical insights later, but this brief survey of the development of shame studies helps set the stage for an introduction to the topic itself.

What is shame?
It is necessary to begin with a note of caution. Shame is too complex to be reduced to a single, unifying meaning or expression. It is more helpful to hold together a range or family of meanings. Pattison, in his recent, masterly study of shame, speaks of the "ecology" of shame.[5] That being said, the experience of shame, at heart, is the experience of exposure. This is why our reaction to shame is the desire to be covered or hidden. Thus shame is a by-product of self-awareness (which is why shame is a uniquely human experience). As Charles Darwin said, "Blushing is the most peculiar and the most human of all expressions."[6] Kaufman captures well the essence of shame:

---

⁵ Pattison, *Shame*, 39, 78.
⁶ Quoted by Carl Schneider, *Shame, Exposure and Privacy* (Boston, MA: Beacon, 1977), 3.

To feel shame is to feel *seen* in a painfully diminished sense. The self feels exposed both to itself and to anyone present. It is this sudden, unexpected feeling of exposure and accompanying self-consciousness that characterize the essential nature of the affect of shame. . . . To live with shame is to experience the very essence or heart of the self as wanting.[7]

Thus it becomes apparent that shame is not primarily about *doing* but *being*.

Shame does have a physiological expression. Blushing, sweating, increased heart rate may be signs of shame. But something much deeper is going on. The Chinese character for shame brings together the two symbols for ears and heart. Red ears reveal the condition of the heart. What the heart is suffering from is a sense of diminished worth. So though shame, at first, may be regarded as a minor issue, thought of perhaps in terms of embarrassment, it turns out to be much deeper, relating to our very sense of identity. This is why shame is so painful. It is not just our actions that have fallen short, but our very selves. Not only that, but the self has fallen short in the eyes of others as well as its own eyes. Shame is a negative regard, in the same way that honor is a positive regard. Both are relational, and both are dynamics of relational systems. So we expect to find, and do find, that shame appears in family systems and extended family systems (e.g., clans, villages, and churches).

Since shame is the sense of being diminished, it is portrayed in body language that reflects smallness and non-worth. Shamed people have poor eye contact, their heads hang

---

[7] Gershen Kaufman, *Shame: The Power of Caring* (Cambridge, MA: Shenkman, 1980), 8.

down, their shoulders slump, spontaneous movement is limited, they may not care well physically for themselves. Shamed people may also experience a paralysis of language. If they do speak it is characterized by self-doubt or condemnation, defensiveness, apology, little emotion. The self is reluctant to peep out of hiding. Donald Nathanson writes:

> Shame affect operates to reduce interest—excitement and enjoyment—joy, just the affects that make us vital, lively, charming, fun, interesting, enjoyable, exciting, charismatic, thrilling, inspiring, and appealing. If you wonder why someone lacks vitality look first for the nearness to shame.[8]

Thus it is easy to see how shame undermines intimacy. The shamed person is deeply torn. On the one hand he or she longs for meaningful relationships. At the same time, however, that same person shrinks back, unable to take the risk. L. A. Burton notes: "The Indo-European root from which the word 'shame' is derived is 'shem' or 'sham,' and it means 'to hide.'"[9] C. S. Lewis expressed it this way: "I sometimes think that shame, mere awkward, senseless shame, does as much towards preventing good acts and straightforward happiness as any of our vices can do."[10]

Good shame

But is shame always bad? Here the limited English vocabulary is a hindrance. Some, especially those recovering from severe shame, argue that there is simply no helpful role for shame. But

---

[8] Donald L. Nathanson, *Shame and Pride: Affect, Sex, and the Birth of the Self* (New York: Norton, 1992), 155.

[9] Laurel Arthur Burton, "Respect: Response to Shame in Health Care," *Journal of Religion and Health*, 30 (1991): 140.

[10] C. S. Lewis in *A Grief Observed*.

there is widespread acknowledgment that shame does have a positive side. This is evident in the disparagement the term "shameless" expresses. No one wants to be known as shame*less*!

So shame is often subdivided into two categories: disgrace shame and discretionary shame or modesty. Robert Albers lists other languages that do have vocabulary to differentiate disgrace shame and discretionary shame: in Greek, *aischyne* and *aidos*; in Latin, *foedus* and *pudor*; in French, *horte* and *pudeur*; in German, *Schande* and *Scham*.[11] Social commentator James Twitchell argues that the loss of "good" shame is contributing to cultural deterioration in the United States.[12] This is, in fact, an old theme. James and Evelyn Whitehead note the god Apollo's denunciation of Achilles in Greek mythology: "He has no shame—that gift that hinders mortals, but helps them too."[13]

Thus there are two sides to shame. This is an important point as pastors look at ministering grace for shame. The goal is not the total removal of shame. If shame is exposure, the goal is appropriate exposure. Thus "shame is like a thermostat," helping human beings maintain the appropriate level of closeness and distance from others.[14] Shame helps distinguish self and other. Shame (sometimes painfully) sees

---

[11] Robert H. Albers, "Shame: A Dynamic in the Etiology of Violence," *Dialog*, 36 (4) (1997): 255.

[12] James B. Twitchell, *For Shame: The Loss of Common Decency in American Culture* (New York: St. Martin's Press, 1997).

[13] James D. and Evelyn Whitehead, *Shadows of the Heart: A Spirituality of the Negative Emotions* (New York: Crossroads, 1994), 91.

[14] Suzanne Retzinger, "Shame in the Therapeutic Relationship," in *Shame: Interpersonal Behavior, Psychopathology, and Culture,* eds. Paul Gilbert and Bernice Andrews (New York: Oxford University Press, 1998), 209.

self through the other. Thus shame guards the boundaries of self and affirms differentiated identity. Without shame there is no proper individuation, and consequently no possibility of meaningful relationship. Bonhoeffer writes: "The destruction of the sense of shame means the dissolution of all sensual and conjugal order. . . [shame preserves] the mystery of human corporeality."[15] Even the long-married approach each other with modesty, reserve, and a moment of shyness. Otherwise sex is reduced to an act, a service. As Fowler comments, "Privacy creates the moral capital that is spent on friendship and intimate relations."[16]

This concept of good shame will arise a number of times throughout this study. The point being made here is that good shame serves as protection against bad shame. Disgrace shame follows us, but discretionary shame precedes us. Good shame restrains us. It preserves us from grandiosity. As Bradshaw says: "It lets us know we are not God."[17] In so doing it preserves us from disgrace shame. Many writers are now describing multiple categories of shame, or a continuum that moves from healthy shame to pathological shamelessness. But for the scope of this study, the division into disgrace shame and discretionary shame or modesty, is sufficient.

Shame and guilt

What then is the difference between shame and guilt? This turns out to be a very important question and one that has not been asked enough. It is a core theme of this study that the

---

[15] D. Bonhoeffer, *Ethics* (New York: The Macmillan Company, 1965 edition), 184.
[16] Fowler, "Shame," 817.
[17] Bradshaw, *Healing the Shame that Binds You*, 9.

church must learn how to ask and answer this question in order to minister the grace of Christ in all its fullness. Fortunately there is considerable agreement in the literature. Asa Sphar writes: "Guilt is a value judgment on a person's behavior. Shame. . . is a value judgment on the person."[18] Robert Albers refers to "one who makes mistakes (guilt). . . one who is a mistake (shame)."[19] Donald Capps writes: "we *perform* guilty actions, but we *are* our shame."[20]

In brief, shame is a negative emotion relating to defective *personhood*, in contrast to guilt, which is a negative emotion relating to defective *behavior*. In other words, shame is about who I *am*, guilt is about what I *did*. Shame is a negative assessment of my very being.

Thus not only is there a difference in focus between guilt and shame, there is a difference in extent. Guilt applies to specific behaviors, whereas shame is a negative *global* evaluation of the self. Guilt can be compartmentalized. Shame affects the whole person.

There is also a difference in terms of resolution. Overcoming guilt results in righteousness, i.e., right behavior. Overcoming shame results in a clearer sense of identity.[21] The self has come back out of hiding.

Shame and guilt are concerned with others, but in different ways. Shame's burden is that others are spectators. Guilt's burden is that others are victims, having suffered from one's

---

[18] Asa Sphar, "A Theology of Shame as Revealed in the Creation Story," *Theological Educator: A Journal of Theology and Ministry,* 55 (1997): 68.

[19] Robert H. Albers, "The Shame Factor: Theological and Pastoral Reflections Relating to Forgiveness," *Word and World,* 16 (3) (1996): 347.

[20] Donald Capps, *The Depleted Self: Sin in a Narcissistic Age* (Minneapolis, MN: Fortress Press, 1992), 74.

[21] Lynd, *On Shame and the Search for Identity,* 209.

actions.[22] Both shame and guilt damage relationships. But the breach in relationship caused by guilt is more easily repaired because it is more external, more accessible—relief comes from reparation or atonement, or at least, apology. The breach in relationship caused by shame is more difficult to recover from because it is deeply internal, affecting the core of the person. Some immediate measure of relief comes from withdrawal, but true relational recovery is complex and costly, as we will see later.

There may even be biological differences between shame and guilt. Evidence for this emerges when shame and guilt lead to depression. It is reported that shame depression is considered atypical and responds to a different kind of medication.[23]

Notice again how we talk more readily about guilt than shame. Guilt is more objective. It can be dealt with rationally. Confessing guilt begins the journey to resolution. On the other hand, people are reluctant to talk about shame. It is more personal, more relational, messier, nonobjective. Confessing shame seems to exacerbate the problem rather than mitigate it. This is a critical point for pastors wanting to minister grace for shame. Consider the following vignette:

> For years Dorothy had wondered about talking to a pastor about what had happened on that dark afternoon so many years before. She had confessed her sin to God many times, but she still had no peace. No matter how she prayed she still felt unforgiven. It occurred to her that she needed to hear the words of forgiveness spoken by a human being. But phoning the pastor was not easy. She tried three times before she had

---

[22] Takie Sugiyama Lebra, "Shame and Guilt: A Psychological View of the Japanese Self," *Ethos,* 11 (1983): 193.

[23] Nathanson, *Shame and Pride,* 22, 147f.

the courage to let it ring. She made the appointment. And then, to the pastor, she told her painful story.

With kindness and firmness the pastor directed her to the promises of Scripture he knew so well. He assured her of God's forgiveness. They prayed together and she left. But Dorothy only felt worse. She found herself avoiding the pastor. She was seriously considering leaving the church. When her grandmother got sick in England, she was more than happy to spend two months there helping her recuperate. Perhaps, when she returned, she would look for a new spiritual home...

In distinguishing shame from guilt we see that ministry for each is different. What guilt seeks is forgiveness. What shame seeks is acceptance. This is not to say that acceptance means denial of guilt. The road to acceptance does not bypass sound judgment. This is precisely why acceptance is grace—it is *grace* for shame. This acceptance is in spite of guilt and anticipates forgiveness. The joy, as we shall see, is that the "varied grace" of God (1 Peter 4:10)[24] addresses both guilt and shame. It does, however, need to be administered differently in each case. Though we are rightly cautioned against asserting too rigorous a distinction between shame and guilt, shame must be recognized as a distinct sickness requiring its own medicine.

It may be unreasonable to expect a concise theory of shame given the complex cluster of emotions and understandings that converge on the subject; nevertheless we can become more familiar with the different faces of shame

---

[24] Bible quotations are from the *English Standard Version* unless otherwise noted.

and learn some of its byways. In our ministry we can work harder on distinguishing shame from guilt. We can become more alert to the signs of shame and work not only to reduce shame generation but to open doors of release for shame-burdened people.

When Shame Is Destructive

Yes, there is good shame, and an appreciation of the importance of good shame is vital to a holistic approach to shame, but our particular concern here is disgrace shame. What are its roots? What is its impact? And where is the way of recovery?

The feel of shame

Shame is no small burden to carry through life. Shame is marked by its intensity, evidenced by the way it persists in memory over long periods. Most of us have no problem recalling shaming incidents from long ago. Since it is so painful, huge amounts of energy are poured into compensating for and defending against shame. For people heavily burdened with shame, few resources remain for normal creative expression.[25] Bradshaw suggests that while abstract thought may be unaffected by shame, reason and judgment applied to practical and personal events may be seriously impaired.[26] Shame consumes capacity. Shame paralyzes. Shame steals hope.

---

[25] Albers, *Shame,* 69.
[26] Bradshaw, *Healing the Shame That Binds You,* 136.

As shame moves up the scale and becomes chronic, or toxic, people become shame based in the core of their being. Their very humanity is being eaten away. As Pattison puts it: "Those who live beyond the shame boundary inhabit the realm of the unclean and inhuman. They may be less valuable to self and others than domestic pets."[27] As a result they may be strangely willing to allow themselves to be used (i.e., treated as a commodity), or even engage in self-harming. _? addiction_

Here are just some of the recognized characteristics of shame-based people: continued low-grade depression, a world seen through a negative lens, the inability to receive criticism, a feeling of not belonging, painfully self-focused, a tendency to addiction, the world seen as black and white, out of touch with feelings, a sense of powerlessness, passivity, poor communication, and isolation.[28]

Underlying all this is the belief that one is simply defective as a person. The normal mistakes of life register as yet more evidence of global failure. It is a feeling, not so much of falling short of the ideal, but of falling short of what is simply adequate or good enough. Where guilt is felt as offense or debt, shame is felt as defilement or pollution.[29] In addition, while guilt can be motivating, shame spirals inwards and change becomes too much to hope for. With guilt there is something to be done. With shame there is no significant "I" to do anything.

The shame-based person finds it hard to accept praise. It is too dangerous to be lifted up. The subsequent fall has come too

---

[27] Pattison, *Shame,* 183.
[28] Marie Powers, *Shame: Thief of Intimacy* (Ventura, CA: Gospel Light, 1998), 19f. and Pattison, *Shame,* 71f.
[29] Pattison, *Shame,* 88.

often. Better to keep your head down.[30] So the "I" is kept out of sight. Shame-based people speak about themselves as if standing back and observing, rather than speaking out of themselves. There is a scarcity of "I" statements. Pattison notes that shame-based people "may find it hard or impossible truly to be present to themselves or to others."[31] What presence there is is fragile. Suddenly one feels exposed, out of place, incongruent; but the reason for the abrupt change is not readily apparent. Group settings are awkward and unpredictable. The shame-based person knows from experience how contagious shame is and lives in horror of the moment when shame answers to shame and the room turns deadly still. One is likely to see guilt coming, but shame catches people off guard.[32]

Shame is about exposure of the self and the shame-based person lives with a constant awareness of that exposure which is so unpredictable and so unforgiving. For this reason human torture often makes use of overexposure—nakedness, lights on twenty-four hours a day, and constant observation. The psychological damage is devastating and long term.

Lebra adds: "Exposure takes a dramatic form in a situational conflict where a double-status occupant is exposed simultaneously to two groups of audiences whose expectations are mutually incompatible."[33] So, for example, one man (from a "no-dancing" church background) talked of dancing with his peers when his family unexpectedly walked through the door!

---

[30] Nathanson, *Shame and Pride*, 384.

[31] Pattison, *Shame*, 156.

[32] Neil F. Pembroke, "Towards a Shame-Based Theology of Evangelism," *Journal of Psychology and Christianity*, 17 (1) (1998): 19.

[33] Takie Sugiyama Lebra, "The Social Mechanism of Guilt and Shame: The Japanese Case," *Anthropological Quarterly*, 44 (1971): 248.

He was suddenly and painfully exposed in different ways before the different groups.

The roots of shame

What can we say about the roots of shame? Shame appears to be the risk associated with the journey to becoming a separate person. This journey involves becoming an "I" in relation to other "I"s. It is a process of the gradual exposure of the self. Shame occurs when the process of uncovering the self goes wrong. A person becomes shame based as the intensity or frequency of shaming incidents is such that shame becomes internalized. So that, as Kaufman observes, "Shame originates interpersonally, primarily in significant relationships, but later can become internalized so that the self is able to activate shame without an inducing interpersonal event."[34]

The first few months of life are critical to the development of a healthy self. The response of the parents is highly significant in this process. In a healthy relationship the mother's loving gaze mirrors back the baby's feelings. Thus the baby sees its emerging self reflected back in an affirming way, and a positive self-image grows. The eye contact between mother and child is central. Eye contact exposes the inner self. This is why we avoid such exposure except in very limited circumstances (with babies, between lovers). As Noble points out, "Only when love and trust exist between persons is eye contact positive. In such situations, exposure of the self is desired and safe."[35] How often we have seen mothers interacting happily with their infants, smiling deeply back into their eyes. As the child discovers itself it experiments with new

---

[34] Kaufman, *Shame*, 7.
[35] Noble, *Naked and Not Ashamed*, 2.

expressions. The delighted mirroring of the mother instills a deep sense of worth.

As this new person grows and matures with a robust sense of self worth, he or she is able to "self-mirror" and becomes increasingly less dependent on external positive mirroring. Allan Schore describes the process whereby infant emotional experience plays a strong role in the development and maturation of the brain. Thus early shame experiences influence "patterns of neuronal connectivity in the infant's brain" that shape the unconscious responses to relational stress through life.[36] Kaufman calls this mirroring the "interpersonal bridge." He sees it as critical in the development of a sense of self and worth.

Shame develops when the interpersonal bridge is broken. Thus, if a child experiences abandonment, at least in the sense of loss of positive mirroring, the development of shame is likely. Though shame may also develop later in life, the early months and years are formative in establishing a robust self. Kaufman argues that shame is overcome, even later in life, as someone is willing to reach out and establish a new interpersonal bridge—a relationship that allows bonds to form.[37] It will be important to return to this point because it is critical for the recovery process.

Though this concept of early positive mirroring is insightful, it is not the whole picture. Shame is a complex story. Remembering that there is a contagious quality to shame, we can see that children of parents who are themselves shame-

---

[36] Allan Schore, "Early Shame Experiences and Infant Brain Development," in Gilbert and Andrews, eds., *Shame*, 57-77.

[37] Gershen Kaufman, "The Meaning of Shame," *Journal of Counseling Psychology*, 21 (6) (1974): 570.

based will identify with them. Thus shame can appear across generations in families. Other factors present in the early years may help form a shame-based identity: an angry home (children take it personally), being different (stuttering, hearing problems, etc.), or the deep devastation of sexual abuse. Children have little defense against boundary violation. They cannot raise the drawbridge on their soul. Shame penetrates to the deep, hidden places. Adolescence is a particularly vulnerable time. The highly sensitive person[38] may be more liable to internalize shame than another person given the same circumstances. The key point in all this is that in the emergence of the self, the self becomes distasteful to itself. Kaufman again:

> The important link between shame internalization and the formation of a shame-based identity lies in a process by which the self within the growing person begins to actively *disown* parts of itself, thereby creating splits within the self. The consequent internal strife waged against disowned parts of the self becomes the foundation for all later pathological developments.[39]

Coping with shame

Shame is a form of grief. It is grief at the loss of self. But this is not like the grief of a widow who can hope to find some resolution over time. It is more like the grief of the divorced person who never knows when he may bump into his former lover. For the shamed person the self has not really gone, it has

---

[38] See Elaine N. Aron, *The Highly Sensitive Person: How to Thrive When the World Overwhelms You* (New York: Broadway Books, 1996). Her chapter on childhood is especially helpful.

[39] Kaufman, *Shame*, 91.

only been pushed aside. The self will never get over the loss of self. The only alternative to the ongoing grief of shame is to begin to recover the split-off self.

The connection between shame and grief suggests that we can expect to see familiar patterns of grief processing in the processing of shame. The splitting itself is a form of denial: "That is not really me." Shame may manifest itself in anger or, more likely, rage. Michael Lewis writes: "I distinguish between anger, a response to a blockage of goal, and rage, a response to an attack on the self."[40] Rage is the protection reaction in a shamed person. Rage slams relational gates shut, while at the same time the shamed person longs to restore the relationship.[41] James Harper and Margaret Hoopes report that shame-prone people tend to get stuck on one emotion. Their emotional field is narrowed down to, say, anger, or fear. They have difficulty feeling and expressing other emotions[42]—further evidence of a stalled grieving process.

Since the pain of shame is so great we also see the use of blaming as an attempt to transfer the shame to another. For example, if a child makes a mistake and the parent feels shame, the parent may use blame to transfer his or her shame to the child. Perfectionism is another attempt to cope with shame. It is a type of bargaining (also familiar from the grief cycle). Perfectionism says, "If I never make a mistake, then I will have worth." But perfection is unattainable. The project is self-defeating and shame only deepens. Nevertheless, such is the

---

[40] Michael Lewis, *Shame: The Exposed Self* (New York: Free Press, 1992), 11.

[41] Kaufman, *Shame*, 11.

[42] See James M. Harper and Margaret H. Hoopes, *Uncovering Shame: Integrating Individuals and Their Family Systems* (New York: Norton, 1990), 13.

power of shame that a person may be driven to extraordinary achievements as he or she attempts to be "adequate."

Shame is also resisted by grasping for power. It is as though a sense of power and control will restore the respect for the self. In the home, the wife or the husband may put the other down. Either may bully the children. The pastor may ride roughshod over church members. All this in a futile attempt to build self-esteem. Albers notes that one of the factors in substance abuse is the artificial reversal of shame. "Grandiosity becomes a drug-affected device of compensation for the ingrained sense of deficiency. When the person is sober, he or she returns to the silent realms of increased low self-esteem."[43] All these attempts to inflate self-worth as a way of compensating for shame are doomed to failure. They in fact function to increase shame.

It is no surprise that shame-based people are marked by persistent low-level depression. The sparkle is missing. The sails hang limp. Kaufman asserts that shame is a vital factor in the development of depression, paranoia, and paranoid schizophrenia. Michael Lewis adds multiple personality disorder to this list.[44] Perhaps the most devastating effect of shame is that we simply give up on ourselves and live a life (if we continue to live) that is not authentic. Such a life is only a shadow of a life.

---

[43] Albers, "Shame and the Conspiracy of Silence," 55.

[44] Gershen Kaufman, *The Psychology of Shame: Theory and Treatment of Shame-Based Syndromes* (New York: Springer Pub. Co., 1989), 105. M. Lewis, *Shame,* 168f.

Relational systems

This is the place to say a word about healthy and unhealthy relational systems in regard to shame. Insight from this field will be important as we explore the concept of churches as places of healing for shame later in this study. Shame undermines trust. It says: "I cannot trust myself. I am inadequate. Furthermore, I cannot trust the external world to respond as I need and expect." Hence, as Harper and Hooper point out, shame-based people have difficulty doing something *with* others. They tend to be either victims (something is being done *to them*), or victimizers (doing something *to others*), or they may be overly dependent (doing things *for me*). "Because intimacy and mutual sharing are incompatible with hiding and covering their core of shame, these people have difficulty thinking in terms of "doing something *with* others.'"[45]

Shame is a problem of the "I" before the "other." Since the human race is incurably social, shame appears, therefore, as a characteristic of families and other family-like systems. Shame-based systems are deeply problematic.

Here briefly are some characteristics of shame-based relational systems. There is a culture of control; boundaries are unclear; there are few common goals; communication is poor; secrets multiply; chaos abounds; stress and crisis are poorly handled; there is a culture of perfectionism and blaming; and real intimacy is undermined.[46] Shame-bound systems are powerful. The impact of the shame-bound family on the children continues into adulthood, where adults remain plagued

---

[45] Harper, *Uncovering Shame*, 13f. (my emphasis).

[46] See Harper, *Uncovering Shame*, 71f.; Merle A. Fossum and Marilyn J. Mason, *Facing Shame: Families in Recovery* (New York: W. W. Norton and Co., 1986), 8; and Sarah Hines Martin, "Shame-Based Families," *Review and Expositor*, 91 (1994): 25f.

by inadequacy and all the ineffective learned responses to that (perfectionism, blaming, etc.).

In contrast, here are some characteristics of healthy systems. Variety and difference are encouraged; a sense of closeness is apparent; talk is open; being needy is OK; judgments are about events, not people; crisis and stress are handled well; and the group has consistent values and surplus capacity, and adapts well to change.[47] I will expand on this in chapter five as I look at what makes for a shame-healing congregation.

Avenues of recovery

Although we are looking at shame from the perspective of pastoral ministry, in closing this section on harmful shame it is helpful to look briefly at strategies for recovery from a psychological perspective. First of all we remember that the goal is not to take away good shame. Discretion shame needs to be affirmed. In addition, cultural differences need to be taken into account that may make discerning good shame from bad shame difficult. Secondly it is important to remember that shame is by nature a hidden emotion. It may be difficult, initially, to recognize that shame is the problem. Thirdly we must accept that recovery from shame is far more difficult than recovery from guilt. It may be that deep shame cannot be fully uprooted in this life. But we can expect to come to terms with shame. We can know it for what it is. We can walk around it. In this way shame loses its grip and becomes at least manageable, no longer all encompassing. Laughter and joy and singing reappear.

---

[47] See Harper, *Uncovering Shame*, 55f.; and Fossum, *Facing Shame*, 20.

James and Evelyn Whitehead introduce the concept of "befriending" our negative emotions. Rather than trying to ignore or bury our emotions, "befriending points the way to the ordinary disciplines of emotional life—naming and taming."[48] There is common agreement that we take a major step towards recovery when shame is named. When we begin to name shame we begin to separate the feeling and experience of shame from the rest of life. It becomes possible to envision a different kind of life, a life colored by more positive emotions than shame. The act of *naming* leads to conscious control, the power of shame begins to weaken. In this vein, Martin says, "Adult children need to "give back their shame" to their parents."[49] It could mean writing a letter (even if the parent is no longer living). This does not need to be confrontational or judgmental. What is needed is simply to name the past for what it was—to get the secret out onto the table.

Beyond this, there is also common agreement that we need others to help us with our shame. As the friends and relatives reached forward to unbind Lazarus at Jesus' command, so we too may allow our brothers and sisters to unbind us and set us free.[50] *Shame is a relational problem and needs a relational response.* Capps writes: "Our real self is not inaccessible, but we need the assistance of another to find it. . . . The source of our knowing is not private introspection but the mutual

---

[48] James D. Whitehead and Evelyn Eaton Whitehead, *Shadows of the Heart: A Spirituality of the Negative Emotions* (New York: Crossroads, 1994), 17.

[49] Martin, "Shame-Based Families," 27.

[50] Karen A. McClintock, *Sexual Shame: An Urgent Call to Healing* (Minneapolis, MN: Fortress Press, 2001), 147f.

mirroring of selves. . . . [we must let go of] the vicious cycle of self-repair."[51]

But the nature of the help from outside is critical. There must be a relationship of trust and warmth. Nathanson insists that the attitude of "therapeutic passivity . . . will always magnify shame."[52] Kaufman also argues that what is needed is not psychotherapy as technique but psychotherapy as "relatedness or connectedness, essential belonging."[53] As the shame-based person begins to open up the hidden recesses and expose again the inner self, what is needed is positive mirroring of the kind that was lost originally. Neither the exposure nor the effective positive mirroring will take place outside of a relationship of warmth and trust. John Patton puts it well:

> The therapeutic experience involves assisting a person to talk about and experience shame within the empathetic relationship, gradually expose the grandiose self that was created to push the shame away, and substitute a more realistic and related self.[54]

It is within this warm and trusting relationship that sinful pride (hubris) can begin to be separated from healthy pride—a sense of worth, accomplishment, and joy in strength and abilities. Hubris is a global overevaluation. Good pride relates to specific qualities and actions. So recovery occurs within authentic, respectful, appropriately affirming relationships, whether formal or informal. It feels, for the shame-based person, like a terrible risk. But the way forward is to reconnect

---

[51] Capps, *The Depleted Self*, 166f.

[52] Nathanson, *Shame and Pride*, 325.

[53] Kaufman, *Shame*, 160.

[54] John Patton, *Is Human Forgiveness Possible?* (Nashville, TN: Abingdon Press, 1985), 59.

with the human community and so find a larger meaning and purpose that is lifegiving and carries shamed persons beyond themselves.

I have already said that this study is not intended to be a manual for psychotherapy. Nevertheless, some awareness of these processes is helpful in understanding the dynamics of shame from a pastoral perspective. What we as Christians offer is the most empathetic, warm, trusting, and appropriately affirming therapist of all, God himself. Without question he is much more than a therapist, yet surely not less. But more of this later.

We must, eventually, own ourselves. This is me. This is who I am. This is how I am feeling. As shame dissipates, the body too will become acceptable again, along with the rest of the whole person. We will begin to taste more, to sing more, even perchance, to dance! We will recognize and revel in the beauty of the natural world. We will begin to be at ease in our own skin, content to be ourselves with others. We will discover deep joy. And, Bradshaw adds, we will recover a sense of humor, perhaps "the ultimate criterion for measuring a person's recovery from internalized shame."[55]

The Cultural Connection

Over the past fifty years in the West the trickle of secular research and writing on shame has grown to a flood. It seemed best for the purposes of this study to begin to sketch in a framework for understanding shame from within this Western

---

[55] Bradshaw, *Healing the Shame That Binds You*, 238.

context, which is the context of this present study. Nevertheless we should remember that it was cross-cultural inquiry that initially exposed shame to the light of day and made it a topic of modern academic discourse in the West.

So we return now to that anthropological spade work. We do this in part because in the global village of the twenty-first-century pastors and church leaders need to begin to think and feel outside of their own mother culture if they are to build effective Gospel bridges to their increasingly culturally diverse congregations. And secondly because, if it is true, as we will argue later, that the West itself is undergoing a major cultural shift in regard to shame, what is learned from other cultures may help us be better equipped for more effective ministry in our own cultures in the days to come. In order to minister grace for shame, we must begin to understand how shame works differently for different cultures. Unfortunately, except for some missiological studies and academic exegetical inquiries, discussions of shame from a faith perspective, have so far largely ignored the cultural dimensions of shame.

Other ways of being

A 1974 study reported that "The Caucasian-Americans and the Chinese-Americans rated [shame] as significantly more serious than did the Japanese-Americans." In addition shame appears to be "less clearly identifiable" (or perhaps understood) for the Caucasian group.[56] Why were the Japanese-Americans not as concerned about shame? Why did the Caucasian group have more difficulty identifying shame? Is shame not a cultural

---

[56] A. J. Marsella, M. D. Murray, and C. Golden, "Ethnic Variations in the Phenomenology of Emotions: Shame," *Journal of Cross-Cultural Psychology*, 5 (3) (1974): 323.

constant? For answers, it is helpful to attempt to step for a moment outside the cultural world of the West.

We begin by remembering that shame is not all bad. It is simply one dimension of human experience that serves a healthy function but can also go terribly wrong. It turns out that, in some cultures, good shame has a much higher profile than it does in the West. This is a reminder, as Augsburger rightly points out, that simply writing off either guilt or shame as "repressive forces to be exorcised" is not helpful. Both emotions have a constructive role. As we observe the vastly different worldview of the Orient that effects everything from child-rearing and home design to religious commitment, we have an opportunity to reread and reevaluate our Western perspective on life. May both East and West together adjust to the values of the Kingdom of God, which is owned by neither East nor West.

But though we in the West may give intellectual assent to such observations, are we really aware of the extent of our own cultural captivity? Augsburger is pointed and startlingly relevant in this comment:

> "Deep within, all people yearn to be English," the colonial empire-builders once assumed. Today a western assumption is: "Scratch any person on the globe, and underneath you'll find an American longing for freedom, democracy, individual rights, and Coca Cola." Perhaps every culture has such bizarre ethnocentricity secretly tipping its scales of justice. But its rightful place is in our humor, not our honor; in our history, not our present values.[57]

---

[57] David W. Augsburger, *Conflict Mediation Across Cultures: Pathways and Patterns* (Louisville, KY: Westminster John Knox Press, 1992), 206.

Malina, perhaps more politely, but no less firmly, underlines the difficulty of the road ahead:

> When you do not share speech patterns, you simply do not understand a language. When you do not share behavior patterns, you simply do not understand what another is doing.[58]

For "behavior patterns" we could insert the word culture.

The simplest definition of culture is, "the way we do things around here." This is not something consciously learned. We absorb it, we catch it, we breathe it in. Just as we often know little about the grammar of our own language until we begin to learn another language, in the same way our eyes are opened to our own culture as we study the cultures of others. For those of us who grew up in a culture where questions of right and wrong are primary, it is very difficult even to imagine a society where alternate values take precedence. The work of Ruth Benedict has been very helpful at this point.

Benedict's inquiry

In June of 1944, with Japan and the U.S. at war, Benedict, a respected American anthropologist, was assigned to study Japan. The U.S. wisely realized it was dealing with people who saw the world through a very different lens. Benedict writes: "The question was how the Japanese would behave, not how we would behave if we were in their place."[59] She goes on to add: "The job requires both a certain tough-mindedness and a certain generosity. . . . The tough-minded are content that differences should exist. . . . Their goal is a world made safe for

---

[58] Malina, *The New Testament World*, 13.

[59] Benedict, *The Chrysanthemum and the Sword*, 5.

differences."[60] What Benedict in her honest and fair-minded examination discovered was a "singular" system, a cultural unity. "It was not Buddhism and it was not Confucianism. It was Japanese—the strength and weakness of Japan."[61] Perhaps the fact that Japan is an island nation helped create such a distinctive and unified culture. In any case her research brought to the table a description of a culture vastly different from the experience of the West. What Benedict was describing was a dependence, or contextual, or group culture, something quite different from our individualist culture.

The contrast can be illustrated by comparing child-raising beliefs and practices in individualist cultures with Japanese child-raising. Simply put, the goal of child raising in Japan is to bring an independent newborn into a proper dependency on the group. Whereas the goal of child raising in Western culture is to bring a dependent newborn to independence.[62] The implications of such contrary views are profound. People in dependency cultures experience differently what it is to be a person. Yes, they are individuals, but that individuality is heavily context dependent, "like an egg without a shell."[63] Benedict writes, for example, that "behavior that recognizes hierarchy is as natural to them as breathing. . . . Every greeting, every contact must indicate the kind and degree of social distance between men. . . . The Japanese have, in other words, what is called a 'respect language,' as many other peoples do in the Pacific."[64] Thus, "It is not merely necessary to know to

---

[60] Ibid., 14f.

[61] Ibid., 19.

[62] Millie R. Creighton, "Revisiting Shame and Guilt Cultures: A Forty-Year Pilgimage," *Ethos,* 18 (1990): 299f.

[63] Ibid., 294.

[64] Benedict, *The Chrysanthemum and the Sword,* 47.

whom one bows, but it is necessary to know how much one bows."[65] This is a way of being that is *field oriented*. Each individual is very conscious not only of who he or she sees but of how he or she is seen. Here is the point of this piece for this study: *since shame, by definition, is about how one is seen by others, shame is highly significant for group cultures.*

We must not underestimate the profound cultural differences. Independence cultures value autonomy, disengagement, individuation. Dependence cultures value connecting, affiliation, engagement. Self is understood differently in each. Emotions play out differently in each. For example, pride of personal achievement is of much higher value in independence cultures. Feelings of respect, for example, are highlighted in dependence cultures. From the perspective of group-oriented cultures, Westerners often appear insensitive and overbearing. In short, the self-conscious emotions are culturally scripted.[66] So James and Evelyn Whitehead speak of the "social construct of emotion." Emotions are not simply private phenomena. They write: "Our impulses always come 'cooked,' part of the cultural stew of expectations and prohibitions that prevail in each society."[67]

Consider again child-rearing. Japanese children are disciplined with ridicule or embarrassment or even temporary withdrawal (of the mother's presence). Western mothers are shocked at this! On the other hand, Japanese mothers are

---

[65] Ibid., 48.

[66] See Shinobu Kitayansa, Hazel Rose Markus, and Hisaya Matsumoto, "Culture, Self and Emotions: A Cultural Perspective on "Self-Conscious" Emotions," in *Self-Conscious Emotions: The Psychology of Shame, Guilt, Embarrassment, and Pride,* June Price Tangney and Kurt W. Fischer, eds. (New York: Guilford Press, 1995), 439f.

[67] Whitehead and Whitehead, *Shadows of the Heart,* 30f.

shocked by American mothers who spank or yell at their children! However, each type of sanction is appropriate within its own culture.[68] In the Japanese family children learn that the best decision is that which maintains the family honor.[69]

The focus in group cultures is not on maintaining a *clear conscience* but on maintaining a *good reputation*. As Creighton puts it: The moral goal in Japanese society is to become a *jinsei no tatsujin*, a "master of life," a person who "never errs in judging the right behavior at any particular moment, given the particular situation."[70] Benedict highlights the contrast with Western, individualistic culture: "In Japan the constant goal is honor. It is necessary to command respect. The means one uses to that end are tools one takes up and then lays aside as circumstances dictate." This is very different, she says, from the Western notions of sticking to principles, win or lose.[71] Thus we see that the sanction, that which keeps people on the straight and narrow in Japanese society, is shame; in the West it is guilt. As a result, it has become common to speak of *shame cultures* and *guilt cultures*.

Some of the implications of this distinction are very relevant for ministry in cross-cultural situations. For example, in high-context (shame) cultures, face-to-face confrontation is avoided if at all possible. A go-between is used. The risk of shame is too great. In low-context (guilt) cultures, face-to-face meetings are encouraged. Competition also works differently in the different cultures. Benedict notes that Americans find competition stimulates effort. Whereas Japanese are extremely

---

[68] Creighton, "Revisiting Shame and Guilt Cultures," 299.
[69] Benedict, *The Chrysanthemum and the Sword*, 56.
[70] Creighton, "Revisiting Shame and Guilt Cultures," 297.
[71] Benedict, *The Chrysanthemum and the Sword*, 171.

concerned about the shame of loss and thus avoid competition.[72] Westerners are concerned when politeness seems to mask true feeling. Japanese, for that very reason, have developed politeness to a fine art. For them, smooth relationships and the cohesion of the group are more important than individual differences and personal expression.[73] There is great caution around expressed sincerity. "It is a shame to any man to 'blurt out his feelings,' it 'exposes' him."[74] This is not the place to pursue further the contrasts between Japanese and Western culture. But we must not underestimate the differences. The dynamics of group culture are pervasive. This is a very different way of living and we who attempt to work with different cultural groups need to take note.

Evaluating Benedict

Has Benedict's work stood the test of time? Answers vary. In 1990 Millie Creighton reviewed the debate.[75] Overall, she sees strong support for Benedict's analysis. Some critics wrote Benedict off as a pejorative account by an outsider, but a careful rereading refutes this view. At times she seems more critical of American than Japanese culture. A key question for this study is whether or not it is valid to speak of "shame cultures" and "guilt cultures." It now seems best to nuance the concept by using the terms "shame-oriented" and "guilt-oriented." Benedict herself does acknowledge the importance of guilt in Japanese culture but argues that the emphasis falls on shame.[76]

---

[72] Ibid., 153f.
[73] Ibid., 158.
[74] Ibid., 216.
[75] Creighton, "Revisiting Shame and Guilt Cultures."
[76] See Benedict, *The Chrysanthemum and the Sword,* 222.

Benedict's contribution to the understanding of culture differences, and especially to the differing roles of shame and guilt, is of great value. Her work exposed new veins of inquiry that are still being mined to this day. While Benedict's study provides an intriguing account of human experience in a group culture, it is important to note (as she herself does) that this is an extreme case (on the independence-dependence scale). Though Asian cultures generally have a group orientation (and thus a shame orientation), they vary in kind and degree from group to group.

What is important here is to begin to accept the broad East-West differences. For one reason, as Noble rightly points out, when Western guilt-oriented Christianity is imposed on a shame-culture people it tends to rob that people of key elements of their identity.[77] Furthermore, it is also necessary to withhold value judgments. For example, as Augsburger observes:

> One culture's belief system is another's disbelief system. Members of low-context cultures view the indirect way of handling conflict as a weak, cowardly, or evasive act, while members of high-context cultures view the direct way of handling conflict as lacking in politeness, or good taste.[78]

In fact both the dependence model and the independence model gain and lose. Creighton argues that the dependence model gains harmony and cohesion but loses individual autonomy. The independence model promotes self-reliance and autonomy but at the cost of a loss of belonging. She notes that both shame and guilt are necessary features of all cultures.

---

[77] Noble, *Naked and Not Ashamed*, 81.
[78] Augsburger, *Conflict Mediation Across Cultures*, 91.

"Because they function as mechanisms of social control it is unlikely that any society could be maintained without them." She helps us integrate a more comprehensive cultural appreciation:

> A conceptual analogy to explain the asymmetrical balance between shame and guilt likely in an individual (or culture) may be drawn from right- or left-hand dominance. It is preferable to have two hands than none, preferable to have two hands than one. Having some dexterity in both is optimal. However, most of us are right-handed or left-handed and the truly ambidextrous person is exceptionally rare. Finally, it is inappropriate to think of either left- or right-handedness as superior to the other.[79]

A composite understanding of shame?

We have explored shame from two perspectives, namely as a psychological reality within Western culture and as a corporate characteristic of high-context cultures. Is it possible to bring these two lines of thought together in some kind of "unified field theory" of shame?

To begin with, it is important to underline once again that shame is not always bad. Shame is a necessary dynamic of human life that functions in both bad and good ways. Shame operates at the interface of the individual and the group, monitoring and managing the balance between individuality and togetherness. (Marie Powers's already helpful recovery guide, *Shame: Thief of Intimacy*, could perhaps be improved by being reworked under the title *Shame: Foe and Friend of Intimacy*.) Shame operates on a continuum from modesty (good

---

[79] Creighton, "Revisiting Shame and Guilt Cultures," 291f.

shame) at one end to toxic shame at the other. But we must accept that the crossover point between good and bad shame is not easy to define. In part this is because shame is a complex ecology that does not easily accommodate to the continuum metaphor and in part because shame, like all emotions, is culturally shaped. The point at which shame becomes a problem can only be determined from within a particular cultural context.

From the perspective of ministry, once pastors begin to understand the nature of high-context cultures we quickly realize that people from these cultures tend to be much more shame-healthy than people from low-context cultures. These people talk more easily about shame and understand more clearly its functioning. In highly individualistic societies, however, shame development is inhibited, often retaining its infantile, cosmic, and narcissistic qualities through adulthood.[80] Thus the term "shame-oriented" refers not only to people who are individually *burdened* with shame now, i.e., "the shamed," it refers also to those who are culturally *sensitized* to the reality and risk of shame in interpersonal settings and who thus live (consciously or not) with shame as a powerful driving and shaping force. Both groups are increasingly represented in the Western church.

Seeing shame through this kind of composite, cross-cultural lens will help the church in at least three specific areas. We will be in a better position to know when shame has gone wrong and needs healing grace (and thus, for example, not rush to "heal" good shame). We will be more astute in understanding how relationships function well in varying

---

[80] Augsburger, *Conflict Mediation Across Cultures*, 82.

cultures (e.g., not forcing face-to-face meetings in culturally inappropriate settings). Thirdly, and significantly, we will learn to frame the Gospel message in ways that are better at touching the hearts of people who are shame-oriented at the level of culture. We will not assume that the Western, guilt-oriented Gospel is the only, or even the best way to present the Christian message in all situations.

Honor and Shame in Biblical Cultures

This brief introduction to the world of high-context cultures may leave us with a strange sense of disquiet. Ways of being that we considered fixed turn out to be relative. We are not sure we still know what it means to be normal! Nevertheless, perhaps it is now possible to begin to understand better why transplanted people experience culture shock. Imagine a world where workers go on "strike" by locking out the bosses and then so boosting production that the owners are shamed into granting a raise![81] It turns out there are other ways of being human, and other ways of being human together, that are alien to us in the West.

And so we come to the disturbing realization that Jesus was raised by foreigners. He was raised in a high-context culture. He was raised to be dependent, mother oriented. The matrix of his emotions was forged in the furnace of a shame-oriented culture. If Jesus were to emigrate to North America he would undergo a profound cultural adjustment that would shake his very sense of being. There may be a few Western

---

[81] Benedict, *The Chrysanthemum and the Sword*, 310f.

Christians who, for a little longer, are able to avoid the cultural mixing that is the hallmark of twenty-first-century cities, but none of us can escape the fact that to pick up "our" Bible is to cross into an alien cultural place. *If we only see Scripture through our low-context, individualistic, Western-culture lens, our understanding will be very superficial.*

Here the prominent application of the social sciences to the study of the Bible in recent years is very helpful. Anthropology in its exploration of human life and culture has built a fruitful partnership with biblical studies. Matthews and Benjamin note that for too long the biblical world was "reconstructed as if it were a European or an industrial world driven by capitalism and individualism." Anthropology serves well when it corrects such misunderstandings. Matthews and Benjamin write:

 "Culture is always a delicate blend of story and daily living, of mythos and ethos. Mythos is the story a people tell, ethos is the way a people live. Biblical scholars study one; anthropologists the other. It is impossible to understand any culture, ancient or modern, without studying both."[82]

Mediterranean cultures, including biblical cultures, are now widely described as honor-shame cultures, honor and shame being the two sides of the emotional currency of these cultures.

In an early 1926 study Johannes Pederson noted the role of honor and shame in Israelite society.[83] Since then Julian Pitt-Rivers and others have examined more closely the honor-shame theme running through the cultures and subcultures of

---

[82] Victor H. Matthews and Don C. Benjamin, "Social Sciences and Biblical Studies," *Semeia* (68) (1996): 7f.

[83] Johannes Pederson, *Israel, Its Life and Culture I-II* (Copenhagen: Dyva and Jeppesen, 1926).

the Mediterranean. In the last twenty five years Bruce Malina has been prominent in bringing these sociological insights to the attention of Bible students generally. In order to discover the depths of Gospel resources for shame-oriented people it is necessary to examine again how the Gospel played out in its own backyard. The Good News came first to shame-oriented people, not to guilt-oriented people. Here is a brief look at the characteristics of honor-shame cultures.

Profiling honor-shame cultures

The cultural unit of Mediterranean societies is the family or kinship group. Individual identity is tied to the group. The smooth functioning of the group depends on the maintenance of appropriate relations between the individual and the group. The rules of this game are rooted firmly in the values of honor and shame. Shame is the loss of honor. And when shame is avoided, honor, dignity and glory accrue. In honor-shame cultures identity is not freestanding. Identity, which is linked to honor (i.e., being a "somebody"), is *in the eyes of others*. This is known as a "dyadic" understanding of personality that has profound implications for what it means to be a person within such settings.

While it is necessary to acknowledge variations on the theme, honor and shame cultures appear to have a remarkable consistency through time, even to the present. Thus it is possible to sketch a general profile. Malina defines honor in Mediterranean societies: "Honor is the value of a person in his or her own eyes (that is, one's claim to worth) *plus* that person's value in the eyes of his or her social group. . . . It is something like our credit rating." Honor can be *ascribed* (by birth or inheritance) or *acquired* (by winning the honor game of "challenge and response").[84] But the point is:

> The person. . . does not think of himself or herself as an individual who acts alone regardless of what others think and say. Rather the person is ever aware of the expectations of the others, especially significant others, and strives to match those expectations. This is the group-embedded, group-oriented, dyadic personality, one who needs another simply to know who he or she is.[85]

Thus we use the term "dependence" culture, in contrast with "independence" culture. Or, in the words of Jerome Neyrey, this is a "face to face" society, in contrast with our "face to space" society.[86]

Another key to understanding honor and shame culture is the concept of limited good. In these settings the size of the "pie" is fixed. As one person's honor increases, another person's honor must decrease (i.e., the other becomes shamed). When good is seen as limited, the person who makes "progress" (valued so highly in the West) becomes a threat to the rest of the community. (John the Baptist's acceptance of Jesus' increase and his own decrease is radically countercultural.) This concept of limited supply leads to a constant sense of wariness—one's honor is always on the line. No small matter when honor, on the street, is better than cash. *Honor-shame culture is always competitive.*

In Mediterranean societies honor is linked to blood. Blood relatives share honor and distrust outsiders. Hence the

---

[84] Malina, *The New Testament World*, 31f.

[85] Ibid., 81.

[86] Jerome H. Neyrey, *Honor and Shame in the Gospel of Matthew* (Louisville, KY: Westminster John Knox Press, 1998), 27.

importance of the kinship unit. Honor resides in the physical person, especially the head (hence the king's crown). Respect is conveyed by bowing, touching, uncovering or covering the head, as prescribed by custom. Slapping, hitting, spitting on the head is a challenge to honor. Any threat to the face is a threat to honor.[87] Since the name represents the person, the name also carries honor. In addition to the honor of individuals in the group, the group itself carries a collective honor. The head of the group carries the burden of honor for the group, both preserving honor and establishing the level of honor. Honor is not about possessions, though it is about how possessions are used to maintain or acquire honor. The currency of these cultures is honor itself.

Since honor is always under threat, a man must know how to defend his honor. "To leave an affront unavenged is to leave one's honor in a state of desecration and this is therefore equivalent to cowardice."[88] Noble notes that in Judaism, embarrassing one's neighbor in front of others was on a level with spilling blood.[89] Furthermore, each man must maintain his own honor. By the nature of the situation another cannot defend it for him (that would be shameful). The final defense for honor is the threat of violence. In high-honor cultures this threat is strong enough to enforce a façade of politeness.[90] Ridicule destroys honor, especially public ridicule.[91]

---

[87] Pitt-Rivers, "Honour and Social Status," 25.
[88] Ibid., 26,
[89] Noble, *Naked and Not Ashamed*, 44
[90] D. Cohen, J. Vandello, and A. Rantilla, "The Sacred and the Social: Cultures of Honor and Violence," 261-282, in Gilbert and Andrews eds., *Shame*.
[91] Pitt-Rivers, "Honour and Social Status," 47.

As I waited in line at the checkout, an older Asian man indicated he would like to slip through from the other direction. As I backed up my cart I said, "That will cost you a dollar!" With hardly a pause he countered, "Do you have change for a hundred?" As I reflected on this later, I realized we were sparring for honor. I had placed myself over him, an older man, by jokingly controlling the passage and claiming a fee. His honor was now on the line. Instinctively he regained his position with the implication that he carried nothing less than a hundred dollar bill, making my fee look insignificant. I left it at that. As an older man it was appropriate that he should come out ahead. Besides to "up the ante" would be to push the exchange precariously close to anger if not actual violence. We left off with humor in the air. But the weight of honor was just below the surface.

It is important also to note a kind of division of labor in honor and shame societies. It is the work of the men to maintain honor. To a great extent the honor of the man resides in his ability to maintain the sexual purity of the women in his life (mother, wife, sisters, daughters). This gives women much indirect power through the threat of shameless action. Thus it is axiomatic that gender differences are clearly marked in honor-shame societies. Dress, role, space, are clearly differentiated along gender lines. Men do not wear women's clothing, do not take on women's functions (spinning, weaving, childrearing), and do not hang around the home. Women rule the private sphere; men rule the public sphere. Paul echoed his cultural context when he wrote: "Does not nature itself teach you that if a man wears long hair it is a disgrace for him, but if a woman has long hair, it is her glory?" (1 Corinthians 11:14-15).

Malina draws some contrasts between Mediterranean cultures and U.S. culture. On the matter of child rearing, Mediterranean cultures see the infant as selfish (as opposed to "dependent" in the U.S.). They see the parents as having the responsibility of molding the child (rather than respecting and allowing self-regulation). They require the child to conform (as opposed to helping the child understand). The authority of the parent is not to be questioned (in contrast to the willingness of U.S. parents to tolerate questioning). In regard to social structure, subordinates in Mediterranean cultures prefer superiors to simply make decisions and give orders. They are uncomfortable with superiors who expect participation and consultation in the decision making. They like superiors to maintain their social distance (as opposed to being chummy or intimate). They expect those in power to have privileges and "look like a leader." Lastly, "societal upheaval is always due to some 'underdog,' who must be punished by force and shame."[92]

Pitt-Rivers points out the fundamental conflict between honor and legality. Formal justice is simply not very satisfying for honor claimants. Each must guard his own honor (not call the police). Furthermore, court cases risk further humiliation.[93] Hence the persistence of the duel (and its modern version of: "Hey, do you want to step outside and say that?") as a dispute settlement mechanism. This is not to say that disputes are settled privately. This is about honor, and honor must be seen or it is nothing. Honor is maintained or lost publicly. (In the checkout-counter vignette above, the whole exchange was monitored by the others waiting in line.) The only court that

---

[92] Malina, *The New Testament World*, 56f., 82f., 93.
[93] Pitt-Rivers, "Honour and Social Status," 30.

matters is the opinion of the group. Thus gossip is a powerful force in honor-shame societies. Gossip communicates the verdict. It is the threat of shame hitting the gossip network that keeps individuals from actions disadvantageous to the group, not regard for legality.

Thus it becomes obvious that honor is not necessarily the equivalent of moral righteousness in honor-shame cultures. Malina notes: "To lie in order to deceive an outsider, one who has no right to the truth, is honorable."[94] (Think, for example, of the Hebrew midwives in Exodus chapter 1.) Furthermore, since honor is about reputation, it is the word out on the gossip network that is important, not necessarily the truth.[95] Honor has more value than truth. Conversely, shame is a reaction to the criticism of the group, not necessarily to a break with an abstract moral standard. In this way the individual evaluates his or her behavior through the eyes of the group.

Malina points out that this echoes the etymology of the word conscience (Latin con-scientia—"with-knowledge," thus "common knowledge").[96] Nevertheless, etymology is not a sure guide to current usage. In fact "conscience," as it is understood today, has a low profile in honor-shame cultures. A good reputation carries more weight than a clear conscience. Group-oriented people simply do not struggle with personal guilt and inner criticism the way individualist, low-context people do. For the former, "wrongness" is in the eyes of the group. That which loses honor is wrong.

In a low-context, guilt-oriented culture if I am guilty I am expected to feel guilty even if no one else believes I am guilty,

---

[94] Malina, *The New Testament World*, 43.
[95] Pitt-Rivers, "Honour and Social Status," 64.
[96] Malina, *The New Testament World*, 63.

since guilt is breach of principle, not relationship. But if I belong to a high-context, shame-oriented culture my "wiring" is very different. If I am innocent but the group believes I am guilty, I am shamed and dishonored already. On the other hand, if I am guilty but the group believes I am innocent I am not ashamed, since shame, by definition, is about how I am seen.

In summary

What then are the key features of honor-shame cultures? First, they are group cultures (the individual is embedded in the group). Second, kinship is everything (strangers, by definition, have no honor). Third, conflict is always in the air (honor is always at risk). Fourth, honor resides with the men (who preserve honor by guarding the purity of their women). Fifth, the honor of the group resides in the leader (as the leader goes, so goes the honor). Sixth, honor is weighed in the court of public opinion (and the verdict is broadcast through gossip). Seventh, honor does not equal truth or virtue (honor is defined by public opinion, not principle). Eighth, personal guilt is not the concern (the negative emotion is shame).

We should note also that while in traditional honor-shame cultures shame plays a major policing role, it does not necessarily lead to shame-based identities. Shame is to be avoided and is devastating if unavoidable. Nevertheless, it is episodic and incident focused in such cases, not permeating and defining of the inner person.

This is sufficient to introduce some of the key characteristics of honor-shame cultures. There are, as I have indicated, differences from group to group around the Mediterranean. Nevertheless, the key elements persist geographically and chronologically. Those knowledgeable in the field agree that these cultural dynamics (of kinship groups) have not changed much since New Testament times. In fact, since my original research in this area, my wife and I spent almost three years living in Turkey, where we experienced firsthand the dynamics of life in an honor-shame culture. We were much closer to experiencing the world of the Bible than we could ever be in Canada.

Why have we taken the time to explore the honor-shame cultures of the Mediterranean in a book written for Christian pastors and leaders? Here are three reasons. Firstly, this is another window on the topic of shame. In particular there is much to be learned about relationships and values in shame-oriented settings. Secondly, an awareness of honor-shame dynamics sheds much helpful light on Scripture. Bible culture is honor-shame culture. We discover that many of the questions we are just beginning to ask about shame have answers waiting to be heard in the biblical text.

And thirdly, as western observers examine the honor-shame dynamics of kinship groups we may well discover ourselves in the process. As Pitt-Rivers points out, *however much the religious world promotes principle, ordinary people cling to honor.*[97] Thus Peristiany, in reviewing the collection of essays on this subject concludes:

> Honor and shame are the constant preoccupation of individuals in small scale, exclusive societies where face-to-face personal, as opposed to anonymous, relations are of

---

[97] Pitt-Rivers, "Honour and Social Status," 24.

paramount importance and where the social personality of the actor is as significant as his office.[98]

Peristiany includes in his face-to-face communities groups like "school groups" and "street corner societies." We cannot ignore the reality that Christian congregations are also small-scale, face-to-face communities. Because of this, honor-shame dynamics are an inescapable factor in the life of the church. *Regardless of how we might feel about "sticking to principle," honor and shame continue to play a large role in the life of the congregation.*

---

[98] Peristiany, *Honor and Shame*, 11.

2. A New Context for Ministry

With this psychological and cultural introduction to shame we are now in a better position to assess the significance of shame in our own North American ministry contexts. Given the increasing ease of mobility in recent decades most Western pastors can now expect to be living and working with people from shame-oriented cultures. But what about people born and raised in the West? What is the role of shame in Western culture? Is it true that the West is a guilt-oriented culture? Or is shame a more present issue than we thought?

Acknowledging Shame in the West

One way to study shame in the West is through the arts. The popular *Lord of the Rings* movie series is steeped in honor-shame themes. In fact poets and novelists have long wrestled with the subject. In a recent article, John Deli-Carpini illustrates this using the novel *The Minister's Black Veil* by Nathaniel Hawthorne. In this story the minister wears a veil as a way of exposing the shame he has inherited from his extended family.[1] For Shakespeare, shame was simply part of life. He reportedly uses "shame language" ten times as

[1] John Deli-Carpini, "Preaching and Feelings of Shame: 'The Minister's Black Veil,'" *Preaching,* 16 (3) (2000): 47f.

frequently as "guilt language." His works are as popular today as they have ever been. The arts reflect back to us our honor-shame orientation, but do we recognize what we see in the mirror?

A reluctance to reevaluate

I begin here with the assertion that shame is indeed a force to be reckoned with in our Western contexts. It is present, and there are reasons to believe it will increase. But it is odd to find within ourselves a resistance to admitting cultural currents of shame and its traveling companion honor. Perhaps we are embarrassed (!) to see in ourselves manifestations of honor-shame culture. We feel we should align our behavior along poles of right and wrong, justice and injustice, principle for principle's sake, and so on; but we discover that the undercurrents of honor-shame dynamics are significant and tenacious.

Perhaps the grammar of honor and shame culture is most readily seen in marriage, where role differentiation and male dominance stubbornly persist. A few years ago I watched a presentation in support of egalitarian marriages by a panel of three hand-picked couples. In each case, before the couple presented, there was either a verbal or nonverbal exchange as the wives requested and received permission from their husbands to speak first!

Part of the difficulty in recognizing shame patterns at work in the West, is the persistent combination of ignorance and prejudice about other cultural maps. One of the urgencies of this study is that Western pastors and church leaders must find the honesty and courage to step back from their own birth culture and begin to see the larger picture. Benedict could see the difficulty sixty years ago:

> The study of comparative cultures. . . cannot flourish when men are so defensive about their own way of life that it appears to them by definition the sole solution in the world. Such men will never know the added love of their own culture which comes from a knowledge of other ways of life.[2]

It is imperative to bring to the table an even-handedness and an openness in the inquiry into the varieties of cultural experience, otherwise, as Benedict suggests, we will be blind not only to the validity of other cultural options, but also blind to the true nature of our own culture.

Can we recognize and accept the reality of shame in the West? We could begin by accepting the validity of both guilt- *and* shame-oriented cultures. Already in 1953 Piers was questioning the idea that so-called guilt cultures would be more capable of progressive change than "shame cultures," the latter supposedly "static, industrially backwards, and dominated by "crowd psychology."[3] It is recognized historically that highly developed civilizations have emerged (e.g., Sumer and Egypt, and more recently Ottoman) among group-oriented cultures. Augsburger argues that in traditional societies shame matures into the "functional, responsible, outer-directed protection of one's own social persona and the careful integration of one's own needs, drives and goals with those of a community of peers," whereas in Western societies shame does not mature beyond the "global self-negation of early childhood" and is

---

[2] Benedict, *The Chrysanthemum and the Sword*, 16.
[3] Piers and Singers, *Shame and Guilt*, 45.

repressed as too painful to face.[4] In our cross-cultural explorations, our challenge is to set aside ignorance, inertia, discomfort, and prejudice and begin to address the issues thoughtfully.

The question being asked here is where, on the spectrum of dependency-independency models of culture, does the West really sit? On the surface, individualism is highly valued. The song, "I Did It My Way," seems to capture the mood, though ironically, the self-made man expects to be "honored" for his achievements. (And the self-made woman still receives mixed reviews!) We also need to ask whether the West is experiencing a cultural *shift* in this area and if so, in which direction. We may not feel at home in our present culture because it has changed from the culture into which we were born. Societies do change. For example, historians have documented the shift from shame to guilt as the emotion of social control in early New England.[5]

A chorus of commentators is now arguing that in our generation the West is shifting from a guilt orientation to a shame orientation. Benedict saw it coming. She notes the early Puritan influence towards guilt, then adds: "But shame is an increasingly heavy burden in the United States and guilt is less extremely felt than in earlier generations."[6] A decade later Piers noted a shift in the West from a high emphasis on guilt (that had climaxed in the Reformation) towards dynamics that tended to highlight shame.[7] Pembroke notes the shift, beginning in the late 1950s, in commonly presented

---

[4] Augsburger, *Conflict Mediation Across Cultures*, 131.
[5] Pattison, *Shame*, 34, 137.
[6] Benedict, *The Chrysanthemum and the Sword*, 223.
[7] Piers, *Shame and Guilt*, 37.

psychological disorders. Borderline conditions and character disorders were replacing neuroses and psychoses. Narcissism (cousin to shame) was one of the emerging presenters.[8] Rodney Clapp is another voice (1991), "Ours [U.S.] is a shame-based culture ashamed of shame."[9] Michael Lewis asserts (1992), "Our culture has become more shame driven as we have turned towards personal freedom and beyond it to narcissism."[10] It is also worth noting that when Patton wrote his helpful book on forgiveness in 1985 he felt he could not do justice to the subject without dealing extensively with shame.[11]

So as we reexamine the West with eyes now open to shame, we discover that the Western emperor also has no clothes! The so-called guilt orientation of the West turns out to be more myth than reality. Shame is an integral part of Western cultures. But if so many cultural observers are recognizing such a shift why is shame not on the church's radar? When did we last preach or hear a sermon that dealt helpfully with shame? This blindness to shame is, of course, the burden of this study as a whole. But it bears repeating that one of the problems with shame is this very hiddenness. Shame is ashamed of shame. So it is kept out of sight behind protective barriers.

Signs of the times
In honor-shame cultures, challenges to honor carry great weight. One of the signs of honor-shame dynamics in the West is unexpected levels of anger attached to seemingly minor conflicts. The phenomenon of road rage is a good example.

---

[8] Pembroke, "Toward a Shame-Based Theology of Evangelism," 16.

[9] Rodney Clapp, "Shame Crucified," *Christianity Today*, March 11, (1991): 26.

[10] M. Lewis, *Shame*, 216.

[11] Patton, *Is Human Forgiveness Possible?* 40.

Here we see the public threat to honor (and therefore nearness to shame). The intensity of road rage reflects the feeling of "global affront" (affront to person, not just behavior) typical of honor-shame culture. There is the need for immediate, public settlement. The settlement is face to face and despises legalities. (We don't need to call the police!) What is missing are the restraint mechanisms built into traditional group-oriented societies. Road rage may be compounded by the burden of disgrace shame. The enraged person feels his or her fragile sense of worth threatened. Unrestrained violence is the instinctive attempt to shake free from shame.

Speaking specifically of the United States, James Fowler argues that unacknowledged shame is one of the key factors in the American love affair with guns. Gun power supplies a sense of presence and authority that the deeply shamed person lacks.[12] Here Jewett's description of what he calls the "American monomyth" is helpful. The threat of evil on a helpless society is overcome by the redemptive violence of the superhero. The evil is manifest in the depth of shame imposed and drives the violence of the response.[13]

Osama bin Laden, following, naturally, the long-established honor-shame scripts of his own culture, struck at the honor of the United States, the "face," symbolized by the World Trade Center towers and the Pentagon. Curiously, the American response seems to have been to follow a similar honor-shame script. Honor had to be restored. Afghanistan (a terrorist stronghold), was taken, but little honor was regained from conquering such a humble enemy. The Iraq venture

---

[12] James Fowler, *Faithful Change: The Personal and Public Challenges of Postmodern Life* (Nashville, TN: Abingdon Press, 1996), 216f.
[13] Jewett, *St. Paul Returns to the Movies*, 154.

(though likely irrelevant to the so-called "war on terror") seems to have been driven in part by a need to reclaim honor.

The fact that the venture may not have seemed honorable to outsiders is irrelevant. Honor has its own internal logic. As J. Davis points out: "Honor is local, it cannot be measured or assessed except very roughly, by an outside observer."[14] Honor is manufactured and consumed locally for local tastes. Translated into the language of modern politics this means that the only verdict that counts is the verdict of the voter. Thus outsiders are puzzled by the term "un-American." They cannot give more than an approximate definition. They realize they are encountering honor language.

A confusing place for men

One of the areas where shame is surfacing is in the so-called men's movement. Men are admitting to a hollowness that bravado will not mend. In the book *Men Healing Shame*[15] various writers discuss shame that is peculiar to men. In part, they claim, this arises from inappropriate expectations placed on men from childhood. One interpretation of this is that the rules have changed because the culture has changed. While some psychologists point out that women tend to be more shame prone because they are more *field* or *context* oriented than men, shame clearly is a big problem for men.[16] John Everingham asserts: "American men are particularly vulnerable to shaming, and almost oblivious to its pervasive presence and

---

[14] J. Davis, quoted by John K. Chance, "The Anthropology of Honor and Shame: Culture, Values, and Practice," *Semeia,* 68 (1996): 145.

[15] Roy Schenk and John Everingham, eds., *Men Healing Shame: An Anthology* (New York: Springer Pub. Co., 1995).

[16] M. Lewis, *Shame,* 10; Pattison, *Is Human Forgiveness Possible?*, 87.

effects."[17] Francis Baumli suggests that one way to get men talking about shame is to simply ask, "Why are you ashamed?" The floodgates open.[18]

As the culture of the West shifts, it is not necessarily the man of integrity who will make an attractive leader. What matters is that the leader be strong, or heroic. Thus a man like Arnold Schwarzenegger, first elected governor of California in 2003, emerges as the perfect leader in a culture increasingly oriented toward honor and shame. As the head of the tribe, he promises to uphold the honor of the tribe. Moral purity is not the primary concern for voters unless misdemeanors undermine the ability to hold power. In fact sexual prowess increases honor. One of the paradoxes of unconverted honor-shame scripts is that men preserve their honor by guarding the purity of their own women, but they accumulate honor by sexual conquest out on the field. No wonder men are confused.

Goodhue asks, "Why is Christianity so irrelevant to masculinity?" His answer is that the church's emphasis on sin and guilt and a neglect of shame are key factors. He argues that society's expectation of men—to succeed, to achieve goals— sets men up for the shame of failure. The church does not meet their shame needs.[19] What can now be added, two decades later, is that the emergence of an honor-shame orientation has so changed the rules of the game that men are threatened at the point of identity. What does it mean to be a man? Nevertheless, the Christian message properly understood, does bring hope. As we will see, the Gospel *rewrites* human cultural scripts and

[handwritten margin notes: "Donald Trump?", "??", "and women are used"]

---

[17] John Everingham, "Some Basics About Shame," in Schenk and Everingham, eds., *Men Healing Shame*, 3.

[18] Francis Baumli, "On Men, Guilt, and Shame," in Schenk and Everingham, eds., *Men Healing Shame*.

[19] Goodhue, "Shame," 57f.

in so doing provides a renewed foundation for identity and sustainable models of leadership.

Exposing the myth

Creighton, in her evaluation of Benedict's Japanese study, makes this observation:

> Americans are more likely to view morality in absolute terms based on principles of right and wrong that are not considered to vary with the situation. Japanese morality tends to judge the value of an act in a situational context based on its impact on significant relationships.[20]

If this observation were broadened to contrast Japan with the West generally, there would be widespread nodding of heads. But again, this needs to be challenged. Is Creighton describing things as they really are? Or is she describing the way we like to think we are? Is the individualism of the West and its concomitant guilt orientation more myth (perhaps wish) than reality?

The truth is that shame never did disappear. It was simply driven underground. It was too messy for the tidy categories of modernity to manage. But the West has gone through a kind of cultural mid life crisis and shame will no longer be hidden. The time has come to admit complexities that are deeper than guilt, that question not merely human actions, but human identity. Though twenty years ago shame could be described as taboo,[21] today it is on the table. Or at least it is on the table in the secular world. It now needs to become table talk in the church.

---

[20] Creighton, "Revisiting Shame and Guilt Cultures," 297.

[21] Gershen Kaufman and Raphael R. Browne, "Shame as Taboo in American Culture," in *Forbidden Fruits: Taboos and Tabooism in Culture,* Raphael R. Browne, ed. (Bowling Green, OH: Popular Press, 1984).

The Western church has woken up to find "the bed is too short . . . the covering too narrow" (Isaiah 28:20).

The road to understanding and recovery begins with naming shame. Thankfully the work of recognition and acceptance has begun. Now it is time to move forward. But first it is helpful to examine some of the factors that have led to the prominence of shame in the West, in order to broaden our perspective.

The Roots of Shame in the West

I believe we must not only become more aware of shame themes in Western culture, but we must also be more alert to the *increase* in the role of shame. A cultural shift is under way. Here now, under three headings, are comments on the roots of this cultural shift. First some general considerations, then a brief look at the effects of modernity and its collapse, finally: What part has the church of the West played in this?

General considerations

If shame orientation is, as I have suggested, the default setting of human communities, why did the West venture into guilt orientation? And why now this move back? It is helpful to remember that culturally, shame orientation emerges in face-to-face settings, in other words, small groups, extended families, kinship and tribal groupings. As Western society developed, traditional groupings were increasingly fragmented, especially with the increase in mobility and the rise of nationalism. Modern industrial times brought large cities, increasing diversity and easy mobility. These populations may have been grouped under one flag, but they were much too large to be face-to-face communities. As Pitt-Rivers notes: "The force of public opinion is diminished when it is no longer omniscient."[22] In addition, there was the growth of political, financial, and personal freedom. The tightly prescribed roles of the kinship group gave way to seemingly endless possibilities for personal choice and opportunity. Individuality and low-context dynamics began to predominate, giving shame a lower profile.

Nevertheless, this venture into individualism was a venture into unknown territory. How far could it be pushed? Fast forward now to our present generation. It seems there are limits beyond which individualism becomes unhealthy. Christopher Lasch, observing the United States context, speaks of a "failure of nerve." Economics, history, philosophy all give up the attempt to describe what is, to tell only "how I feel about things." Individualism has collapsed into narcissism.[23] And narcissism is near neighbor to shame. Capps lists some characteristics of narcissism including: a pervasive pattern of grandiosity, a hypersensitivity to the evaluation of others, a feeling of unworthiness, and an impairment of relationships.[24] Thus, ironically, as the cultural pendulum swung across to individualism, shame moved from social function to psychological dysfunction. Furthermore, while, at the personal level shame was raising its ugly head in the form of narcissism, at the level of popular culture some honor-shame values were also returning. So, for example, the story of the rescue of U.S.

---

[22] Pitt-Rivers, "Honour and Social Status," 61.

[23] Christopher Lasch, *The Culture of Narcissism: American Life in an Age of Diminishing Expectations* (New York: Routledge, 1979), 17f.

[24] Capps, *The Depleted Self*, 12f.

soldier Jessica Lynch in the Iraq war in 2003 was rescripted to fit the honor-shame tastes of home consumption.[25] And, as we have already observed, there is the shift to more "heroic" leadership styles.

We could ask, why do Western nations now seem to behave like honor-shame societies when they are too large and complex to fit the traditional pattern? It may be that mass media, in particular TV, has created a pseudo-face-to-face community. For example, an estimated 5 million people watched the final episode of the TV show *Friends*. Each viewer became part of an intimate extended family! So whole nations live in a virtual village, watching and weighing the actions of their chief. Will he maintain honor for the tribe? Thus, at the same time as individualism is taking its toll at the personal level, leaving people lost, relationally disconnected, fragile as persons and vulnerable to shame, at the macro level, cultural honor-shame dynamics, perhaps aided by modern mass communication, reemerges.

Modernity and postmodernity

It is helpful to consider shame and its shifting cultural role against the backdrop of discussions of modernity and post-modernity. The ethos of modernity with its idolatry of reason, science and individualism was barren ground for the study of shame. Shame would not even surface before the impersonal, detached, objective gaze of modernity's observers. And if it had, shame would have been too messy and personal to fit modernity's rigid categories. Shame intercepts the defining

---

[25] See, for example, *The Guardian*, Thursday, May 15, 2003.

qualities of human life: speech, disclosure, acceptance, intimacy, and community.

Schneider comments that modernity's reductionist world left shame out. He illuminates this from another angle. Shame and awe are closely connected. The modern world saw everything through the lens of technology and utility, thus to be explored without restraint. Earlier times recognized mystery that needed to be respected. That recognition, however, was lost in modernity: "We are caught up in limitless self-assertion—that is, shamelessness." He adds: "A sense of shame . . . respects the veiled nature of truth."[26] And so, curiously, while shame as a *topic* was off the table, shameful *behavior* was the order of the day in the immodest rush to pull back every last curtain.

But human nature rebelled at the straitjacket of modernity. A metanarrative built on such a reductionist foundation had to be deconstructed. Thus both at the philosophical level and at the level of popular culture, the West has entered a postmodern phase that has proven to be a more congenial environment for the study of the paradox and mystery of shame. A book such as this would have been very difficult to write thirty years ago.

There are two sides to this coin, however. As the emphasis has shifted from the individual life (in modernity) to the relational life (in postmodernity), shame, a fundamental dynamic of the relational life, has resurfaced. Thus while post-modernity opened the way for a greater *awareness* of shame, it appears also to have contributed to an increased *experience* of shame.

---

[26] Schneider, *Shame, Exposure and Privacy*, ix, 111, 121.

This is the argument. In postmodernity, ontology was replaced by hermeneutics. We no longer, at the level of culture, have the courage (or audacity) to simply declare what is. What we see depends on our interpretation. Truth becomes a matter of perspective. The problem here is that we ourselves are inside the circle. Within this hermeneutical atmosphere, our own human identity loses its fixity. Our identity now rests on the interpretation of others. How am I seen by my group? This is the big question. But it is also a place of great vulnerability, for to be seen negatively is to be shamed.

To take this a little further, it is often pointed out that one result of this cultural development we call postmodernity has been the "retribalization" of society as common interest groups huddle to establish a private context in a fragmented, post-metanarrative landscape. The postmodern loss of the center and suspicion of institution raises again the importance of the small group and face-to-face relationships.

At street level this is reflected in the proliferation of "communities": the gay community, the ex-con community, the diplomatic community, the homeless community, the various ethnic communities, and the like. If honor-shame orientation is the default setting of tribal cultures, this retribalization will further contribute to the rise in shame orientation in our day. As small, manageable common-interest groups are carved out of mass society, "face-to-faceness," the context of shame orientation, reemerges.

Shame is a crisis in personal ontology. And the hermeneutical environment of postmodernity simply favors shame. The burden of postmodernity is that "I" have the terrible, lone responsibility for defining reality, including the reality about myself. The bedrock of absolutes has melted away. There is no wall to put my back against. I am painfully exposed. Naturally, against this we rebel. We long to be an "I am," consciously or unconsciously echoing the great "I Am" in whose image we are made. The answer to this ontological crisis, at the level of the individual as well as the level of culture, is to rediscover the good news that, in a relational knowledge of God, made possible through Jesus Christ, it is possible to rediscover a secure place of being—an anchorage. The context of postmodernity, and the reemergence of shame, prompts us to reexamine a widely discarded narrative—the Christian faith.

The role of the church

We cannot understand the emergence of the West without taking into account the influence of the Christian faith. Christianity has been a major player in shaping every aspect of the culture of the West. So it is important to probe the relationship between the Christian faith and the role of shame in Western culture. But first a word on the impact of mono-theism on the relation of the individual to the group.

In high-context (shame-oriented) groups the individual is embedded in the group. The identity of the individual has little significance outside the context of the group. The early civilizations of Sumer and Egypt were high context. The individual was not differentiated from the group. As one, they lived before the gods, who were also a high-context group. But the Jewish experience was different. They were confronted with one God. This personal God called forth the personhood of the individual who could and must stand forth from the community (for example: Abraham, Moses, and Job). This does not mean Israel was already an individualist society. This is a relative change. Biblical cultures retain their group orientation and exhibit the typical honor-shame dynamics of such groups, but there was a pulling away from deep embeddedness towards the emergence of the individual.

Jump ahead to the 1500s. Here, with the rise of Protestantism, the pendulum is pushed sharply towards the individual and thus low-context culture. Luther is a key figure in this shift. Luther's own personal searching and agonizing over guilt shaped the DNA of the Protestant world. So we have, for example, the studies of Wallbott and Scherer that connect guilt orientation to "Protestant ethic" countries ("Sweden, Norway, Finland, New Zealand, U.S.") and shame orientation to "not Protestant ethic" countries ("Mexico . . . France, Spain, Portugal, Greece.") They also describe the non-Protestant-ethic countries as experiencing a clearer distinction between shame and guilt, with shame being acute but short-lived and having less long-term effect. In the Protestant ethic cultures, shame blends into guilt and has a more lasting effect on self-esteem.[27]

Protestant theology followed Luther's lead and emphasized guilt and the Gospel response of justification by faith and imputed righteousness. It was a needed emphasis. But in the process, shame dropped out of sight. In fact shame is almost totally absent in Western theology. Bonhoeffer makes a small contribution. Besides this there is little else.

But there is another twist to this plot. Protestantism developed a symbiotic relationship with the emerging condition of modernity. Protestants somehow felt obliged to play by the reductionist rules of modernity. So Christianity was presented

---

[27] Harald G. Wallbott and Klaus R. Scherer, "Cultural Determinates in Experiencing Shame and Guilt," in Tangney and Fischer, eds. (1995), 465f.

in increasingly rationalistic and individualistic terms. Since guilt is easier to manage, it was natural for the managerial ethos of modernity to nudge pastors into being managers of guilt. (It only takes four spiritual laws to resolve guilt!) Shame was ignored. It did not make it onto the Protestant agenda. Melba Maggay, writing insightfully out of the Filipino (high-context culture) perspective, comments on the way Western Christianity has centered on guilt. "Over time, the Christian religion increasingly became the means by which guilt could be relieved, a sort of 'laundering venture,' as Camus put it."[28] Thus Protestantism and modernity conspired together to move western culture towards individualism and guilt orientation.

But this was not to last. We have already commented on the waning of modernity. At the same time, as the twentieth century was drawing to a close, Christian influence and presence in the West also declined dramatically, particularly in its Protestant manifestation. The center of gravity of Christendom shifted to the Southern and Eastern hemispheres. Hultberg is just one voice attributing the movement from a guilt culture to a shame culture (in the West), to the "decline of conventional Christianity in the western world."[29]

One silver lining in the dust cloud of departing Christendom is the wonderful opportunity to rethink theology and ministry in terms of grace for shame. Indeed it is an imperative. Clapp may overstate his case when he writes: "Christian theology has well-developed theologies of guilt, while the majority of its constituency is struggling with the

---

[28] Melba P. Maggay, "Towards Sensitive Engagement with Filipino Indigenous Conscience," *International Review of Mission,* 87 (344) (1998): 364.
[29] Hultberg, "Shame—A Hidden Emotion," 114.

debilitating, demoralizing, and even de-humanizing effects of shame."[30] Nevertheless, there is a need for a theological repentance, given the way Protestant formulations and practices have contributed to the problems of dysfunctional shame. The passing of both modernity and Western Christendom has opened new doors for the ministry of God's grace.

Though Christians may mourn the loss of modernity, and the good that came with it, there is reason to believe that the postmodern environment is encouraging some healthy correctives in the Christian world. For example, insofar as modernity recognized God, the emphasis was on the unity of God. This echoed the individualism of modernity. It is interesting to note in this new climate the upsurge in the study and awareness of God as Trinity, a concept emphasizing both interrelatedness and paradox. This relational, eternally self giving Trinitarian God is much more attractive (and healing) for the shamed person.[31]

There is a widespread concern in the Christian community today over shallow conversions and stalled spiritual transformations. It is sometimes put this way: "Why is the church 1000 miles wide and only ½ inch deep?" For some the problem is the lack of a "good beginning" (i.e., shallow conversions.)[32] For some the answer is revival. Some call for a return to the practice of spiritual disciplines.[33] Surely all

---

[30] Clapp, "Shame Crucified," 35.

[31] See Jung Young Lee, *The Trinity in Asian Perspective* (Nashville, TN: Abingdon Press, 1996).

[32] Gordon T. Smith, *Beginning Well: Christian Conversion & Authentic Transformation* (Downers Grove, IL: InterVarsity Press, 2001).

[33] For example, Dallas Willard, *The Divine Conspiracy: Rediscovering Our Hidden Life in God* (San Francisco, CA: HarperSanFrancisco, 1998).

address the problem. But to these we add the need to come to terms with shame in all its manifestations.

It now appears that a significant cause of spiritual shallowness is our fixation on guilt, and our corresponding neglect of shame, in ministering the Gospel. As Noble pointed out, this may well lie at the root of Bonhoeffer's concern over "cheap grace," which is "the justification of sin without the justification of the sinner."[34] Again we ask: When will sermons be preached that deal helpfully and healingly with shame? When will church leaders understand the power of church communities to be places of healing (or harm) for shame? There is an urgent need to recover the fullness of the Gospel both at the level of theological formulation and at the level of practical ministry. We have good news for shame. Let's get the word out!

Insights from Missiology

We are almost at the point where it is possible to re-examine life in the church and parish from the perspective of shame. The questions that need to be asked are now becoming apparent. We have gained valuable insight from studies of other cultures, as well as from a review of psychology and more broadly a review of Western cultural and religious shifts. But before we turn back to reexamine Western ministry settings, there is help to be gleaned from one more corner. This is the field of missiology. It turns out that the missiologists, because the nature of their work compels them to think from

---

[34] Noble, *Naked and Not Ashamed,* 80.

the perspective of other cultures, have made great strides in understanding what the Gospel means for shame. Here are five helpful questions missiology has taught us to ask.

1. Are we willing to accept the reality of other perspectives?
As we have already seen, the challenge of accepting that there are other cultural perspectives, and that they are just as valid as our own, is no small matter. To quote Benedict again in her wisdom:

> The lenses through which any nation looks at life are not the ones another nation uses. Any country takes them for granted, and the tricks of focusing and of perspective which give to any people its national view of life seem to that people the god-given arrangement of the landscape.[35]

Here is a simple example. A number of students come from the U.S. to study in Canada. The transition appears simple. The language is the same, the food is the same, the currency works the same way, the electrical voltage is the same. Then November comes around, and U.S. Thanksgiving Day is just another day of classes. Nobody knows or cares that it might be an important day for these foreigners. It is at this point that many U.S. students suffer classic culture shock as they are forced to give up the fiction of sameness and come to terms with difference.

It may take this kind of cultural shock treatment to open our eyes to deeper, subtler variances of other cultures. Furthermore, as I have already argued, we need to come to terms with the fact that not only has the Western cultural world changed because of immigration of other cultures, the West's

---

[35] Benedict, *The Chrysanthemum and the Sword*, 14.

own culture has shifted. We may still be living in the same house but our cultural context has changed.

Do we have eyes to see this new world? There is no simple formula here. It will take time to learn to read other cultures. For example we cannot assume similar emotions will be expressed in similar ways in other social contexts. What are the major topographical features we should be on the lookout for? Two important clues are the level of connectedness and the importance of the group in relation to the individual.

2. Can we distinguish the Gospel from Western culture?

As we have already seen, Filipina theologian Maggay offers some hard-hitting but necessary advice in her valuable article entitled "Towards Sensitive Engagement with Filipino Indigenous Consciousness." This is a wake-up call for those Western missionaries who have been blind to the extent their Gospel has been embedded in Western culture. By ignoring the complexities of Filipino culture and worldview, Christianity has achieved only a superficial engagement in the Filipino consciousness.

Maggay reviews the Western emphasis on intellectualism, individualism, clock-time, and the secular-sacred split, that are more western than biblical and do not connect with the Filipino mind. She specifically addresses the Western Christian emphasis on guilt. She writes: "The Filipino conscience is not tortured by the kind of guilt known by Martin Luther." For Filipinos the sense of wrongness focuses on ruptured relationships. She suggests framing a theology of sin as "rupture of koinonia" rather than rule breaking. Maggay's analysis ranges beyond the present topic, but what is relevant here is her insight into the need for a reexamination of the role guilt plays in different cultures and her contention that the Gospel story is so "rich" that no one summary will capture its essence.[36] Here is missiological insight from the other side. We need to pay attention.

Roland Muller models the kind of cultural awareness needed. In his book *Honor and Shame: Unlocking the Door*, he argues that the reason the Gospel has made such small inroads into the Muslim world is not so much that the people are particularly resistant but that we have preached a message better suited to Western culture. For example, he points out that the "Four Spiritual Laws" and the "Roman Road" presentations of the Gospel, while working well, at least in the past, in Western, guilt-oriented cultures, have little meaning for people in shame-oriented cultures.[37] Muller's careful study of honor and shame in both Scripture and Middle Eastern settings should be required reading for Western pastors also in the third millennium.

3. Do we understand the difficulty of being different?
Here is a very practical matter. We need to think about the challenges involved for individuals in high-context cultures to "come to the front," or to "stand up for Jesus" in any sense. People of high-context, shame-oriented cultures are by definition highly attuned to how others see them. Feelings of shame occur when an individual fails to meet the approval of

---

[36] Maggay, "Towards Sensitive Engagement with Filipino Indigenous Conscience," 361f.

[37] Roland Muller, *Honor and Shame: Unlocking the Door* (Bloomington, IN: XLibris Corporation, 2000), 36f.

the group. The others do not even have to be present. The fear is of separation and abandonment.[38]

These cultures place a high value on group harmony and "smooth relationships." Decisions of individuals are strongly affected by the impact of the group. Individuals are highly uncomfortable making decisions that deviate from the norm. In group-oriented cultures individuals will find it difficult to stand apart from the group and call Jesus Lord in a way that means something for them as individuals. This is a major ministry challenge for Western pastors serving in a mixed-culture context. The answer is not to try to turn everyone into Western individualists. (That won't happen anyway!) But it does mean we have to acknowledge these practicalities of high-context cultures.

The other side of this coin is that if the "tribe" converts, all of the individuals are swept along with the group. Is this a problem? It was not for Patrick in fifth-century Ireland, evangelizing a whole country village by village. And it was not for Paul with his "household" conversions (e.g., Acts 16:31). What we need is at least an awareness of the undercurrents, in our mixed and changing culture setting.

4. Are we able to present the "Old Old Story" in fresh words?
As Malina writes, the "theological problem has been and continues to be how to make known the goodness of Jesus in terms of the ever-kaleidoscoping cultural scripts that cover the world like a crazy quilt."[39] For some cultures it is simply difficult to appreciate the need for the Savior we offer. In Asian

---

[38] Young Gweon You, "Shame and Guilt Mechanisms in East Asian Culture," *The Journal of Pastoral Care,* 51 (1) (1997): 58f.

[39] Malina, *The New Testament World,* 184.

homes, for example, the child grows up within a well-defined extended family structure. The child is never out of touch with the external authority. Korean writer Young G. You suggests that as a result, the conscience is undeveloped. Behavior is molded by group acceptance and belonging.[40] How does this affect Gospel preaching? It is not obvious to these people that they need to be forgiven for their sin. They do not feel guilt as a problem.

What happens to the traditional categories of Gospel presentation in a shame-oriented culture? Again Benedict is very helpful:

> In a culture where shame is a major sanction, people are chagrined about acts which we expect people to feel guilty about. This chagrin can be very intense and it cannot be relieved, as guilt can be, by confession and atonement . . . Where shame is the major sanction, a man does not experience relief when he makes his fault public even to a confessor . . . confession appears to him merely a way of courting trouble. Shame cultures therefore do not provide for confessions, even to the gods. They have ceremonies for good luck rather than for expiation.[41]

In fact, in shame cultures to *forgive* someone may well be a way of reinforcing the shame, since it is a way of acknowledging the other's badness.[42] Goodhue concurs: "Unlike guilt feelings, which may vanish upon confession, shame often increases with exposure."[43] It is the burden of

---

[40] Young Gweon You, "Shame and Guilt Mechanisms in East Asian Culture," 60.

[41] Benedict, *The Chrysanthemum and the Sword*, 223.

[42] E. G. Singgih, "Let Me Not Be Put to Shame: Towards an Indonesian Hermeneutics," *Asia Journal of Theology*, 9 (1) (1995): 78.

[43] Goodhue, "Shame," 59.

shame, not guilt, that is their point of need. They feel the need of a savior, but a savior to deliver them from shame, not guilt.

Almost three decades have passed since Timothy Boyle wrote about his attempts to communicate the Gospel faithfully in the shame-oriented Japanese culture. He notes the difficulty in even finding a meaningful translation for terms like sin and forgiveness. But he did find it helpful to emphasize the role of shame in Genesis chapter three. Christ's covering of righteousness is thus the final answer to human nakedness. God takes responsibility for human shame (as a parent would do on behalf of children's shame.) God took a "deep bow" humbling himself in the incarnation and death, even laying down his life, to "restore face" to humanity.[44]

Moving to another arena, Bruce Thomas asks, "Have we failed to reach Muslims at their point of deepest insecurity?" In working with Muslims, he came to realize that their major concern is not sin but defilement. Thus guilt (which relates to sin) is less of a concern than shame (which relates to defilement). (Interestingly, Pattison, in his study of shame, frequently makes this link between shame and defilement, although he does not seem to be aware of this missiological connection.) From his understanding of the Muslim mind-set Thomas began rereading Scripture and discovered much that speaks to the Muslim concern. He writes: "Could it be that the purpose of these [Levitical] laws was to draw attention to man's defiled condition in the same way that the sacrifices drew attention to his sinful condition?"[45] Hebrews 9:13-14

---

[44] Timothy D. Boyle, "Communicating the Gospel in Terms of Shame," *Japanese Christian Quarterly*, 50 (1984).

[45] Bruce Thomas (pseudonym), "The Gospel for Shame Cultures: Have We Failed to Reach Muslims at Their Point of Deepest Insecurity?" *Evangelical Missions Quarterly*, 30 (1) (1994): 289.

indicates that Jesus' work on the cross removed human defilement as well as human sin. Thus Thomas relates the Gospel to shame by relating it to deliverance from defilement. Summing up he writes: "This defilement may form the basis for shame, insecurity, and a felt need for the Gospel in shame cultures."[46]

Bill Musk also addresses the problem of how the Gospel connects for Muslims.[47] He argues for the importance of understanding the primacy of honor and shame in ministry among Muslims of the Middle East. He lists the sources of honor: hard earned prosperity brings honor, age brings honor, sexually pure women bring honor, and generosity and hospitality bring honor. In the lives of Middle Eastern people, shame avoidance, or saving face, is central. Gossip is the policing mechanism, since public exposure is the very nature of shame. In fact a lie, or a promise of the impossible, is an acceptable way to maintain honor. There can be no talk of peace until some sense of honor is regained.

From his acquaintance with Middle Eastern culture Musk notes the importance of honor in the Bible:

> 'Sinning' tends to be perceived according to the evidence of the Bible, as the violation of honor. Such a perception is not just a fact of popular culture but is part of the authoritative teaching of the revealed text.[48]

He notes how the death of Jesus is presented in terms of honor and shame (e.g., Hebrews 12:2). Musk observes that the Western emphasis is on the "horizontal relationship" between

---

[46] Ibid., 288.
[47] Bill A. Musk, "Honor and Shame," *Evangelical Review of Theology*, 20 (1996).
[48] Ibid., 162.

Jesus and humanity: in other words, God's *agape* love. He argues, however, that an emphasis on the "vertical relationship" demonstrating Christ's loyalty to the Father resonates more deeply with the Muslim heart: *Christ vindicates the Father's honor.* Musk points out that this vertical relationship is in fact the dominant theme in the Gospels and in the missionary sermons of Acts.

In these and other ways the frontline evangelists challenge us to be more creative in presenting the Old Old Story. This is not about departing from Scripture. It is essential that our salvation theology rests on a strong biblical foundation. Yet, as we will see, it turns out that we can bring new questions to the Scriptures and discover there new answers and fresh ways of presenting the Christian Gospel.

5. Are we willing to be 150 percent culture persons?
These missiological perspectives are valuable because they help Western pastors and church leaders feel cultural differences. This is necessary because in the twenty-first century, the West itself has become a mosaic of cultures. Modern cities are becoming increasingly diverse. Furthermore, Western culture is beginning to feel alien to home-grown people, as deep shifts are under way.

Judith and Sherwood Lingenfelter's concept of the "150 percent culture person" is helpful at this point. This is a call to begin to live and think beyond the perimeters of our own culture. It involves two movements: first an attempt to reduce the expression of one's own culture (say to 75 percent); and second to stretch aggressively towards the understanding and behaviors of the target culture (never fully achievable, but possibly 75 percent over time). Jesus, in his incarnation, is the great model in this.[49]

In terms of ministering grace for shame, this kind of cultural recalibration is essential. How easy it is to *generate* shame in cross-cultural situations! As Augsburger points out, "Routine behavior in one culture can be ruthless behavior in another."[50] Opportunities for miscommunication are endless. Musk notes the ambiguity of a servant spirit in different cultures. Honor-shame cultures see menial work as shameful. Pastors who roll up their sleeves and wash dishes may be seen as squandering their honor and thus an embarrassment to the members of the church![51] True, such aversion to servant leadership will need to be challenged by Gospel values. The culture of the Kingdom of God, and here the example of Jesus' own servant-leadership, must be allowed to confront all cultures. But the astute pastor will be sensitive to the cultural dynamics and pick his fights wisely!

The 150 percent culture person will read the Scripture in new ways. As Maggay asserts, "Third World Christians insist that there is no 'unengaged' reading of Scripture; all need to exercise some degree of 'hermeneutical suspicion.'"[52] We must ask, "Whose glasses are we wearing?" as we pick up the Bible.

But this counsel must not be heard as restrictive. It turns out, in fact, to be a journey of discovery. As Scripture is read through the eyes of brothers and sisters from other cultures, we discover new Gospel riches we never knew existed. We stumble on streams of grace for which our own hearts have

---

[49] Lingenfelter, *Teaching Cross-Culturally*, 23.
[50] Augsburger, *Conflict Mediation Across Cultures*, 112.
[51] Musk, "Honour and Shame," 157.
[52] Maggay, "Towards Sensitive Engagement with Filipino Indigenous Conscience," 361.

been thirsty. A sensitivity to different cultures compels us to re-read the Gospel and rediscover the extent of its fullness.

Shame in the Life of the Church

Consider this snapshot from the life of one urban pastor:

> The first call of the morning came from Roberto. "Pastor, do you have time? I need to see you." The pastor remembered that Roberto had arrived in the city nine years earlier. He had come as a refugee from Nicaragua, but he had adapted well to his new home. What could be the problem? A half hour later Roberto was sitting across from the pastor. He had never seen Roberto this subdued. Usually he was confident, even cocky, always smiling, ready with a quick word. Now he seemed broken, struggling to get his story out, head down, no eye contact. Was he losing his English?
>
> Roberto worked nights at a seniors' home doing security, janitorial work, and odd repairs. In his office he had the use of a computer. During maintenance to that computer it was discovered Roberto had accessed an internet porn site. He had been called in to the supervisor's office over the matter. Roberto claimed he had not intended to click on that page and exited as soon as he realized what was going on. The supervisor made it clear that viewing internet sex sites was incompatible with a job with this level of responsibility. Roberto assured her that he would be very careful in future.
>
> As Roberto told his story the pastor listened and prayed, wondering how to respond. Clearly Roberto didn't need to have the problem of internet pornography explained to him. And he wasn't coming with a confession. Furthermore there was no need for anxiety about losing the job. Yet there he was,

shaken to the core; he hadn't slept for 24 hours. The pastor was puzzled. They prayed together, but the pastor wasn't sure how to pray. He felt uneasy, a little embarrassed, even somewhat irritated. He had a sense of unfinished business. Something was still hanging, but he didn't know what. More than two years went by before the pastor saw Roberto again. . .

Our goal is to minister the grace of God with greater wisdom. In particular we are seeking to understand what grace means for shame-oriented people. Shame is a multi-dimensional concern. Thus we have tried to broaden our perspective through a multidisciplinary approach. We have already seen that not all shame is bad. Yes, there is toxic or dysfunctional shame that cries out for relief; but there is also good shame, which operates as a kind of modesty that is more or less prominent, depending on cultural type. With these thoughts in mind, it is time to probe the undercurrents of shame in the local congregation.

Toxic shame in the church

One way to unearth toxic shame in the church is simply to ask about it. One man, now in his fifties, talked about growing up in a home that was Christian but was filled with shame. The roots of his shame went back at least two generations. His grandmother had divorced her first husband, an alcoholic. She remarried, but the first child from this relationship was born before the wedding took place. In the early 1900s this was scandal upon scandal. The grandparents had to leave town.

The family attempted to cope with the shame by a code of secrecy. The children were not aware of their biological parentage until well into their adult years. The grandmother lived with the constant threat of exposure. Furthermore, the family also attempted to relieve shame with perfectionism. Family life ran according to strict rules aimed at being "better Christians." There was love, but it was always conditional. This man felt that the influence of this shame extended to the great-grandchildren. He even wondered if being Christian might have been part of the problem. "If they had not been Christians then the idea of divorce might not have been such a terrible thing. It is hard to forgive yourself if you believe that you have done such a terrible thing that God will not forgive you."

What would the ministry of grace look like for this family? This question will be addressed more fully later. The first step, however, is to be aware of the problem. And, once again, it is precisely here that shame is so difficult to deal with. Shame, by definition is about hiddenness. Though people may speak easily, even at times eagerly, about guilt, driven by the need to confess and make restitution, they are reluctant to talk about shame. They may not even be aware that they have shame. They may not have the vocabulary or the concepts to express themselves in terms of shame.

The first step in assessing shame in the congregation is realizing that it does not live on the surface. The above story came to light in a situation where trust was developed and shame was already out in the open as an acceptable topic of conversation. Though a few stories will emerge in this way, we can assume there is much that lies hidden behind the pain of shame.

Nancy Ramsay reports that in the U.S. thirty percent of girls and fifteen percent of boys are sexually molested before the age of eighteen. By "molest" she means not only explicit intercourse. She defines the term to also include covert sexual seduction that violates personal and sexual boundaries. Sexual abuse is psychologically crippling and shame is a central factor. Ramsay writes:

> Shame organizes the psychological reality of adults molested as children. . . . Sexual abuse is particularly destructive for spirituality because the locus of violation and shame is the body itself. Alienation from one's bodied self is crippling for any experience of spirituality. . . .[53]

Ministry for shame calls for an awareness of the effects of sexual abuse, as well as other abuses. Simply acknowledging that not every home, even a Christian home, was perfect, can give permission for people to talk. Healing begins when the secret can be brought out into the open.

It may be noted here, too, the difference age makes. Older generations are still strongly shaped by the atmosphere of modernity that informed their youth. It will be very difficult for these good folk to come to the point of awareness and expression of shame. The children of postmodernity will deal with shame more freely.

Shame clogs the arteries

One indication of shame is that confession and forgiveness seem to exacerbate the problem instead of relieving it. In these circumstances confession is functioning as a further exposure of self, rather than a way of dealing with specific actions. This is part of what is going on with Roberto in the vignette above.

---

[53] Nancy Ramsay, "Sexual Abuse and Shame," in *Women in Travail and Transition,* Maxine Glaz and Jeanne Stevenson, eds. (Minneapolis, MN: Fortress Press, 1991), 110f., 112f.

We must also be alert to toxic shame when people speak in terms of global negative self-valuation. For example, rather than saying, "I did something wrong," they say, "I always mess up," or simply "I am a mess." Shame-bound people lump everything into their being. They cannot separate who they are from what they do. It is also important to be tuned in to the physical symptoms of shame, the lack of eye contact, the body curved in on itself, the person slipping in and out of a back pew. In conversation we may notice: a difficulty in expressing who "I am" directly, a scarcity of "I" statements, feelings of alienation, rejection, inadequacy, pollution, and a limited ability to vocalize.

We quickly discover as we talk to people that although some shame is the direct result of sin, some is not. It may be the result of another person's sin, or it may simply be the result of distorted values (e.g., the shame of baldness, or short stature). Many in the congregation will identify with Roberta Bondi:

> "Hardly any of my misery from childhood on had come from my own badness. Rather it came from my shame at not living up to harmful yet typical family standards, shame at being female in a world that curled its lip at women, and shame over my unworthiness of the sacrifices that had characterized my mother's life as a divorced woman with children."[54]

We notice too that not only do shame-based people find it difficult to receive forgiveness, they also find it difficult to forgive others. They demand a scapegoat. They project their own global self-evaluations onto others. A shame orientation

---

[54] Roberta Bondi, "Out of the Green-Tiled Bathroom: Crucifixion," *Weavings*, 9 (1994): 26.

lies behind the letter to the pastor that offers a negative global assessment ("you are a 'such-and-such' kind of a person") rather than dealing with issues and specifics.

Shame ranges from the sense of a loss of honor in the eyes of others to a sense of profound unwantedness. When people withdraw from interactive participation in the life of the congregation we must be alert to shame as a likely underlying issue. Shame is destructive to community. Shame may well be hiding behind other behaviors: indecisiveness, excessive people pleasing, unrealistic pride, power hunger, rage, and flat emotions. Shame reduces risk tolerance, failure is too costly. Thus there is a loss of a sense of adventure, inner fire, enthusiasm. The shamed life is a "constricted life."[55]

Since shame is a relational dynamic, it helps to be aware of the role of shame in the relational *system*. Shame-prone adults will continue to gravitate towards relationships and situations that feed their own shame and promote shame in others. Pastors and church leaders need to be alert to group dynamics that promote shame, such as the proliferation of secrets and inside information, a climate of perfectionism and legalism, and difficulty separating issues from people.

Since shame-based people have no clear sense of self, they have difficulty with differences. Differences invite comparison and are potentially threatening. Shame-based congregations will attempt to create an artificial uniformity. Racial and cultural diversity are threatening for shame-based people and systems. Since pastors are unavoidably part of the church-

---

[55] Pembroke, "Towards a Shame-Based Theology of Evangelism," 23.

family system, we need to be alert to our own shame and how this helps form the life of the congregation. More on this later.

And so we see that becoming alert to the undercurrents of bad shame in the congregation will take time and conscious effort. This is like learning a new language. But the work needs to be done. To a guilt-centered theology, this shame discussion seems like an evasion. But for people divided at their core by shame, guilt resolution takes a back seat. Forgiveness has to be appropriated by someone. But for shame-based people, no one is really at home yet to answer the door. To rework the metaphor: Grace-for-shame must come first and unlock the door for grace-for-guilt. Or to put it another way, shame has clogged the arteries that deliver grace for guilt.

Shame and culture in the church
The cities of the twenty-first century are becoming more and more culturally diverse. Healthy, growing, "open-door" churches will reflect this diversity in their membership. What we discover in sharing congregational life with people of other cultures is that often people of non-Western cultures are more sensitive to shame. With this greater sensitivity often comes a greater maturity in this regard. Shame is more easily talked about, is better understood, and is generally more skillfully handled. So the presence of people from shame-oriented cultures changes the life of the congregation. This emerges in many ways.

Think of decision making in the church. Shame-sensitive people are reluctant to engage in public confrontation where one party risks losing face. The use of "go-betweens," so irritating to Westerners, is normative in shame-sensitive cultures. Pushing individuals to take a public stand will generate great discomfort. The decision-making process needs to adjust to this new reality. Robert's Rules of Order are a distinctly Western invention! New and more flexible processes need to be developed that allow people of other cultures to sit at the table. We may find these processes are healthier for all of us.

Since shame-oriented cultures are group or high-context cultures, social hierarchy is highly significant, and leadership roles take on new dynamics. Shame-oriented cultures are sensitive to proper respect. Shame arises when people are not treated with the respect required by their place in the social hierarchy. Likewise, shame arises when people behave in ways considered inappropriate to status. Thus pastors are seen differently in shame-oriented cultures. Pastors carry the honor of the community. If they are shamed, the whole community loses face. In a mixed-culture setting, conflicts arise when pastors are seen and treated in different cultural ways. What one culture understands as open debate may feel to another culture like an explicit "honor challenge." This partly explains the sometimes unexpected vigor of response to what others might perceive as a minor matter. Leaders need to temper their response to honor challenges. Grace is the order of the day.

But shame is not only a relevant issue because of cultural migration. *Shame orientation is a specific characteristic of church life.* Churches are, as has been noted, by nature, small face-to-face communities. It is characteristic of such communities that honor-shame dynamics are strong. Saving face and preserving honor are paramount as lives are lived out in the context of the small, intimate community. Behavior is weighed by the community. Is it appropriate to status and role requirements? Special behavior is expected of pastors' children (and wives). Christian parents are shamed by their children's sins, especially sexual sins.

In theory, the church adheres to eternal moral standards. In practice, the selection and prioritization of moral values is determined by the group. The Christian ideal of finding honor in virtue is amazingly illusive. Honor clings to wit, ability, money, power, even sexual prowess. Churches have a propensity for rewarding charisma over character. Why is the church board slow to pursue justice for a girl who has been sexually abused? Is it because we don't want to shame the abuser, who is a pillar in the church? We are hospitable to "respectable" outsiders (but not the "shameless"). We are, in fact, uncomfortable with a crucified (dishonored) leader. We prefer a sanitized cross. We are embarrassed by a foot-washing leader.

We can expect enthusiasm for the church to decline as we move further into this post-Christian age, where Christianity is not longer honorable. With this loss of honor will come loss of appeal (why join a church?), loss of commitment (it will take less to leave), loss of dollars (I don't care so much), loss of nerve (the hostility of the world seems too threatening), and loss of men (the church is a women's place). Issues of honor and shame are unavoidable in church culture.

Finding a way forward

At the start of the twenty-first century, shame is emerging as an important category of ministry. In part this is the result of a greater *awareness* of shame. In part it is the result of a greater *prevalence* of shame. Unfortunately, the church is unprepared for ministry to people suffering from shame. Theology, whether systematic or applied, is only just beginning to grapple with this matter. So far in this study we have begun to look at our ministry contexts with a greater understanding of shame, and a sharper eye to the urgencies of shame. The question pressing now is: What can we do?

But before we explore strategies for ministering grace for shame, I want to first turn back to Scripture. What is the biblical understanding of shame? What is the biblical answer to shame? How does Jesus minister grace for shame? It is in returning to the Scriptures that we find the foundation we need for ministering grace for shame in twenty-first-century churches. We turn now to the Bible with our new questions.

Part Two

The Bible and Shame

3. A Survey of Shame in the Biblical Story

What does the Bible say about shame? This study is written for the church. The biblical text is foundational for us. It must inform our theology at every point. It is God's Word that must be preached if our preaching is to be effective. But reading Scripture faithfully demands mental alertness. It is human nature to bring to the text a hatful of hermeneutical prejudices, for the most part blissfully unaware. We see what we are conditioned to see. We Westerners may be completely surprised at the prominence of shame in the Bible.

I want to begin this chapter by simply surveying the vocabulary of shame. Then I will follow with a look at some examples of Old and New Testament passages that have been reexamined in the light of the new awareness of honor-shame cultures. I will close with a return to Genesis and a re-examination of the Fall in terms of shame.

The Vocabulary of Shame

Noble expresses the surprise of many when he writes:

I was amazed when I discovered that the word shame occurred much more often than guilt. Guilt or guilty occurs twenty three times in the King James version whereas shame, ashamed and derivatives are found 224 times.[1]

Statistics will vary according to the lexical range of words included, and of course with different English translations. Nevertheless, the fact remains, overall (and particularly in the Old Testament) the vocabulary of shame is far more prominent than the vocabulary of guilt. In the Old Testament, noun and verb forms on the Hebrew root *bos* (shame) occur about one hundred and fifty times, and on the root *kalam* (shame) about forty times. Most of the Old Testament references to shame are in the Psalms and the prophets.

The most common use of shame in the Old Testament is to describe the humiliation that results from breaking God's law. For example, Jeremiah 3:25:

Let us lie down in our shame,
  and let our dishonor cover us.
For we have sinned against the Lord our God,
  we and our fathers,
from our youth even to this day,
  and we have not obeyed the voice of the Lord our God.

The relationship between shame and exposure sometimes emerges in the explicit linking of shame and nakedness (e.g., Jeremiah 13:25f. and Micah 1:11). But shame is not just our reaction to sin, it is also the punishment for sin. For example:

Let them be put to shame and disappointed altogether
  who rejoice at my calamity!
Let them be clothed with shame and dishonor
  who magnify themselves against me! (Psalm 35:26)

---

[1] Noble, *Naked and Not Ashamed*, ix.

In wonderful contrast, the removal of shame is one outcome of the promised salvation:

> Instead of your shame there shall be a double portion;
>> instead of dishonor they shall rejoice in their lot;
> therefore in their land they shall possess a double portion;
>> they shall have everlasting joy. (Isaiah 61:7)

Moving to the New Testament, it can be seen that the balance of shame and guilt vocabulary is more even. Bultmann[2] and Kee[3] give detailed introductions to the vocabulary, though missing from their analysis is the relatively new insight arising from the study of honor-shame cultures. The place to begin in Greek is with *aischuno* and its cognates. The meaning ranges from embarrassment to deep disgrace and humiliation. The concept of "semantic field" developed by Louw and Nida also suggests the inclusion of *aschemoneo* (to behave disgracefully, dishonorably or indecently), *atimazo* (to dishonor, treat shamefully or insult), *deigmatizo* (to expose, make an example of, or disgrace), *entrope* (shame, humiliation), *tapeinoo* (to humble or humiliate), *theatrizo* (to put to shame or expose publicly), and more. Thus it is evident that the vocabulary of shame is well developed in the New Testament. There is also a similar well-developed vocabulary for honor.[4]

---

[2] Rudolf Bultmann, "Aischuno," in *Theological Dictionary of the New Testament*, G. Kittle and G. Friedrich, eds., B. W. Bromley, translator (Grand Rapids, MI: Eerdmans, 1964, vol. I), 169f.

[3] Howard C. Kee, "The Linguistic Background of "Shame" in the New Testament," 133-148, in *On Language, Culture, and Religion: In Honor of Eugene A. Nida*, Matthew Black and William Smalley, eds. (The Hague: Mouton, 1974).

[4] Johannes P. Louw and Eugene A. Nida, eds., *Greek-English Lexicon of the New Testament Based on Semantic Domains* (New York: United Bible Societies, 1998).

Not all New Testament shame is the direct result of sin. Jesus (Luke 14:7f.) advised dinner guests to avoid humiliation by selecting a "lower" seat. Better to be bumped up than down! Nevertheless, for the most part shame and sin are intimately and directly connected. This is illustrated by the following Scriptures:

> But what fruit were you getting at that time from the things of which you are now ashamed? The end of those things is death. (Romans 6:21)

> Wake up from your drunken stupor, as is right, and do not go on sinning. For some have no knowledge of God. I say this to your shame. (1 Corinthians 15:34)

> Take no part in the unfruitful works of darkness, but instead expose them. For it is shameful even to speak of the things that they do in secret. (Ephesians 5:11-12)

> And now, little children, abide in him, so that when he appears we may have confidence and not shrink from him in shame at his coming. (1 John 2:28)

> I counsel you to buy from me gold refined by fire, so that you may be rich, and white garments so that you may clothe yourself and the shame of your nakedness may not be seen, and salve to anoint your eyes, so that you may see. (Revelation 3:18)

Much of the shame vocabulary in Scripture reflects the honor-shame dynamics of biblical cultures. This becomes especially important as the shame of the cross is examined. Crucifixion was deeply shaming by design, but Jesus "despised its shame" (Hebrews 12:2), as did his followers (Romans 1:16). Thus we see that an important aspect of the life-transforming effectiveness of the Christian faith lies in its ability to rewrite honor-shame scripts in such a way as to remove shame and restore honor (more on this later).

Furthermore, as might be expected at this point in this study, the vocabulary of "good shame" or "modesty" is also evident in the Scriptures. Schneider notes the connection between shame (modesty) and awe in both the Hebrew and Greek traditions.[5] The shameless person knows no fear of God, but the modest person falls down in awe before the all-seeing gaze of God (Ezra 9:6, 1 Timothy 2:9,10, Hebrews 12:28). The important word here is the Greek *aidos* (modesty or reverence). Cairns argues that "*aidos* includes concern both for one's own *time* [honor] and for that of others. As a result, part of the function of *aidos* is to recognize the point at which self-assertion encroaches illegitimately upon the *time* of others." Thus *aidos* monitors personal boundaries.[6]

Even five minutes with a good concordance is enough to impress on the Bible student the significance of shame. It is indeed a puzzle as to how such a prominent concept should have escaped the eye of the Western church. But we need to dig deeper to appreciate the complexity of the subject. Here now is a sample of some of the recent exegetical studies that highlight the role of shame in Scripture.

---

[5] Schneider, *Shame, Exposure and Privacy*, 109f. See also Ceslas Spicq, *Theological Lexicon of the New Testament,* James D. Earnest, translator (Peabody, MA: Hendrickson, 1994, vol. I), 44.

[6] Douglas L. Cairns, *Aidos: The Psychology and Ethics of Honor and Shame in Ancient Greek Literature* (Oxford: Clarendon Press, 1993), 432.

New Directions in Old Testament Studies

Esther

Timothy Laniak's 1998 study, *Shame and Honor in the Book of Esther*, is a good example of the way sociology and anthropology are being brought into play in the exegesis of biblical texts.[7] Laniak demonstrates that, in the extensive scholarship on the book of Esther, honor and shame themes have been almost totally neglected, despite being, as he intends to show, central to a proper understanding of the text. This gap is the result, he says, of reading from the perspective of the West, where honor and shame have a low profile. Once we recognize these themes in Esther, new patterns emerge that help us understand the ongoing significance of the book.

The plot, which Laniak also sees in a number of other Old Testament narratives, is one of honor granted, challenged, vindicated, then enhanced. The book of Esther begins (chapters 1-2) with Esther and Mordecai chosen, surprisingly, by God and also receiving unanticipated human favor. In the second phase (chapters 3-5) this grant of honor is challenged as Haman plots to kill the Jews. In the third phase (chapters 6-7) Haman himself is disgraced as his plot is turned back on himself. In the final phase (chapters 8-10) the plot reaches its climax, with the status of the Jews, led by Mordecai and Esther, greatly enhanced.

Laniak argues that the way the story is told, and the values that are inherent in the story, compel us to recognize the rising honor of the exiled community. The book of Esther speaks to their crisis of identity. Esther, the orphan child, represents the

---

[7] Timothy S. Laniak, *Shame and Honor in the Book of Esther* (Atlanta, GA: Scholars Press, 1998).

entire nation in their disinherited state. "Exile in the ancient world was considered a state of shame."[8] The book of Esther enhances the honor of God by demonstrating, in culturally appropriate ways, how God was able to honor the Jews even during their time of exile.

The importance of Laniak's work is his careful analysis of the way honor and shame are portrayed in the details and construction of the story. The Word of the Lord in Esther will speak more powerfully to our own twenty-first-century experience of a people in exile as we incorporate these insights in our teaching and preaching.

Job

The book of Job is a remarkable literary accomplishment. It continues to grip the reader even today with its interwoven themes of human suffering, injustice, the cry for God, and the mystery of the divine. William Morrow, in his article "Toxic Religion and the Daughters of Job," presents a fresh interpretation of Job as the story of a man caught in the grip of toxic religion ("perfectionist retribution theology") but who appears to emerge with some sense of recovery and resolution. Morrow notes the shame-producing dynamics of that theology: abuse of power, overcontrol, the "no talk" rule, perfectionism, and blaming. How is this resolved? Is it resolved? The ending of Job is notoriously ambiguous. But this very ambiguity is itself an escape from the overstructured toxic religion of early Job and his three friends.

I include a summary of Morrow's article here as an example of the way old and familiar texts yield new insight in

---

[8] Ibid., 173.

the light of recent shame studies. Morrow makes use of psychological studies that describe the toxic role of shame in dysfunctional relational systems. This is seen in family systems where problems exist with overcontrol, perfectionism, and denial of feelings, and where all members are at risk for shame. Similar dynamics occur in religious systems. What is toxic in Job's religion, Morrow argues, is the "Wisdom" doctrine that "God is the guarantor of a cause and effect relationship between order and chaos, justice and suffering." This appears to leave no room for human initiative and decision making. It is the ultimate case of "over-control." Morrow continues, "A great deal of the poet's skill is invested in making readers of Job feel its shaming potential."[9]

Thus the readers of Job are told unequivocally that Job is a morally upright man. Job himself knows this, yet he suffers. Job's shame is apparent with his opening words. He wishes he had never been born (Job 3:1-10). His suffering indicates moral failure, according to his theology. Job's humiliation drives him to regret his own birth. Morrow argues that it is the presence of the three friends that prompts Job's outburst. Job's shame is "activated" as he is exposed as defective in front of his friends.

Morrow goes on to point out the tactics of perfectionism and blaming that are typical of shame-based systems. In chapters 4 and 5 Eliphaz rebukes Job for his weakness (4:5-6); he attempts to overrule Job with his claim to special revelation (4:12-16); and if Job will admit his errors and humble himself, God will restore his fortunes (5:1-27). Morrow quotes Fossum and Mason, who note the unconscious rules of the shame-based systems that conspire against authentic relationships and drive

---

[9] William S. Morrow, "Toxic Religion and the Daughters of Job," *Studies in Religion*, 27 (3) (1998): 268.

shame deeper "regardless of the good intentions, wishes, and love that may also be a part of the system."[10]

Morrow notes, too, the "rupture of the interpersonal bridge" evident in chapter 6 as Job replies. They are reluctant to look him in the eye (6:28). Furthermore, as Job turns to God in Chapter 7 there is illustrated the typical ambivalence of the shamed person who "almost in the same breath" yearns for God's absence (7:19) as well as an increased presence that will bestow forgiveness and the possibility of reconciliation (7:21).[11] Bildad "invokes the no-talk rule (8:2) and more perfectionist blame."

In Job's response in chapters 9 and 10 he begins by acknowledging God's omnipotence, but then argues that such a god must be capricious (9:22-24), for who can restrain him? "In effect Job describes a toxic relationship characterized by the abuse of power . . . divine over-control and the complete silencing of Job's capacity to protest his suffering and assert his innocence."[12]

As the dialogue proceeds, Job becomes more and more alienated from his friends. Their rigidity and "compulsive abuse" is typical of shame-based systems. As Job later says, they attack him "shamelessly" (19:3). Conversely, "Job renews an appeal for accountability and dialogue [with God] (13:17-28; 14:13-17), characteristic of the antithesis of the shame-based system, a system of respect."[13]

Morrow now summarizes the resolution of the plot:

---

[10] Ibid., 269.
[11] Ibid., 270.
[12] Ibid., 271.
[13] Ibid., 272.

Recovery from the wounds of toxic shame can be described as "moving from shame to respect" and "restoring the interpersonal bridge." The fact that YHWH responds to Job suggests the restoration of the interpersonal bridge. YHWH's response also initiates a movement that ends in the recovery of Job's social respect (42:7-17).[14]

While acknowledging the ambiguous nature of the conclusion of the book, Morrow does direct attention to the three beautiful daughters of Job, who are not only named (their brothers are not) but receive an inheritance (unique in Scripture). Morrow sees in this evidence of Job's revisioned theology. Morrow argues that the speeches of YHWH "challenge the shaming beliefs of the toxic religion which Job and his friends have shared." Reading these speeches from the perspective of shame-based family systems yields the following, says Morrow.

First, the YHWH speeches challenge the anthropocentric nature of Job's toxic religion. The description of weather patterns and wild animals opens up a much broader religious outlook with categories unrelated to human values. "A view of the cosmos that does not have humanity at its centre relieves suffering persons from having to interpret every situation as a potentially blameworthy response to their own actions." This is analogous to the need for adult children to "refuse to make themselves the centre of their family dysfunction."[15]

Second, the toxic religion of Job and his friends included a sharp distinction between chaos and order. The idea that chaos must also come under God's rule was repressed. This allowed the possibility of an ordered, predictable, tidy world. The

---

[14] Ibid.
[15] Ibid., 272f.

YHWH speeches that include God's control not only over the untamed, wild animals, but even the monsters of the chaotic deep, forced Job to make room in his theology for both order and chaos. We live in a world that is not fully understandable. Our own experiences and emotional lives will include chaotic elements that we will not always understand or control. But God is still God and Lord of all.

Third, Morrow adds that such passages as 38:12-15 and 40:7-14 highlight the moral ambiguity in the created world. There is wickedness loose in the world that God, from our perspective, seems unable to remove. This runs contrary to the doctrine that God is so perfect and powerful that creation must mirror that perfection. "Somewhat similarly sufferers of chronic shame must come to terms with the moral ambiguity of their primary caregivers. Giving up the fiction of the perfect parent is an important step in arresting the syndromes of self-blame and shame which inhibit recovery."[16]

Morrow's treatment of Job from this perspective of the psychology of shame is insightful and provocative. It sheds new light on this book and explains in part why Job is so exhilarating and freedom generating for many readers. Unfortunately Morrow does not incorporate the insights gained from the study of honor-shame cultures. This would add more depth and appreciation of the shame dynamics of the book. For example, there is the burden of the loss of honor symbolized by Job's relocation to the ash-heap (outside the city wall), and the re-honoring (de-shaming) of Job as he is given the priestly function of praying for his friends at the conclusion of the story. Nevertheless, Morrow's article is a fine example of the

---

[16] Ibid., 274.

way recent shame studies have brought new questions to the biblical text that reveal new and helpful insights.

The book of Job does not replace one closed, airtight theology with another. It ends with an uncircumscribed God. It moves from a tidy, mechanical, "Newtonian" theology to an open-ended, mysterious, more humble, "quantum" theology. In so doing, it removes the burden of uncovering every consequence and determining all blame.

Here we can only sample this rich vein of fresh investigation. But it is helpful to be aware of the considerable body of literature that is accumulating on the role and function of shame in the Old Testament. Much work has now been done on examining the honor-shame dynamics of Hebrew life and nuancing the concept. A sampling is listed in the bibliography at the end of this book. Any one of these will open the door to valuable resources for further study. As Laniak and Morrow demonstrate, we are able to gain precious insight on grace for shame by examining both cultural and psychological themes in the Hebrew Scriptures.

New Directions in New Testament Studies

What are the roots of the Western emphasis on guilt? Krister Stendahl, in an article originally published in 1960, argues that Western theology is unaware of the extent to which it has been shaped by Luther's personal struggle with conscience. Thus, for example, reading the central focus of Romans to be "justification by faith as the answer to the troubled conscience" is a westernized interpretation of that letter that does not accurately echo Paul's major concerns. It is a Reformation interpretation that emerged in the context of an overemphasis on works in the established church of the time. That overemphasis on works was then read back into first-century Judaism.

Stendahl argues, however, that in fact Paul, the faithful Jew, was not conscious-stricken but on the contrary could declare his conscience clean (e.g., Acts 23:1). He argues that Paul's major concerns in Rome focus on (a) the effect of the coming of Christ on the law and (b) the relationship between Jew and Gentile. Thus: "Romans 9 to 11 is not an appendix to Chapters 1 to 8, but the climax of the letter."[17]

Stendahl's interpretation has, of course, been much debated and the discussion has moved on. Nevertheless, he did helpfully flag the problem of allowing modern Western concerns to distort our reading of Paul. In so doing, he helped open the way to fresh readings that offer Western Christians new perspectives on the Gospel. Here is a quick look at two examples.

In 1988 Halvor Moxnes argued that reading Romans through the lens of the honor-shame culture of the Mediterranean yields new insights and reveals a greater unity and consistency within the whole of the letter than an emphasis on justification, a reading he says is shaped more by late Western individualism.[18] He notes that terms for honor, honor claims (boasting), and shame "are found in all sections of [Romans] and are more evenly distributed than terms for

---

[17] Stendahl, *Paul Among Jews and Gentiles*, 85.
[18] Halvor Moxnes, "Honor and Righteousness in Romans," *Journal for the Study of the New Testament,* 32 (1988): 61f.

justification and righteousness."[19] Moxnes suggests that Paul, in Romans, has a strong interest in the relationship between Jew and Gentile, thus his concern for "the creation of new groups and marking off new identities and borders."[20] This redistribution of boundaries includes some who were formerly shamed (since they were outsiders) and excludes others (who claimed insider status on inadequate grounds).

At some points Paul appears to be aligning his teaching with local honor-shame values. Moxnes argues, for example, that Paul's discussion of homosexuality in Romans 1 is not primarily about ethics but about gender confusion. Clearly defined sexual roles are critical in an honor-shame society. God is honored when approved sexual roles are maintained.[21] Yet Paul does challenge local cultural values by redefining the distribution mechanism for honor (e.g., Romans 12:9f.). Moxnes writes: "There is to be no connection between service performed in leadership, and honor and recognition above others. Honor is to be awarded solely on the basis of "brotherly love." In fact "the weaker should receive more honor."[22]

Thus he sees Paul writing within the context of his own honor-shame culture, building on it where helpful, but challenging it when needed. Moxnes concludes that while the Western application of Romans may have been helpful for Westerners, this kind of reexamination of Paul's historical context helps pave the way for a more fitting application of Romans to other cultures and the concerns raised by those cultures.

---

[19] Ibid., 63.
[20] Ibid., 64.
[21] Ibid., 67.
[22] Ibid., 74.

A decade later Robert Jewett confesses his awakening to the impact of the new shame perspective in New Testament studies: "Although I have been working intensively on Romans since 1980, it has only been in the last several years that the awareness of the theological significance of honor and shame has begun to dawn."[23] Thus he now can write:

> When the frequency of honor and shame terminology is compared with the single allusion to pardon in Romans 3:25, it now seems clear that a mainstream has been confused for a minor current in the tradition of interpreting Pauline theology. It is time to move beyond the paradigm of individual guilt and forgiveness in understanding Paul. This book represents my first extended effort to articulate a new assessment of the triumph of grace over shameful status as the new organizing center of Paul's thought.[24]

Jewett's approach is novel. He uses the story lines of ten movies to illustrate themes of honor and shame in Romans. He argues that movies allow the observers to gaze on shame and its hiddenness, while at the same time allowing them to retain their own privacy. Thus, he suggests, movies can provide a new window into the difficult but critical concern of shame in Paul's writings. It is human nature to contrive to look good and to hide shame; but attempts to hide shame leave people antagonistic towards God who, by definition, knows what is really going on. Jewett argues that Paul "developed a critique of the various methods people develop to hide their shame."[25]

Jewett is also helpful in highlighting the way the death of Christ addresses a wide range of human concerns, as seen in,

---

[23] Jewett, *St. Paul Returns to the Movies*, 15.
[24] Ibid., 19.
[25] Ibid., 31.

for example, Romans 5:1-11. He notes "the references to "peace with God," to "reconciliation" with God, to "boastings," and to "affliction." Paul's approach is grounded in the "effectiveness of Christ's death on behalf of the vulnerable and undeserving."[26] Elsewhere Jewett has also argued that "righteousness" is synonymous with "honor" and "glory." To be justified is "to be set right." This honor is not dependent on a human court of opinion but on the eternal, heavenly court of opinion and is thus a permanent gift of grace.[27]

These studies by Moxnes and Jewett are two examples of rereading the writings of the apostle Paul with a deeper awareness of local cultural concerns. Given that Romans has historically played a central role in the explication of a theology of guilt, can we now allow this letter to speak also to a theology of shame?

Other areas of the New Testament

David Desilva explores the problem of dishonor experienced by the recipients of the letter of Hebrews. Where does this dishonor come from? It comes from being part of a maligned, marginal group following a crucified leader. He asks this question:

> How does the author of Hebrews solve the dishonor of Christians, thereby permitting honor-sensitive people to continue in Christian activity, worship, and community

---

[26] Ibid., 124.

[27] Robert Jewett, "Honor and Shame in the Argument of Romans," in *Putting Body & Soul Together: Essays in Honor of Robin Scroggs,* Virginia Wiles, Alexander Brown, and Graydon F. Snyder, eds. (Valley Forge, PA: Trinity Press International, 1997), 270.

(indeed to satisfy their desire for honor specifically through Christian activity)?[28]

Desilva argues that the author of Hebrews points to an alternate system of honor centered in the ascended Christ, who occupies the greatest position of honor at the right hand of God. God's people do not need to be bound by shame.

Thus Hebrews offers examples of earlier saints who overcame shame by despising it: Abraham (who became a dishonorable sojourner), Moses (who left the honor of the Egyptian court), plus others who suffered dishonor for God. What the author of Hebrews is doing is arguing persuasively for a new view of reality. "Because they have such a hope for honor from the higher court of opinion, namely God's, the author may exhort them to disregard the opinion of unbelievers, who serve a lower court."[29] The application of such a reading of Hebrews for Christians today, burdened by loss of honor in a post-Christendom world, is readily apparent.

K. C. Hansen's similar approach in his analysis of the "blessings" and "curses" of Matthew 5:3-10 and Matthew 23:13-36 is worth noting here. Hansen argues that these "makarisms" (from the Greek *makarios*) and "reproaches" should not, in fact, be translated "blessings" and "curses" but rather, "how honorable" and "how shameful" (or "shame on"). These passages then function as a realignment of honor and shame at the start and conclusion of Jesus' public ministry.[30]

[28] David Desilva, "Despising Shame: A Cultural-Anthropological Investigation of the Epistle to the Hebrews," *Journal of Biblical Literature,* 113 (3) (1994): 439.

[29] Ibid., 458.

[30] K. C. Hansen, "How Honorable! How Shameful! A Cultural Analysis of Matthew's Makarisms and Reproaches," *Semeia,* 68 (1996): 81f.

What is Jesus' ministry? It is inviting people to be part of God's Kingdom, where this world's honor-deprived discover much honor and find a place of belonging.

Two years after Hansen's study of the "makarisms" and "reproaches" in Matthew, Jerome Neyrey published a book-length study, *Honor and Shame in the Gospel of Matthew.* Neyrey provides not only a detailed description of honor-shame dynamics in Mediterranean culture, he also shows how Matthew's book is itself an example of a rhetorical style of writing designed to display the praise and honor of the individual being portrayed. Neyrey argues that proficiency in this kind of writing was part of the basic training of students of that era. Matthew follows the conventions of his day in presenting the honorable aspects of Jesus' life: his background and birth, his upbringing, his deeds, and his death. Neyrey examines in detail just how Matthew can present the crucifixion of Jesus, normally the most shameful of deaths, as an honorable death. We will return to this concern a little later, but here is a sample of Neyrey's provocative approach from his cultural analysis of the Sermon on the Mount:

> In the Sermon on the Mount, Matthew presents Jesus reforming the fundamental value of his culture, namely, honor. His reform consists not only in refining and correcting the Torah of Israel, but in engaging the values and consequent social structures of his social world. Jesus did *not* overthrow the honor code as such, but rather redefined what constitutes honor in his eyes and how his disciples should play the game. The person who declared that last is first and least is greatest is surely redefining the criteria for worth and respect (see Matt. 23:12). . . .

Jesus, then, changed the way the honor game was played and redefined the source of honor, namely, acknowledgment by God, not by neighbor. As a result, by conforming to the image of the Master, disciples are shamed in the eyes of their peers and become least and last before their neighbors. But Jesus honors them himself with a grant of reputation and respect that far surpasses what could be hoped for in the public arena of the village. . . .[31]

Note Neyrey's assertion that Jesus did not set aside the honor-shame code, but he redefined it. The critical question is, Where does our honor come from? Does it emerge from local culture values or Kingdom of God values? If it is true, as we argue, that honor and shame play a significant role in church culture, and increasingly in secular Western culture, then such a cultural analysis of the New Testament is not only of historical interest, but speaks to our life together now. In the family of Jesus, the game of honor and shame is fundamentally redefined. But sustaining this redefinition takes vigilance. The Sermon on the Mount needs to be preached regularly in all its radical and startling countercultural freshness. Otherwise the family of Jesus will revert to the default honor-shame settings of the unconverted, face-to-face communities of this world.

While these studies demonstrate the "human level" honor-shame sensitivities of the New Testament, it is helpful to note an earlier (1977) observation by Schneider that shame in relation to God almost disappears in the New Testament. There is a breaking free from the Old Testament awestruck attitude towards God. The unpronounceable YHWH becomes Abba.[32]

---

[31] Neyrey, *Matthew*, 164f.
[32] Schneider, *Exposure and Privacy*, 115f.

Schneider points out that part of Nietzsche's problem with Christianity was that the emphasis on an intimate identification with Christ appeared to mean the loss of the holiness, the otherness, of God—it was too familiar, immodest, shameless.[33] Thomas addresses this same concern from the perspective of ministry to Muslims. He writes "the very thing that Muslims object to most in Christianity [is] *syirik*—the identification of God with his creation."[34] Nevertheless this is precisely where Christians must hold firmly to one of the great paradoxes of the Christian faith, God is at once transcendent *and* immanent. Furthermore, not only has God in Christ drawn near to us, we in Christ are invited to draw near to God. Thus, as we will see later, boldness (a kind of good shamelessness) is a gift of God that comes to the fore in the New Testament. The children of God are invited to walk into the very holy of holies.

This is just a sample from the flood of studies now re-evaluating New Testament passages from this cultural perspective of honor and shame. But even this brief survey makes clear that much has been overlooked. It is humbling to discover such a blind spot in biblical studies. We wonder what else we are missing!

Genesis and the Origins of Shame

While a *sensitivity* to shame may be helpful in curbing inappropriate behavior, the *experience* of shame is deep, painful, and damaging to the very core of the self. To

---

[33] Ibid., 11.
[34] Thomas, "The Gospel for Shame Cultures," 286.

experience shame is to be diminished as a human being. It is in fact to live less than God intended in creation. And it is to this creation story that we now turn.

The garden exposure

The beginning of shame is found at the beginning of sin, in that first garden. With our new awareness of shame in mind, it is now clear that the response of those first human beings to the Fall is described in terms of shame rather than guilt. "Then the eyes of both were opened, and they knew that they were naked" (Genesis 3:7). They felt exposed, unbearably so, and improvised coverings for themselves. They withdrew, hiding themselves from God. They demonstrate shame's destructive effect on relationships. They employ the typical defense of blaming as they try to cope with their shame. The story illustrates shame's global response to sin. They do not try to hide their actions: they try to hide their very selves. They do not cover the "apple core," they cover their own bodies. They are not trying to bury evidence, they are trying to bury themselves.

It was in Eden that Satan planted the stubbornly persistent seed of "I am not good enough." In his examination of the creation story, Asa Sphar points to the way the framing of the serpent's question generates a sense of incompleteness or inadequacy in the hearers.[35] This sense of ontological shortfall is the essence of shame. Sphar rightly indicates the flaw in the serpent's words: "Some comparisons are not rightfully made.

---

[35] Asa Sphar, "A Theology of Shame as Revealed in the Creation Story," *Theological Educator: A Journal of Theology and Ministry,* 55 (1997): 65.

Persons were never created to be 'like' God."[36] As Powers points out, Satan's original tactic was to convince Eve she was inadequate as she was. This was true. But Satan's solution was also part of the problem: seek completion apart from God; do not trust God to do it.[37]

When Adam and Eve fell before the temptation, relational harmony was broken at all levels. Sphar notes alienation from God, others, and self. In addition, however, shame is a dynamic in our fallen relationship with physical creation. No longer are humans in the honorable position of being "namers." Now we are reduced, vulnerable, unrespected, and alienated. From being God's regents, we became rejects, outcasts, small in relation to the universe.

It may not have occurred to pre-Fall Adam to say to God, "When I look at your heavens . . . what is man that you are mindful of him?" (Psalm 8). This is a post-Fall perspective. What is lost is a sense of place and a sense of belonging. Sphar points to the coming resolution. The eventual restoration for shame is revealed in the "grace of unconditional acceptance found in the cross."[38]

As we have already noted, Bonhoeffer provides one of the few theological discussions of the origin of shame in his book *Ethics*. He begins the book with his interpretation of the Fall as the falling away from God as "origin." The knowledge of good and evil was not new knowledge. What was new was knowing *apart* from God, thus the attempt to establish a new origin. Bonhoeffer writes: "Shame is man's ineffaceable recollection of this estrangement from the origin; it is grief for this

---

[36] Ibid., 66.

[37] Powers, *Shame: Thief of Intimacy*, 26.

[38] Sphar, "A Theology of Shame as Revealed in the Creation Story," 72

estrangement, and the powerless longing to return to unity with the origin. . . . Shame is more original than remorse."[39] He sees shame as a longing to recover unity, first with God, then with people.

Paradoxically, a covering is now necessary to conceal the irreparable disunity. Before the Fall, Adam and Eve could be fully exposed before each other and before God, who walked with them in the garden. They felt no shame. But in their attempt to be autonomous, their inadequacy as separate beings became clear. They saw themselves as diminished. Life now is bearable only if the self is covered.

The covering is not only for Adam and Eve before God, but Adam and Eve before each other. Thus even in the intimacy of an exclusive marriage relationship, full exposure is illusive; modesty remains. Even those most "uncovered" moments—sex and prayer—we hide from outside eyes.[40] So Bonhoeffer comments on the "shamelessness" of being too frank and open. He speaks against indiscreet curiosity, even commending the "so-called 'hypocrisy' of the British" in contrast with the "honesty" or "frankness" of the Germans. He adds full disclosure is only appropriate "at confession, i.e., before God."[41] To be bearable, life post-Fall requires a certain modesty or shyness.

The role of modesty

Modesty is a veiling of the person, a way of limiting access. Modesty describes our present human relationship with God, who has withdrawn his direct presence. We know him now by

---

[39] D. Bonhoeffer, *Ethics* (NewYork: Macmillan, 1965), 20.
[40] Ibid., 21.
[41] Ibid., 216.

faith not by sight. Even in his great Visit—his Incarnation—his "god-ness" was mostly kept under wraps. He was known to be God by inference, indirectly, not as later when every eye will see. Even now he knocks at the door and draws near privately.

But at the end of this great story the veil will be removed. God will dwell in the midst of his people again (Revelation 21:3, 23). Full exposure will be bearable because the work of Christ in our restoration will be fully accomplished. Interestingly, marriage will no longer be needed. Perhaps because it is only a present taste of the future transparency that all will experience then before God and each other. On the other hand the punishment of hell will be distance, separation and abandonment—all that shame fears. The pain of hell is not only to be guilt ridden for ever, but also to be shame ridden for ever.

So during this in-between time God gives us space. He shields us from his all-seeing eye. He deals tenderly with our shame. He clothes us. Margaret Hess speaks of "God the seamstress."[42] His garden dressmaking is the beginning of a Gospel motif. We sons of Adam and daughters of Eve need to hear more about "God the seamstress."

This is, of course paradoxical. Is anything really hidden from God? It cannot be. Yet if God does voluntarily absent himself, it helps to know that. Pattison explores this: "The image of the lack, or absence, of God provides a powerful and necessary counterbalance to the image of the immanent, present God who takes a minute and oppressive interest in

---

[42] Margaret B. Hess, "A Portrait of Shame," *Christian Century*, 114 (1997): 509.

human affairs, especially personal inadequacies and wrong-doings."[43]

Job speaks for all who struggle with the all-seeing eye of God:

> What is man, that you make so much of him,
>   and that you set your heart on him,
> visit him every morning
>   and test him every moment?
> How long will you not look away from me,
>   nor leave me alone till I swallow my spit?
> If I sin, what do I do to you,
>   you watcher of mankind? (Job 7:17-20)

As Pattison observes, an absent God "allows people to grow up, to learn to trust themselves and other human beings, to make their own mistakes, to discover the limits of their powers, and to enjoy a proper sense of boundaries and possibilities in relationships."[44]

Shame and sin

What then is the relationship between shame and sin? This discussion of shame is not meant to downplay the concept of sin. Adam and Eve sinned. Since then sin has been an inescapable part of human life. As Paul makes clear in Romans 5, sin "came into the world through one man [Adam]." Christ came into the world to deliver us from sin. Thus I do not argue that the concept of shame should replace the concept of sin, or that we should speak of the Fall as "original shame" instead of

---

[43] Pattison, *Shame*, 305.
[44] Ibid., 305.

"original sin."[45] Shame is one of the *consequences* of sin, and the *origin* of shame is sin.

What I am arguing is that the church has responded much more helpfully to the sin-consequence that we name "guilt" than to the sin-consequence that we name "shame," despite the fact that the initial consequence of the sin of Adam and Eve was primarily the experience of shame not guilt. Objectively they were guilty. We could argue that they were also objectively shameful because of their sin, whether they had experienced the feelings of shame or not. But in fact subjectively, their primary *experience* was shame.

God's ministry of grace to Adam and Eve took the form of a covering. This is what shame longs for. If they had been consumed with feelings of guilt, the covering would not have helped much. But God tailored his response to their need. Yes, in the end sin demands blood. God was going to meet that blood demand once and for all. In fact, even this preliminary covering required the shedding of blood. Nevertheless this divine first aid took particular note of the *shame* injuries received as a result of sin and responded accordingly.

In the end, healing for shame, just as healing for guilt, requires deliverance from the origin of shame, namely sin. But sin is *manifest* as both guilt and shame. The application and appropriation of grace for shame will be different from the application and appropriation of grace for guilt. May the discerning ministry of God in Genesis be our model for ministry in the church today.

---

[45] Cf. Laurel Arthur Burton, "Original Sin or Original Shame?" *Quarterly Review,* 8 (1988); and Boyle, "Communicating the Gospel in Terms of Shame," 42.

The *imago Dei*

In exploring the roots of shame in the Fall it is helpful to remember the concept of the *imago Dei*, the image of God. Shame is the feeling of being diminished. But diminished from what? The Bible describes human beings as created in the very image of God (Genesis 1:27). The image of God has been variously understood as (a) a physical representation of God; (b) the Trinitarian nature of the human soul (memory, intelligence, will); (c) human function (having dominion); (d) holiness (Christ restored what Adam lost); and (e) relationship (man and woman in community). From studies in parallel Eastern cultures, it also appears that the language of image was used to indicate a representative.[46]

It is helpful to draw on all these insights and see human beings in their totality as physically, psychologically, functionally, morally, and relationally representing God on earth. Thus men and women together, as multidimensional persons, represent, on earth, God's being and function in the heavens. This is a "high" view of humanity that underscores the original dignity of both men and women.

What effect did the Fall have on this original dignity? The Bible does not work out a comprehensive doctrine of the Fall. Paul breaks new ground in Romans 5:12-21, but this is not pursued. Augustine spoke of the consequences of the Fall in terms of biological inheritance. True, he was swayed unhelpfully by an undue emphasis on sexual sin; nevertheless, he connected the sin of Adam to the general corruption of human nature. Calvin spoke of the corruption of human nature more broadly as "depravity." This depravity is imputed by God

---

[46] See S. B. Ferguson, "Image of God," in *New Testament Dictionary of Theology*, 328-329.

to all, just as Christ's righteousness is imputed to those who believe.[47] The Reformers expressed the extent of the Fall with the phrase "total depravity." This was not intended to mean the total loss of *imago Dei,* but that the Fall touched every aspect of human nature. They argued there was no central core of untouched good. Thus Reformed teaching asserts that no corner of human life and experience is free from the tentacles of sin.

All of this suggests, then, that deliverance from shame will be connected with a restoration of the *imago Dei* at some level. Paul indicates this in 2 Corinthians 3:18, "We . . . are being transformed into his likeness with ever increasing glory [honor]" (NIV). As Athanasius argued in the fourth century, the purpose of the incarnation was to restore the *imago Dei* in humanity.[48] What was lost in Adam is restored in Christ. What is recovered is the dignity of humanity made in the image of God, with all the richness and potential of that. Though "what we will be has not yet appeared" (1 John 3:2), there is substantial restoration here and now.

The concept of *imago Dei* also underscores the importance of identity being found in relationship. Human identity is not separate from God's identity. When Moses says, "Who am I?" God's answer is to say, "I will be with you." Shame moves in the opposite direction. Relationships are broken until even the self is divided from itself. Restoration of the *imago Dei* is about the restoration of a relationship. The life, death, resurrection, and ascension of Christ is about restoring the relationship between human beings and God.

---

[47] J. E. Colwell, "Fall," in *New Testament Dictionary of Theology,* 249-251.

[48] Athanasius, *The Incarnation of the Word.*

Furthermore the corporate aspect of *imago Dei* must not be neglected. Male and female together image God (Genesis 1:27). The church, as the body of Christ, is to express corporately the restored image of God. Insofar as shame, as we have seen, is a relational problem, recovery from shame will require a relational response. Healthy Christian communities allow people to taste the dignity of *imago Dei* corporately. Life together provides the context for the recovery of true personhood.

Western theology (not least Reformed theology) has rightly emphasized the depth of the Fall. We build on sand if we are naïve in this matter. But a doctrine of original sin needs to be balanced by a doctrine of original dignity. The concept of *imago Dei,* from which humans have fallen and to which we may be restored, brings hope to the heart cowed in shame. If we began with such unity, wholeness, completeness, and such a sense of identity, belonging and place, perhaps we may recover that. And, in fact, for this Christ came.

Thus we remember that Genesis chapter 1 is more foundational than Genesis chapter 3. A renewed understanding of the primacy of *imago Dei* underlines the value and worth of every human being. Here is help for shame. The roots of shame do go back to the beginnings of the human race. Shame is the response to original sin. Yet the concept of *imago Dei* reminds us of a dignity that is more original even than sin. And God's gracious covering in the garden suggests the beginning of a recovery of that dignity, a hope that is fulfilled in the person and ministry of Christ.

4. Hope and Healing in the Biblical Story

Jesus in His Honor-Shame Culture

It is my conviction that hope and healing for both sin and the fallout of sin are to be found in the person and ministry of Jesus Christ. Shame is the particular consequence of sin being addressed in this book. We have laid a foundation for understanding shame and we have surveyed shame in Scripture. We are now ready to ask: What does the coming of Christ mean for shamed people?

From glory to shame and back

Philippians 2:5-11 is a profound and succinct summary of Christ's ministry:

> Have this mind among yourselves, which is yours in Christ Jesus, who,
> though he was in the form of God,
> did not count equality with God a thing to be grasped,
> but made himself nothing,
> taking the form of a servant,
> being born in the likeness of men.
> And being found in human form,
> he humbled himself by becoming obedient
> to the point of death, even death on a cross.

Therefore God has highly exalted him
    and bestowed on him the name that is above every name,
so that at the name of Jesus every knee should bow,
    in heaven and on earth and under the earth,
and every tongue confess that Jesus Christ is Lord,
    to the glory of God the Father.

Here we can trace the journey from high honor to no honor to high honor. At the beginning Christ bears the honour of God— the very highest honor. Then, in an extraordinary move, he chooses reduced honor, becoming a human servant, then death, "even death on a cross," the place, as we shall see, of greatest shame. Then finally, God restores Christ's honor, his shame is banished, and he is returned to the highest position.

In brief, the ministry of Jesus is this: he sets aside his own honor and glory to identify with human dishonor and shame at its deepest level; but in his own recovery and return to glory, he breaks a path out of shame for all humanity. Each human being is now invited to identify with Christ and to participate vicariously in the depth of his descent and the height of his ascent (Romans 6:3f.).

What an amazing story! God swallowed his pride and became a human embryo. We, who wanted to become like God, find God became like us. The awesome glory of God represents the unapproachable boundaries of his majesty. It is a deceit that created beings could be like him. Yet the wonder of the incarnation is that God laid aside his glory and made his boundaries vulnerable, opening the possibility, then reality, of being shamed himself. In becoming human, Christ was opening the door for our return to true humanity. In laying aside his glory he became, in his humanity, a true image of God. As such he is the firstfruit of restored humanity. He is the antithesis of

Satan, who urged Eve to find fullness of life in becoming like God. He demonstrates fullness of life within the constraints of human flesh. Thus we see in the great sweep of Christ's ministry this parabolic drop-and-return as he authors our salvation. As Japanese parents take on the shame of their children's behavior, God humbles himself and "bows low" to restore human honor.[1]

Subverting the script

Nevertheless, while the overall glory-shame-glory movement is readily acknowledged, complexities within this plot are also evident. On the one hand, long before reaching the depths of the crucifixion, Jesus experiences life as a nobody from nowhere town. Even the legitimacy of his birth is in question (an item never forgotten in village life). On the other hand, he experiences honor in counterpoint to his shame. Though truly he laid aside his glory it was offered back repeatedly. His birth was overshadowed with heavenly glory in the appearance of the angels. At his baptism he was handed the ultimate deposit of honor, "You are my son." In working miracles he accrued great honor. So we see the paradox of shame and no shame in Jesus' life. This is inextricably linked to his dual nature, fully human and fully God. In Luke 5:4f. the glory of Jesus "leaks out" in the miraculous catch of fish. Peter's encounter with this divine Christ evokes discretionary shame (awe, fear): "Depart from me, for I am a sinful man, O Lord." The incident reveals Christ's constant nearness to glory and honor.

Furthermore, Christ *accumulates* honor in the course of his daily ministry. The public appearances of Jesus must be

---

[1] Boyle, "Communicating the Gospel in Terms of Shame," 45.

understood in the light of the omnipresent challenge to honor that marked his society. The interactions surrounding the healing of the crippled woman in Luke 13:10-17 illustrate the pattern. First, Jesus heals the woman. This is an implicit claim to honor. In response, the religious leaders challenge his honor by accusing him of breaking the Sabbath. Jesus defends his honor claim by arguing that, as an ox is untied on the Sabbath and so can receive water, so this woman can be unbound from Satan on the Sabbath. In typical honor-shame culture fashion, the verdict is returned immediately and publicly: "As he said these things, all his adversaries were put to shame, and all the people rejoiced at all the glorious things that were done by him" (Luke 13:17).[2]

It seems that Jesus could not do other than increase in honor as his ministry unfolded. His encounters with the Jewish leaders further increased his honor to their shame. Malina and Neyrey write: "It is truly an understatement to say that the whole of Luke's Gospel, almost every piece of social interaction, should be viewed through the lens of honor and shame."[3] Certainly the crucifixion of Jesus was a final, desperate attempt on behalf of the Jewish leaders to regain honor and shame Jesus. But, as we shall see, the followers of Jesus discovered in the cross even greater glory and honor.

So it is wrong to see in Christianity a disregard for honor. In fact Jesus entered an honor-shame culture and excelled in the honor game. Furthermore, that which brings glory (or honor) to God is of highest value. The Christian concern is not

---

[2] See Bruce J. Malina and Jerome H. Neyrey "Honor and Shame in Luke-Acts: Pivotal Values of the Mediterranean World," in *The Social World of Luke-Acts: Models for Interpretation,* Jerome H. Neyrey, ed. (Peabody, MA: Hendrickson, 1991), 50.

[3] Ibid., 64.

so much about *sensitivity* to reputation (or honor) but the *criteria* driving that assessment. God himself seeks his own glory (a difficult concept for people of guilt-oriented cultures), but his criteria consist of principles of righteousness, justice, and covenant love. The problem with the human honor-shame dynamic is that each human community establishes its own criteria, thus the many variations on the honor-shame theme. Christ comes alongside and says, yes it is possible to work with honor and shame, but the criteria need to be realigned with the criteria of God's honor-shame values.

Christ teaches and models for humanity the honor-shame dynamics of the Kingdom of God. Jesus successfully defends his honor, a point the biblical writers are careful to demonstrate,[4] but at the same time he redefines what it means to be an honorable person. Now the foot-washing role of a servant can be honorable. Jesus even tampered with the distinction between men's role and space and women's role and space. Mary was affirmed in absenting herself from the kitchen and entering man-space (Luke 10:38-42). Even taking up a cross can be honorable in the Kingdom of God!

Joseph Hellerman, in his study of Philippians 2:5-11, highlights the way Paul deliberately counters the extreme status consciousness of the Roman colony at Philippi. Where Romans (and thus Rome-loving Philippians) loved to advertise their *cursus honorum*, the upward trajectory of their career advancement, Paul, in contrast, advertises the *cursus pudorum*,

---

[4] See David M. May, "Mark 3:20-35 from the Perspective of Shame/Honor," *Biblical Theology Bulletin,* 17 (1987); and Jerome H. Neyrey, "The Trials [Forensic] and Tribulations [Honor Challenges] of Jesus: John 7 in Social Science Perspective," *Biblical Theology Bulletin,* 26 (1996).

the downward trajectory of shameful dis-advancement, that Christ pursued.[5]

Thus we see that Jesus is attuned to the reality of shame. He is incarnate in an honor-shame culture. Sensitivity to shame is integral to the conscious and subconscious backdrop of his world. As we reflect upon Jesus' ministry in this setting, it becomes evident that he is offering great hope to people burdened with shame. He does this in two ways.

Ministry in word

We can begin with the teaching of Jesus. Jesus confronted the honor-shame criteria of his earthly culture with radically alternate criteria. For example: "Turn the other cheek!" Hitting the face (the focus of honor) was a great threat to honor, requiring immediate action to defend the honor. But with the in-breaking of the Kingdom of God, the rules of the game changed. Jesus announced a new set of criteria that made turning the other cheek a possible honor response.

But Jesus also challenged the honor-shame values of his culture at a much deeper level. He had a particular concern for the least, the last, and the lost. He loved those who could not even defend themselves in the face of an honor challenge, let alone climb the honor ladder. With the new rules of the Kingdom, hope flooded in for these people too:

> Blessed are the poor in spirit,
>   for theirs is the kingdom of heaven.
> Blessed are those who mourn,
>   for they shall be comforted. (Matthew 5:3-4)

---

[5] Joseph H. Hellerman, "The Humiliation of Christ in the Social World of Roman Philippi, Parts I & II," *Bibliotheca Sacra* 160 (2003): 321-336, 421-433.

What powerful words of healing and release for those on the outside looking in.

In the parable of the prodigal son, Jesus portrays the recovery of the lost son. Kenneth Bailey has painstakingly unpacked the cultural implications of this story.[6] Here are some of the relevant aspects. In acquiring his financial inheritance dishonorably, the son squanders all his honor credits. The story is skillfully told to highlight the young man's shamefulness. The power of the story is felt as the father, in his love for the son, is willing to behave in culturally shameful ways to protect and restore his boy. In his running, embracing, clothing, and celebrating, the father, in effect transfers the shame of the son to himself. What is "parabolic" is that the father is intended to represent God, who takes human shame on himself, thus restoring lost people to their place and identity in the community.

Significant here also is not just the *content* of the story but the *way* of the telling. Parables are veiled truth. They are shy presentations of truth. Not only do parables slip behind the guard of the proud, but they slip behind the guard of the shamed. The full light of truth is too bright for overexposed (shamed) people. Parables slip into the heart as memorable stories and stick. They are deceptively powerful in rewriting deeply etched shame scripts. What we admire in Jesus is the *way* of his words, not just the *what*. We pastors need to follow Jesus and speak grace for shame; but we will need to move beyond lectures on the subject and learn from Jesus' manner of speaking.

---

[6] Kenneth E. Bailey, *Finding the Lost: Cultural Keys to Luke 15* (St. Louis, MO: Concordia Publishing House, 1992).

Ministry of presence

But there is more. It was not only with his *words* that Jesus ministered healing for shame, it was also with his *person*. Shame is about loss of place and stature in the eyes of self and *others*. Shame is a relational problem requiring a relational response. Luke 15 begins with the report that tax collectors and "sinners" were congregating around Jesus. The Pharisees and law-teachers react: "This man welcomes sinners and eats with them." What Jesus is doing is spending time with the least honorable members of society. He is physically with them. He is present to them. Not only that, but he actually *eats* with them. We can almost hear the disdain in the mutterings. To eat with, in that context, was to identify with, to join with, to take the part of. In effect, Jesus says these people are *my* people.

Here is Jesus, a man who has demonstrated his ability (publicly, of course) to defend ably any honor challenges thrown at him. He is an honorable man. Now, however, he shares his honor with those who have none. In telling the three parables of the lost sheep, the lost coin, and the lost son, Jesus is, in fact, jousting for the honor of his shameful tablemates. And his opponents are left speechless.

Yes, the sins of the tax collectors and "sinners" are real and have multiple consequences, but Jesus brings hope *first* at the point of shame. Jesus, by his presence at their table, gives them back themselves. He restores their dignity. They get bragging rights. They have eaten with Jesus! They are some-bodies again, not no-bodies. Yes, lifestyles will need to change. Yes, restitution will need to be made. Yes, forgiveness will need to be appropriated. Nevertheless, Jesus *begins* the healing by loving the "sinner," not just in words, but in a costly giving of himself. Albers puts it well: "Intellectual acceptance and verbal affirmation normally do not carry sufficient power of weight for the shame-based person to shift her or his personal attitude. Grace must be incarnationally experienced."[7] *in relationship*

We discover great hope for shame in Jesus. We find it in his humble approach, the setting aside of glory. We find it in his Kingdom teaching, both in content and form. And we find hope for shame in his self-giving love. He invited himself into the sinners' circle and transformed it into a new community. But the spear-point of Jesus' attack on shame was the cross. And to this we now turn.

The Cross and Shame

> . . . looking to Jesus, the founder and perfecter of our faith, who for the joy that was set before him endured the cross, despising the shame, and is seated at the right hand of the throne of God. (Hebrews 12:2)

He shared our shame

Yes, it is true that Jesus was incarnate in an honor-shame culture. He had a sensitivity to the subtleties of honor and shame that was anchored in the depths of his Palestinian identity. This man knew about the burden of shame. But could he really identify with shamed people? Could he truly minister to shamed people? In the game of honor, Jesus was master. He foiled every shaming thrust. But how would the shame-bound person feel in the presence of such class?

---

[7] Albers, *Shame*, 98.

Berecz and Helm argue that holding up Jesus as a model is unrealistic, thus shame producing. They go so far as to say the answer to shame is to back away from Jesus as the model and refocus on Adam and Eve.[8] But this argument fails in two places. First, shamed people, in fact, were *not* intimidated by Jesus. They were drawn to him in life and found release from shame. Second, and even more significantly, Jesus *did* experience shame. He knew it profoundly in the cross.

Albers describes Jesus' experience:

> [The cross] represents a symbol of God's solidarity with humankind. In Christ the experience of disgrace-shame is epitomized as he suffers the shaming experiences of the passion—mocking, derision, humiliation, scourging, spitting, and the ultimate ignominy and isolation of the crucifixion.[9]

At the cross Jesus draws even nearer to our human condition, and actually takes on shame for love's sake.

Those suffering from shame will not be helped by a focus on God's power alone. For these sufferers the concept of God's suffering love is more helpful.[10] And what deeper suffering than the suffering of shame—a suffering that cuts to the very core of human identity?

The proclamation of the cross was, from the beginning, and still is, foolishness to the sophisticated hearer. Yet it is at the foot of the cross we find God's deepest answer for shame. We still feel awkward around the cross. But to shy away from the brutal reality of the cross, complete with its humiliation and shame is, in effect, to retreat into docetism, that old belief that

---

[8] John M. Berecz and Herbert W. Helm, "Shame: The Underside of Christianity," *Journal of Psychology and Christianity,* 17 (1998): 5f.

[9] Albers, "The Shame Factor," 351.

[10] Ramsay, "Sexual Abuse and Shame," 120.

God only *seemed* to draw near.[11] No, Jesus truly is Emmanuel—God with us. And the painful reality of his crucifixion is pivotal for the followers of Jesus.

So while the resurrection of Christ represents the *final* victory over shame, it is important not to rush past the cross. Shame must be acknowledged before it can be healed. Shame-oriented people will benefit more from Good Friday as they identify with the one who was shamed. Perhaps this is why the Lord Jesus called on the church to focus on the cross, not the resurrection, at the communion table. It takes time to be a resurrection person. Hurrying Easter Sunday will only highlight the failings of the non-triumphal. Indeed, if the message of Christ is to wield its powerful effect, the cross must be presented in all its scandal and humiliation. A domesticated cross will not deliver fallen people from the depths of sin and shame.

The shame of crucifixion

Neyrey, in his analysis of shame in crucifixion, summarizes the "progressive humiliation" of the victims. Crucifixion was a punishment reserved for slaves (it was not even spoken of in polite society). The trials were held in public. The victim was further humiliated by naked, public torture. He was forced to carry his own cross-beam. Clothing was confiscated. The tied or nailed hands left the victim unable to make a defense, thus further shaming. Public execution was accompanied by mocking, often intensified by fastening the victim to the cross in odd positions. Death was slow and involved embarrassing loss of control over bodily functions. The corpse was usually

---

[11] Martin Hengel, *Crucifixion in the Ancient World and the Folly of the Message of the Cross* (Philadelphia: Fortress, 1977), 15f.

left to wild animals.[12] It was this shameful experience of death by crucifixion that Jesus endured.

Let's look in more detail at the shame of the crucifixion. Jesus endured the vulnerability of allowing himself to be arrested. It is a shame to be held and pushed by others. With this came the shame of betrayal. We can imagine the laughter among the soldiers as his own Judas kissed him (Matthew 26:48f.). Then the shame of abandonment as his disciples fled. At the interrogation before the high priest, Jesus is mocked. Others make fun of his prophetic powers (Matthew 26:68).

They hit him in the face and spit in his face (John 18:22, Matthew 26:27), a blatant insult to honor (which has its focus in the head). We can add here the testimony of Isaiah as he records the words of the Servant: "I gave my back to those who strike, and my cheeks to those who pull out the beard; I hid not my face from disgrace and spitting" (Isaiah 50:6). Loss of the beard was shaming (see, e.g., 2 Samuel 10:4).

Jesus suffers the shame of having the crowd prefer Barabbas, the insurrectionist, over him (John 18:40). Jesus is beaten by the soldiers, but the mocking is even more painful. As Neyrey points out, "It produces the most dreaded of all experiences, shame."[13] Again the mocking is aimed at Jesus' head, the seat of his honor, as the soldiers strike him in the face, spit at his face and force a cruel, mocking crown on his head (John 19:3, Matthew 27:30). The blindfolding (Mark 14:65) further "reduces" Jesus. He cannot see to walk or brace himself. He stumbles like a child and is caught off guard by the blows.

---

[12] Jerome H. Neyrey, "Despising the Shame of the Cross: Honor and Shame in the Johannine Passion Narrative," *Semeia,* 68 (1996): 113f.

[13] Ibid., 125.

Jesus was stripped for the scourging. In a modest culture like that of the Jews, nakedness was especially shameful. Captives were often paraded naked (e.g., 2 Samuel 10:4, Isaiah 20:4). Shame is about exposure. Jesus was exposed without mercy. The ground refused to swallow him up.

Jesus, with his quiet and peaceable spirit, was thrown into the center of a public uproar (Matthew 27:24). Both shame and honor come to life before a viewing public, and Jesus is certainly on display. There is nothing secret about the crucifixion. The crowd, in an act of profound rejection and condemnation, cries out, "Crucify him!" (John 19:6). It was not here his *actions* being condemned but Jesus *himself*. This is the "global condemnation" that is both the foundation and fear of shame.

The King of kings suffers progressively deepening shame as his status is reduced to that of a crucify-able person, a nobody. The greater the fall, the greater the shame. Hengel, in his classic study of the crucifixion, gives this assessment: "By the public display of a naked victim at a prominent place . . . crucifixion . . . represented his uttermost humiliation."[14] He who was most high, was brought most low. In all this, Jesus assumes that silent wordlessness that is the hallmark of the shamed (Matthew 26:63).

Carrying the cross was itself shaming (John 19:17). Slaves were punished and shamed by being made to carry a pole around the neighborhood. A cross-pole would invoke even greater shame. But if there was even deeper shame, it was that a man was not able to carry his own cross. Such was Jesus' humiliation (Mark 15:21).

---

[14] Hengel, *Crucifixion in the Ancient World*, 88.

Then, with no allowance for the sensibility of a faithful Jew for matters of religious purity, Jesus is marched onto the unclean site of the crucifixion. Humiliation was deepened by the threat of the lack of burial for the body. The bones and half eaten corpses of earlier victims littered the site. There, on a hill, beside a busy road, he would die. Modesty (discretionary shame) calls for privacy at birth and death. We still pull a sheet over a dead body. Part of the shame of the cross was the public nature of Jesus' dying. No curtains were drawn around his hard bed. But even if human eyes had been averted, the humiliation of Jesus could not be hidden from the spirit world. Jesus was shamed before "rulers and authorities in the heavenly realms" (see Ephesians 3:10), a degree of exposure we cannot imagine.

Shame and honor are conveyed by location. Jesus bore the shame of suffering *outside* the city walls (Hebrews 13:11-13). And to drive home the loss of status, Jesus is hung between two thieves (John 19:18), his last living memory (as thought). All hope of recovery from nakedness is gone as his clothes are gambled away (John 19:23). He is again mocked in his helplessness (Matthew 27:42). He had come to his own and been rejected (John 1:11). And over all this, what shame fears most, the experience of divine rejection. "My God, my God, why have you forsaken me?" (Mark 15:34).

Uncontrolled exposure of body and soul is the fuel of shame. Jesus was publicly stripped of friends, freedom, dignity, clothes, light, life, and even of his Father's acceptance. Could there have been any deeper exposure? In the cross we fast forward to sin's *telos*: exposure and abandonment, utter shame and humiliation.

Gazing on the cross

Don't bother me with polished cross
Or plaster cartoon crucifix
Forget your smoking limping lights
And plaintive hairless kitten prayers

I want my Jesus, man for men
Whose decibels would rouse the dead
Whose parables with fishy breath
Would slap some sense in sleepy heads

Now rainless clouds relentless slide
The whip-wind howls along the hill
The pulpy bloody shadowed man
Howls back but no one answers him

And there he dies in gasps and drips
Naked as a nightmare on his ugly pole
All my worst fears mirrored on him
My Jesus washed in shame for me[15]

As we learn to take seriously the deep shame of Golgotha, unexpectedly we discover this cross to be a place of healing and restoration. One staunchly Protestant woman found surprising release from inner turmoil as she entered a Catholic church and put her hand on a crucifix. She recognized in a new way the depths of Jesus' identification with her suffering.

---

[15] These lines express something of the emotion I felt as I meditated on the shaming of crucifixion.

Feminist theology has opened new perspectives on the death of Christ. It may be that women generally have been quicker to understand the meaning of Jesus' journey into shame. See, for example, Josephine Ford and her examination of the shame of the cross. She sees a Christ who chose to be a friend who would "go to calamity's depths" for his friends. So that even the most abused in this wide world could know him as a real friend.[16]

Roberta Bondi describes her own profound and searching pilgrimage to a new understanding of the crucifixion. The journey begins with the angry God of her childhood demanding payment for sin, which she sees as mirrored humanly in the demand for female subservience. It ends with a new understanding of a God who loved humanity so much that he took on himself the shame that binds and destroys, in order to give freedom. Her portrayal of her own reconversion is powerful testimony to the irrepressible fullness of the Gospel. She puts these words into the mouth of Jesus:

> It is your suffering shame that consumes you with anger, that renders you passive, that swallows you in depression, that keeps you from loving and knowing yourself to be loved. . . . I hate the shame that binds you and destroys you, and I will prove it to you and to the world by casting in my lot with you even so far as to die a death the world finds shameful. By showing you the source and meaning of your shame, I will make space for you to breathe and thrive. This is what I, Jesus, as a human being in the image of God, and as God's own self, chose with great joy.[17]

---

[16] Josephine M. Ford, *Redeemer: Friend and Mother* (Minneapolis, MN: Fortress Press, 1997), 52f.

[17] R. Bondi, "Out of the Green-Tiled Bathroom: Crucifixion," 27.

We experience the consequence of sin as guilt *and* shame. The Western world has long understood the cross as God's answer to guilt. What we are rediscovering is the cross as God's answer to shame. We have forgotten what the ancient church knew well. It was, in fact, in her reading of Athanasius and Gregory of Nyssa of the early Eastern church that Bondi discovered the seeds to her "new" understanding of the cross as healing for shame.[18] As we gather together to gaze on the cross of Christ, many of us will discover that it is the resolution of our shame that unlocks the door for the resolution of our guilt.

Seeds of glory

We must not end this brief survey of the cross and shame without also noting that in entering into the experience of shame at the deepest level, Jesus is already reinterpreting shame. He is already fusing it with glory.[19] This understanding is developed in the thought and writings of the early church, in Acts and the Letters. Neyrey sees this too in the passion narrative. An honor script runs parallel to the shame script. For example, the Apostle John alerts the reader to the honor Christ wins to himself. Thus Jesus knew of his arrest beforehand (he is not taken by surprise); the soldiers fall down; Jesus guards the safety of his followers.[20] The cross becomes a place of "lifting up," an exaltation; it is transformed from a place of shame to a place of glory. As Moxnes writes: "Power in weakness, confidence of honor while seemingly put to

---

[18] Ibid., 20.

[19] Ford, *Redeemer: Friend and Mother*, 95.

[20] Neyrey, "Despising the Shame of the Cross," 119f. See also David Daube, *The New Testament and Rabbinic Judaism* (Peabody, MA: Hendrickson, 1956), 301f.

shame—that was the paradox of Christian existence in a Jewish and Graeco-Roman environment."[21]

So in the end the cross became an badge of honor. In enduring the worst shame humanity could inflict, Christ triumphed over shame and made possible the same triumph for his followers. For each individual, as for him, the answer is not to avoid the shame of the cross but to take up the cross, and find victory in so doing. Or, as Hebrews puts it: "Therefore let us go to him outside the camp and bear the reproach [shame] he endured. For here we have no lasting city, but we seek the city that is to come" (13:13-14).

The Gospel and Shame

The Christian Gospel is, by definition, good news. But is it good news for shame-oriented people? How is the finished work of Christ redemptive for shame? These are the questions we are exploring. What we are discovering is that traditional "Gospel scripts" do not answer the cry of all hearts. Smedes expresses his own longing: "What I needed more than pardon was a sense that God accepted me, owned me, held me, affirmed me, and would never let go of me."[22] For Bondi it became very clear: "I did not need to repent. I needed to be rescued from my shame."[23]

There is, in fact, a tension between the way our Gospel narrative describes human need and the way that need is

---

[21] Moxnes, "Honor and Righteousness in Romans," 73.

[22] Lewis B. Smedes, *Shame and Grace: Healing the Shame We Don't Deserve* (San Francisco: HarperSanFrancisco, 1993), 80.

[23] R. Bondi, "Out of the Green-Tiled Bathroom: Crucifixion," 26.

expressed by many people. This tension exists within the church. Capps's study of committed Christians reveals

> that Christian laity and clergy have conceptions of sin that are generally congruent with a theology of guilt, whereas their actual experience of sinfulness—of a deep inner sense of wrongness—is more reflective of the psycho-dynamics of shame.[24]

And this tension also exists at the interface of the church and the world as Pannenberg observes:

> In modern times a Christianity which takes its bearings from the problem of guilt has increasingly come up against lack of understanding and mistrust among people who do not feel themselves to be sinners and who consequently believe that they do not need the message of forgiveness either.[25]

The argument here is not that the Christian Gospel is irrelevant or artificial but that pastors need to rediscover the breadth of the Gospel, particularly as it relates to shame. If we neglect this aspect of salvation, our message will be irrelevant, for practical purposes, for many people. Furthermore we will not glorify (honor!) God as we might.

Is atonement for everyone?

We have already seen how theological understanding is enriched by fresh perspectives from other disciplines. Psychologist Paul Pruyser makes a helpful contribution at this point in an article entitled "Anxiety, Guilt and Shame in the Atonement." Remarkably, he wrote this in 1964, long before

---

[24] Capps, *The Depleted Self*, 41.
[25] Quoted by Pembroke, "Towards a Shame-Based Theology of Evangelism," 15.

shame had even begun to be a topic of theological conversation. Pruyser divides the various theories of the atonement into three categories:

1. In the "Ransom Theory" (e.g., Origen, Gregory of Nyssa, and Gregory the Great), "the death of Christ is the ransom price which God pays to Satan in order to reclaim the creature estranged from him by original sin." The ransom theory resolves anxiety.

2. In the "Satisfaction Theory" (e.g., Anselm) the death of Christ satisfies God's requirement for justice. The satisfaction theory resolves guilt.

3. The "Moral Influence Theory" (e.g., Gregory of Nazianzus, Abelard, and Crotius) emphasizes the human desire to emulate Christ, who identified with and suffered for us. The moral influence theory highlights the resolution of shame.

Pruyser describes shame as the sense of falling short (of the ideal). The Moral Influence Theory of the atonement offers the possibility of real change for the better, thus resolution of shame.[26]

As indicated in the introduction, this is not the place to pursue a three-dimensioned salvation (for guilt, shame, and anxiety), but we are challenged here to enlarge our Gospel understanding. This is no easy matter. As Pruyser rightly points out, "Each believer is immersed, as it were, in a vast symbol

---

[26] Paul W. Pruyser, "Anxiety, Guilt, and Shame in the Atonement," in *Religion in Psychodynamic Perspective: The Contributions of Paul W. Pruyser,* H. Newton Malony and Bernard Spilka, eds. (Oxford: Oxford University Press, 1991), 99f.

system around a given atonement motif."[27] Our reflex response may be to doubt whether alternate motifs are even Christian!

Pruyser rejects the idea that Christians should tailor their atonement theory to the condition of the hearer. Yet he does argue for a rich, creative, multifaceted, psychologically aware formulation of the atonement that speaks to "the young and the old, the simple and the sophisticated, the well and the sick, the sure ones and the perplexed."[28] In addition, it could be added, to those whose wholeness and sinfulness have been deeply sculpted by cultures other than the cultures of the West.

Alan Mann, in a much more recent study, sends a passionate call to the church to listen more carefully to, and engage more deeply with, the postmodern world. He is concerned that traditional, guilt-oriented readings of the atonement will not make sense to a society where the concept of sin is lost. He calls for a new Pentecost where once again people will hear the gospel in their own language. With echoes of Pruyser he writes:

> [T]he story of atonement needs to be rich and thick so that it can speak meaningfully and sufficiently to every storied-self it encounters: The lost need to be found. The socially excluded need to be welcomed. The sick need to be healed. The oppressed need to be liberated. The divided need to be reconciled. The chronically shamed need to become "shameless." Ultimately, individual and communal needs shape where the emphasis comes in the story of atonement.[29]

---

[27] Ibid., 111.

[28] Ibid., 116.

[29] Alan Mann, *Atonement for a "Sinless" Society: Engaging with an Emerging Culture* (Milton Keynes, U.K.: Paternoster Press, 2005), 97.

The good news for pastors in the twenty-first century is that our gospel truly is "rich and thick." Faithful exegesis of our present *actual* world (not our nostalgically *remembered* world!) invigorates our exegesis of Scripture and opens our eyes to forgotten but hungered-for dimensions of the Gospel. Do we have the courage to preach a Gospel that strikes a chord for more than those who are "just like us"? If we don't, we will find our message increasingly irrelevant for people, including our own children, who are formed by cultures other than our own.

Good news for shame

Again, not all shame is bad. Shame is a healthy sanction for people who have mature shame. Modesty is good. Nevertheless, for people who got stuck with shame, possibly in infancy (and who still feel shame in a global, narcissistic way), there needs to be release. For those who have been deeply shamed, often by the sins of others, for example by sexual abuse, there needs to be healing. For those who have sinned, and respond with more shame than guilt, there needs to be hope of recovery.

Given the multifaceted nature of shame and the way shame is felt differently in different contexts, it is wise to resist generalizations. Moreover we must never forget how difficult it is to empathize with a person feeling shame in another culture. To a great extent shame is culture specific and hard to understand from outside. What is needed is deep respect and careful listening. Nevertheless, it is apparent that the Christian Gospel is grace for shame as well as grace for guilt, and both sides of the Gospel are needed.

So, yes, we need grace as forgiveness. We humans have a righteousness deficit; we have sinned; we are guilty. We need redemption from our moral indebtedness. But we humans also need grace as honor. We have squandered our honor. We have an honor deficit. Hence our shame. Our sin has left us on the outside looking in. God's gracious gift of honor is precisely what is needed. We sinners resist grace in both forms, but we need both to find full freedom. Grace for guilt is unmerited forgiveness. Grace for shame is unmerited acceptance. (And grace for anxiety is unmerited security.)

We may well find that preaching the Gospel of forgiveness is counterproductive for shame-bound people. Or at least it is not the place to begin. Shame-bound people cannot separate out wrong actions from wrong self. Forgiveness for sinful behavior does not yet help. Offering forgiveness simply confirms their misdeeds which, in their shame-bound state, is a confirmation of their unworthiness as persons.

Good News for shamed people is to discover that they are accepted, they are affirmed, they are valued as unique persons, they are included, they are welcomed, they are embraced, and they are loved. As Patton rightly observes, "Guilt can be more nearly dealt with according to rational principle, whereas shame is inevitably relational and personal."[30] Gospel truth for shamed people is that God loves them dearly. So the New Testament paints the picture of the spreading Gospel bringing grace for both guilt and shame around the Mediterranean. Wherever it travels the Gospel rewrites the scripts of shame-bound people and graciously dispenses honor.

---

[30] Patton, *Is Human Forgiveness Possible?* 39.

The healing word for guilt is well known, it is the grace of forgiveness. The healing word for shame is now apparent, it is the grace of acceptance. The good news for shamed people is the embrace of God. The love of God calls the shamed self out of hiding. No more does God have to say, "Where are you?" Now the shame-healed person steps out into the gaze of God saying, "Behold me!"

How is this possible? It is possible because our sins have been removed and we have been clothed with the righteousness of Christ. Here is the gospel according to Isaiah:

> I will greatly rejoice in the Lord;
>> my soul shall exult in my God,
> for he has clothed me with the garments of salvation;
>> he has covered me with the robe of righteousness. (61:10)

This joy anticipated by Isaiah is now available to us all.

From the perspective of honor-shame culture, the Gospel is about displacing shame with honor. Honor accrues from honorable relationships. Who are you the son of? Who are you the daughter of? The Gospel—the Good News—is this: "To all who did receive him, who believed in his name, he gave the right to become children of God" (John 1:12). We are now sons and daughters of the most high God! Who is the chief of our tribe?—none other than *Christus Victor,* the Victorious Christ. Now that is good news for shame-bound people!

Honor also relates to where we are from. The simple question, "Where do you come from?" may elicit honor or shame (think Nazareth, for example). But God's grace for shame reframes our past as well as our future. And we learn to say of our Nazareths, "Surely God was in that place."

In the kingdoms of this world honor is in limited supply and is accumulated only by those who can play the game well. The poor in spirit, the mournful, the meek, get only scraps. But in God's kingdom honor is poured out, shaken together, spilling over. There is more than enough to go around. We, too, are free to give it away. We can choose to be lowly foot-washers, and still honor comes. We can choose to turn the other cheek, and still honor comes. All are special. All are honored. All have the closest possible relationship to the high king. All are blessed.

Wherever two or three are gathered together in this world there is immediately the question of who has most honor! But when Jesus is in the midst he challenges the culture of the two or three. He changes the rules. He redistributes honor according to the Kingdom of Heaven.

Shame fears abandonment, but God covenants himself to nearness, non-abandonment. The notion of covenant is important for people with shame-based identities because the covenant that God establishes with his people does not *depend* on his people. God does not set qualifying standards—he accepts us as we are. Yet for shame-bound people it is hard to accept that the great promise, "I will be with you," is enough to deal with the horror of shame. At first Moses, in his shame, struggled to accept (Exodus 4), but, over time, he did.

Healing for shame is the recovery of face-to-faceness. Capps speaks of this as a kind of "healthy narcissism":

> Mirroring is at the very heart of the Christian Gospel. Quite simply but profoundly, it is the form and means by which the depleted self experiences divine grace, the benediction of God:

"May the Lord's face shine upon you, and give you peace, now and forever more."[31]

Moses came eventually to a face-to-face relationship with God (Exodus 33:11). All humanity is invited to the same. The good news of the Christian faith is that in Christ people may recover true face-to-faceness with both God and other people. The temple curtain is torn open, so that all may draw near to God in confidence (Hebrews 10:19f.). And the human walls of separation have been demolished so that we may gaze upon each other in love (Ephesians 2:14f.).

An incarnational Gospel

Always, the Gospel for shame needs more than words. As shame is a relational problem, God's answer is a relational answer. Shamed people need an incarnational Gospel. And this God has provided. "When the fullness of time had come, God sent forth his Son, born of woman" (Galatians 4:4). So, as we have already seen, Jesus, by his life, demonstrated Good News for shame. He embraced those with no honor and restored their personhood. In his death he identified with the deepest human shame and transformed the cross from a place of shame to a place of glory.

But this relational, incarnational Gospel for shame did not end with the ascension of Jesus. Jesus established a new community, so identified with himself as to be called his body. This new community is the place of acceptance, respect, welcome, and embrace, in Jesus' name, for all who come. In the life of the church this inclusion comes to a focus around the communion table.

---

[31] Capps, *The Depleted Self,* 64.

Why was Paul so upset with the behavior of the Corinthian church around the table (1 Corinthians 11)? He was upset because the very heart of the Gospel was betrayed. The old rules of who was honorable and who was not were creeping back into the church.[32] This is catastrophic for the life of the church.

In the body of Christ all have equal honor, the weak and the strong, the gentiles and the Jews, the slaves and the free, the women and the men, all have a seat around the table. Christ has rewritten the cultural narrative that describes who is honorable and who is not. Yes, there is a setting apart; there is an in and out. But shame is a wrong setting apart; holiness is the right setting apart. And holiness is found in Christ (Romans 6:21-22). Thus Jewett argues that the concept of *justification* in Romans is not simply forgiveness for sins. It is the breaking in of a radically new evaluative reality that has profound implications for who is in and who is out. God's proclamation of "in" overrides previous cultural considerations and becomes the foundation of a new culture.[33] The church is not called to *geographical* separation but to live with its radically rewritten honor-shame rules *in the midst of* the old order, thus existing as powerful and poignant testimony to the Kingdom of God where deposits of honor are dispensed graciously and incontestably.

What is the Gospel to shame-oriented people? It is not so much *guilt* removed (at least not yet). It is the news that transformation of the self is possible—from self seen as deficient, to self welcomed and valued. The Gospel brings

---

[32] Robert Jewett, "Babette's Feast and the Shaming of the Poor in Corinth," *Dialog,* 36 (4) (1997).

[33] Robert Jewett, "Honor and Shame in the Argument of Romans," 270.

healing for shame because it offers redemption for broken *persons* not just broken *actions*. It justifies the sinner, not just the sin. We cross from Adam's line to Jesus' line. We are born again into a new humanity (Romans 5).

Construing human brokenness and the impact of sin more in terms of shame and less in terms of guilt highlights the need to make room for conversion as *process* and not only as *event*. Shame relates to core identity, and the defining scripts will not be transformed overnight. In fact, like all aspects of salvation the grace of acceptance has its eschatological dimension; it anticipates a heavenly completion. Nevertheless, it is also very much a grace for here and now. As Smedes puts it so well, the Gospel for shame "is the discovery that we are in spite of everything accepted by the grace of someone we most need to accept us."[34] This is Good News!

Parresia—Evidence of Recovery

But does it work? Does the Gospel of Jesus Christ in fact bring relief from shame? Is there evidence of recovery? If we ask these questions of the New Testament we get a number of answers in the affirmative.

For example, there is Paul's lack of shame in regard to the Gospel. Within the construct of Mediterranean culture, the idea of a crucified leader was untenable. For the head of the clan to suffer such loss of honor cast a blanket of shame over the whole group. This is observed in the response of the disciples to Jesus' arrest—his clan fled. Yet as the full story of the cross

---

[34] Smedes, *Shame and Grace*, 60.

and the resurrection and ascension comes to light, a marked change becomes evident in the honor-shame rating of the disciples. For example Paul writes: "I am not ashamed of the Gospel" (Romans 1:16). In fact, his so-called shamelessness reaches its zenith as he openly proclaims the "folly" of the cross (1 Corinthians 1:18-31). Furthermore, he invokes shame on himself if he does *not* preach the Gospel (1 Corinthians 9:16).

There is a psychological robustness about each of these post-resurrection New Testament characters. They stand tall. They stand out. They stand against the opposition. These are not diminished, wordless, hidden persons, but vibrant, confident, present, and engaged. They are shame free.

But there is other evidence of recovery. There is one intriguing New Testament word that speaks particularly of the Gospel as grace for shame. This is the Greek noun *parresia* (and the corresponding verb *parresiazomai*). *Parresia* is complex, difficult to express in one English word, but often glossed as "boldness." It stands in opposition to shame. If shame is "a category of hiddenness, wordlessness, abomination and rejection,"[35] *parresia* is a category of openness, public speech, confidence, and face-to-faceness.[36]

Take, for example, Acts chapter four. Peter and John had been preaching publicly about Jesus. The religious leaders were very upset and arrested the two disciples. The next day, in response to interrogation, they declared even more forcefully their allegiance to Jesus, ending with the bold assertion, "There

---

[35] Pattison, *Shame*, 290.
[36] For my extended study of this word, see John Forrester, "*Parresia* in the New Testament: Openness and Confidence in Christian Communication" (Th.M. Thesis, Regent College, 1995).

is salvation in no one else, for there is no other name under heaven given among men by which we must be saved" (Acts 4:12). This is followed by the narrative response: "When they saw the boldness [*parresia*] of Peter and John and perceived that they were uneducated, common men, they were astonished. And they recognized that they had been with Jesus" (4:13). Clearly the leaders intended to shame the disciples. But instead they were taken by surprise at their "boldness." And even they somehow made the link between the boldness of the disciples and their connection to Jesus. Being with Jesus had shame-proofed these men.

Some background

Parresia turns out to have a significant place in the vocabulary of the New Testament. It is one more indication that shame and its recovery comprise a much more salient New Testament concern than we late Westerners may have realized. *Parresia* and *parresiazomai* are together used about forty times in the New Testament with a widespread distribution. In order to tell the story, it is necessary to briefly survey its prior history.

The word came to prominence in the fifth century B.C. as the Athenians began to experiment with a democratic model of government. *Parresia* (from *pan*, "all" and *resia*, "saying") was the "freedom to say everything" that was the privilege of Athenian citizens under this new system. In a world where freedom of speech was rare, this *parresia* was prized. Exiled citizens mourned the loss of this freedom more than anything else.[37]

---

[37] See Euripedes, *The Phoenecian Maiden,* Translated by Arthur Sanders Way (Cambridge, MA: Harvard University Press, 1962), 388f.

As the Athenian dalliance with democracy collapsed *parresia* shifted from the political world to the personal world. For example, it emerged as an aspect of friendship. Plato observed, "Frankness of speech [*parresia*], by common report and belief, is the language of friendship."[38] Where *parresia* did persist politically, the element of courage became more pronounced. It takes a brave man to speak his mind when the political right is gone.

And one more note: the Cynic philosophers pushed *parresia* beyond the edge of decency. L. E. Vaage writes: "In the mouth of a Cynic, *parresia* meant saying whatever whenever however in such a way as to provoke the consistent sensation of 'boldness.'"[39] Just as shame is not always bad, so boldness is no longer good after a certain point.

It is this history that gives *parresia* its richness of meaning. Thus, in addition to the core meaning of freedom of speech, *parresia* carries overtones of truthfulness, openness, frankness, confidence, and courage. It indicates an inner freedom that is particularly expressed in speech.

It is worth noting also that while this word plays a significant role in the New Testament, it is rare in the Septuagint (only twelve occurrences in the whole of the Old Testament). This is unusual. It is common to see New Testament writers taking up the theological vocabulary of the LXX. Not so with *parresia*.

What prompted the New Testament writers to import this largely secular word? The argument is this. As the church began to grow, observers noticed something odd about these

---

[38] Plato, *Laches*, 188. E.
[39] Leif E. Vaage, "Like Dogs Barking: Cynic *Parresia* and Shameless Asceticism," *Semeia* 57 (1992): 26f.

new followers of Jesus. They spoke with a remarkable freedom and confidence. In looking for a word that captured this new phenomenon, they drew in this old secular word and began using it in this new religious context. In support of this argument it should be noted that *parresia* only appears once in the synoptic Gospels yet is a major theme in Acts. Why this distinctive usage? The answer is that *parresia* did not emerge until *Christians* began to emerge: it is a characteristic of born-again people. The church that emerged after the death, resurrection, and ascension of Jesus Christ was a community of shame-healed women and men.

Two dimensions

In the New Testament writings, *parresia* works in two directions. In Paul's letters and in Acts, the word primarily describes a characteristic of human relationships. In particular, *parresia* operates at the interface of the church and the world. When outward circumstances appear to dictate caution in order to avoid shame, Christians exhibit boldness and confidence, particularly in speaking of their Lord. Thus *parresia* is grace for shame *particularly in regard to sharing the Gospel.*

The New Testament, however, also speaks of *parresia* in relation to God. This usage is seen primarily in Hebrews and 1 John. For example, Hebrews 4:16: "Let us then with confidence [*parresia*] draw near to the throne of grace, that we may receive mercy and find grace to help in time of need." Thus rather than coming into God's presence bowed in shame, wordless and broken, God's people are invited and expected to come near with a sense of freedom and confidence. After all, we are no longer servants, but sons and daughters. Christians are to value this gift. Hebrews 10:35: "Therefore do not throw away your *parresia*." It has been purchased at a great price (Hebrews 10:19), the blood of Christ.

Furthermore, in 1 John 2:28 the return of Christ is anticipated with boldness: "And now, little children, abide in him, so that when he appears we may have confidence [*parresia*] and not shrink from him in shame at his coming." Here *parresia* is presented explicitly as the opposite of shame (see also Philippians 1:20). In a similar, way Christians look ahead to the day of judgment, not in shame but in confidence, *parresia* (1 John 4:17).

True, there is still, for now, a veil drawn across our relationship with God. Perhaps a few mystics will come close to the rapture of full openness, but for most people, in this life, it is only possible to bear so much before we fall back in awe. In Christ shame does not disappear entirely but takes its rightful place as modesty. Schneider quotes from the Talmud:

> "A sense of shame is a lovely sign in a man. Whoever has a sense of shame will not sin so quickly; but whoever shows no sense of shame in his visage, his father surely never stood on Mount Sinai."[40]

Nevertheless, though it is not appropriate to seek in this life the complete removal of shame, yet the Gospel of grace for shame is a remarkable gift. This gift of boldness is to be welcomed. Like all Gospel gifts it must be appropriated. But by faith we say "Yes" and stand tall.

Parresia is an intriguing lexical thumbprint on the pages of the New Testament. It highlights the way the Gospel displaces shame. Followers of Jesus face the world with heads

---

[40] Schneider, in *Shame, Exposure and Privacy*, 109.

up. They have something worth saying and are confident about saying it. This impacts not only relationships at the human level but also our relationship with God. *Parresia* speaks of an openness and freedom—the human face gazing up into the face of God, basking in his love. Since we are clothed with the righteousness of Christ we no longer shrink back from the gaze of God. Our shame has been taken away.

And so, as we have seen, it turns out that many familiar texts of both Old Testament and New Testament deal in depth with the concerns of shame for both individuals and cultures. Furthermore, a study of the opening chapters of Genesis reveals that the roots of shame are to be found in the Fall. Both guilt *and* shame are consequences of sin.

But the Bible not only describes shame, it also offers hope and healing. The heart of God's redemptive response to the problem of human shame is found in the ministry of Christ. Both the *words* of Christ and the *works* of Christ offer profound hope for shamed people. We discover that the cross is awash with shame because it is precisely there at the cross that Christ took on himself the shame of the world as well as the guilt of the world. We are now in a better position to understand how the Gospel is Good News for shamed people.

What shamed people long for and need is acceptance, affirmation, and inclusion, precisely what the Gospel offers. The Gospel rewrites the rules about who is in and who is out. The Gospel is about the surprising hospitality of God. As people are restored to God and to each other they are able to then appropriate the grace of forgiveness more deeply.

The Christian characteristic of boldness that is seen in the New Testament is just one piece of evidence that the Gospel does indeed resolve shame. *Parresia* (boldness) describes the shame-healed person, not only in relation to other people, but also in relation to God. This biblical understanding of grace for shame provides a foundation on which we can build a more comprehensive applied theology. With this biblical background we can now begin to speak with authority about a pastoral ministry that responds helpfully to people and communities burdened by shame.

Part Three

Ministering Grace for Shame

5. Words That Heal

So far I have attempted to outline the way in which shame
has emerged as a category of ministry. Because of the elusive
and hidden nature of shame, it has been helpful to explore the
subject from the various perspectives of a range of disciplines.
In this way we are able to return to the biblical text with new
questions and perspectives that broaden our appreciation of the
efficacy of the Christian Gospel. The challenge now is to
translate this into pastoral ministry that more effectively
ministers God's grace. In particular, how do we minister grace
for shame? In this chapter I reflect on the *word* component of
ministry—teaching, preaching, and prayer. In the final chapter
I reflect on the *relational* component of ministry—so critical
for bringing hope to shame-troubled people.

Theologizing Grace for Shame

Western theology of the past five hundred years has
largely ignored shame. If we are going to minister grace for
shame effectively, we need to reintegrate shame into our
theology. It is not enough to add the word "shame" to our
theological vocabulary, or to add "shame ministry" to our
résumé. Shame needs to be firmly embedded in the conceptual
framework of the Christian faith of all who desire to minister

effectively the grace of Christ. Consciously or unconsciously, we minister out of our theology. A ministry that takes shame seriously needs theological substance. I offer what follows as a start to a theology of shame.

Shame and origins

Shame and sin feel like near neighbors, but what is the connection? As we have seen, the Bible teaches us that shame has its roots in the Fall. Adam and Eve sinned. They were objectively guilty of sin. But the narrative makes clear that the primary negative emotion they felt was not guilt but shame. Furthermore, the text implies that this shame was new. They had not experienced shame before. So with the first sin came the first shame. Shame is a result of sin let loose.

Given that Genesis is painting a picture of the origins of the human condition, we expect to see a close association between sin and shame in all people. It is true that not all shame is a direct consequence of sin. For example, a man may feel shame because of where he was born. Nevertheless, all shame has its roots in sin and if the link is not direct, it is, at least, indirect. Thus sinful actions of one (e.g., an abuser) inflict shame on another; and sinful attitudes of a group evoke shame in others.

Comparative cultural studies have established that people experience what it is to be a person in different ways. In group-oriented cultures individuals exist contextually (the "egg without the shell"). Since shame, by definition, relates to how people are seen, group-oriented people are shame oriented. And since, in these cultures, sin diminishes reputation, sin is felt as shame. Now it is true that in group cultures what constitutes "sin" varies from group to group among those not aligned with biblical values. Nevertheless, in general terms, in group cultures sin is felt as a failure of the person. This contrasts with individualistic cultures, where persons are less dependent on others for their identity. How they are seen is less of a burden. When such people sin, their negative feelings will be more guilt than shame. Guilt is sensitivity to rule-breaking and fears punishment. Shame is sensitivity to personal failure and fears rejection. Thus, while sin is universal, the felt consequences of sin vary. It is important to note, however, that statistically, group orientation is the more common way of experiencing personhood. Individualistic cultures are the exception and may be only temporary manifestations of human culture.

A theology that emphasizes guilt will major on behavior. A theology that includes shame will have to develop a theology of self. A study of shame alerts pastors to the reality that an adequate response to sin requires a rebuilding of self. Shamed people want to hide because of the pain of being seen as less. They instinctively draw back from being exposed as diminished persons. This feeling of being reduced begs the question, from what? Thus a theology of shame also calls forth a strong position on what might be called "original dignity." Human beings were created in the image of God. The *imago Dei,* and later the incarnation, are anchor points for the shamed person suffering with a diminished sense of self. Both affirm human worth. A theology of shame must not minimize sin. No lasting help for shame comes from calling particular sins "no sins," nor from backing away from the doctrine of "total depravity" (though we might want to rename it). Nevertheless, while a theology of shame does not flinch from the hard reality of Genesis chapter 3, the tragedy of the Fall is set against the joyful backdrop of Genesis chapters 1 and 2 and a glorious creation. A theology of shame reminds Christians that dignity is more original than sin.

Shame and identity

Just as the leper knows that physical pain is a blessing as well as a curse, so shame has its positive side. True, as we have already noted in this study, not everyone accepts the idea of "good shame." In fact those who resist the concept of "good shame" are often those who deny the pervasiveness of sin. Shame as a help in restraining sin doesn't make sense to those who believe in the "inherent goodness" of all people. But this takes the discussion outside orthodox Christian belief. The position taken here is that fear of shame serves a good cause by encouraging sin-avoidance.

But shame also has a more subtle effect. It helps guard privacy. Without shame, human beings lose their mystery. Shameless people do not know when to stop. Community cannot exist without privacy, nor intimacy without reticence. It takes individuals to make relationships. Sensitivity to shame sustains human *otherness* and preserves differentiation. The creation story can be read as a story of differentiation—light from darkness, up from down, water from dry land, day from night, animal from human, male from female, and, above all, creature from creator. The Fall was an attempt to "de-differentiate" at the deepest level, shamelessly wanting to be "like God." Good shame helps us redifferentiate, not only as created beings distinct from our creator, but as individuals distinct from each other.

But are there limits to the usefulness of this concept of differentiation? Here it is helpful to remember that we are created in the image of a Triune God. And here the relational Trinitarian models of the East (suggested, for example, by the language of John of Damascus, *perichoresis* [lit. "circle dance"] or the table scene in Rublev's famous icon) are more helpful in a discussion of shame than the more mechanical models of the West (triangles, ice/water/steam, and so on). What is the balance between unity and individuality in the Trinity? We take it as axiomatic that the Trinity is the ideal community. What this means for this study is that in the Trinity there is the perfect balance of the individual and the group. The Father, Son, and Holy Spirit are not *only* known by their place in the group, each can be spoken of individually, yet neither are they known *independently* of the group. What then does it mean to be created in the image of this group? It means, in part, that we are truest when our relational life is aligned with the relational life of the Trinity. This calls us back from both extreme individualism and extreme group orientation.

It appears that for humans, in the pre-Fall state, full exposure, both to each other and to God, was normal. Adam and Eve were naked and not ashamed. God walked with them in the garden. After the Fall, however, safe exposure became elusive. Even in the boundaries of an exclusive marriage relationship, couples approach full exposure tentatively. It is desirable but dangerous! It is only possible to *taste* what was. In a similar way, God no longer walks with people. He is known by faith and not sight. Full exposure is not safe. Thus the link between shame and awe. The human who draws near to God drops her eyes and lowers her head. Moses hid his face at the bush (Exodus 3:6). Face-to-faceness is elusive. The promise of the Gospel is a return to unveiled presence. The day will come when God will be with his people, present, sun-like.

In heaven men and women will experience an intimacy that can only be tasted here. But the Christian life on earth only anticipates, eschatologically, this unveiled presence. Thus discretionary shame or modesty is both healthy and necessary in this present life.

Shame and salvation

Christianity asserts that sin is one of the defining realities of our present human condition. It is not the only defining reality, but sin does negatively impact all of human experience. It is from sin and the consequences of sin that the human race needs to be rescued. Human sin is always, at heart, a slap in the face of God. But God plays by his own rules and counters, unexpectedly, with grace. A study of shame broadens our understanding of the human problem of sin and deepens our appreciation of the divine response to sin.

For example, we speak of sins of commission and sins of omission. While all sin results in some measure of both guilt and shame, sins of commission, or transgression, are more likely to register as guilt. These sins are more external and action oriented; they are about rule violation. Salvation here is more helpfully expressed in legal or economic metaphors (such as atonement, ransom, and redemption). In contrast, as Noble points out, "Sins of omission are failures, not transgressions."[1] They represent limitations, lost potential, and reduced presence, and so are more likely to register as shame. Shame is the sense of falling short, or not measuring up. Thus, as Scripture says, "For all have sinned and fall short of the glory [honor] of God" (Romans 3:23). Salvation at this point is more

---

[1] Noble, *Naked and Not Ashamed*, 81.

helpfully expressed in relational metaphors (such as hospitality, adoption, and citizenship). What is lost and restored is a sense of dignity, place, and person.

Salvation from sin and sin's consequences (both guilt and shame) centers in Christ. But, while a theology of guilt focuses on the cross, a theology of shame, though still cross centered, draws a larger circle. The incarnation *as a whole* is healing for shame. God-with-us is deeply affirming. His tabernacling among the human race seeds hope and renewal. On the one hand, his life among us exposes the two-dimensional thinness of both the sinners and the professionally "sinless." On the other hand, his rich, wholesome presence models a humanity that truly images God.

So from shame's perspective the cross is part of a larger package. The shame bearing of the cross is the outcome of a shame-bearing life. Furthermore the resurrection, ascension, and heavenly session of Christ extend the shame-bearing ministry of Christ into the future. For those whose lives are now hid in Christ, the present glory of Christ heralds the anticipated restoration of *our* glory, when salvation will be complete and all shame finally washed away. The delightful boldness of Christians now is a foretaste of greater glory then.

A theology of shame helps us recognize and accept that conversion is often more process than event. Shame relates to deep personal fracture, and healing does not happen overnight. Here the Eastern church emphasis on inner corruption remedied by the transforming work of the Spirit provides a helpful counterbalance to the Western church emphasis on guilt remedied by the great transaction at the cross. We need to hear both.

Various observers note the problem of shallow conversions. Burton's comment hints at part of the reason: "One may. . . be in the position of being forgiven but not experiencing acceptance."[2] What is needed is *accepting grace* as well as *pardoning grace*. Gordon Smith, in his concern over superficial conversion, helpfully explicates seven dimensions of conversion including the particularly shame-healing elements of membership, Spirit filling, and baptism.[3] Out of a broader and deeper understanding and experience of conversion, we can expect to travel further along the road to wholeness. Recovery from shame is an important dimension of this pilgrimage.

The good news for shame is that at last it is possible to come out of hiding. To the God who asks "Where are you?" the shamed person can respond, "*Hineni*" (Behold me). Christ says it is safe to come out now. Believers are free to step out into the loving gaze of God. We are invited in Christ to experience the ultimate positive mirroring. And so we discover that the honor of the Father is ascribed to the children.

Shame and church

A theology of shame highlights the *corporate* nature of salvation. Where guilt points to breach of principle, shame points to breach of relationship. Shame, by its very nature, requires relational healing. And this is precisely what the Gospel offers. Jesus' ministry focused on creating a new community, where those on the outside were now reconnected. Jesus was announcing the Kingdom of God, where honor-shame scripts are rewritten to encompass those who had no

---

[2] Burton, "Original Sin or Original Shame?" 38.
[3] Smith, *Beginning Well*, 140f.

place and were not a people. Churches are called to be living expressions of the Kingdom of God, where the formerly shamed discover belonging and intimacy. Thus baptism is not only the sign of forgiveness, it is the rite of initiation into the new community, where the old honor-shame rules do not apply. The weak, the nobodies, the women, the children, the gentiles, the lepers, the handicapped, are all equally graced with honor. In baptism we receive the gracious deposit of a new identity, firmly embedded in God and his covenant community.

A theology of shame weans Western Christians from an over-attachment to individualism. We gain a deeper appreciation for corporate or church-based evangelism (less of a "soul-winner" emphasis), where people are drawn to Christ through the witness of the corporate life of the church. We may even see the conversion of groups or families. The household baptisms of the New Testament will make more sense to us. After all, it was specifically to the "families" of the earth that God promised blessing through Abraham, not to the "individuals" of the earth (Genesis 12:3). As the postmodern, neopagan West reverts to group orientation (hence shame orientation) George Hunter's suggestion that the church re-introduce St. Patrick's model of corporate evangelism makes good sense.[4]

Adult baptism highlights appropriately the personal and individual aspects of conversion. Thus Luther leaned first to adult baptism. Nevertheless, group-culture dynamics, the apparent default setting of the human race, asserted itself, and Luther reverted to infant baptism! The child is swept into the

---

[4] George Hunter, *The Celtic Way of Evangelism: How Christianity Can Reach The West . . . Again* (Nashville, TN: Abingdon, 2001).

Kingdom along with the parents. Infant baptism plus later confirmation is an attempt to balance the group and the individual. Modern Baptists counter the individualism of believers baptism with a renewed emphasis on baby dedication and the place of the new person within the larger community.

Shamed people shun difference and seek sameness. The church, in contrast, is an ecology of unique individuals, each free to differentiate vigorously yet bound together in love and interdependency. Shamed people, under cover of grace, come out of hiding and embrace their unique identity in the context of the believing community—a community that images the heavenly Trinitarian community. Shame-healthy churches delight in diversity.

Shame and Scripture

To the communication-impaired, shame-bound person, Scripture is a breath of fresh air, a gust of healthy words! This written Word is God's revelation of himself. God exposes his heart, his personal diary published. This cosmic modeling of robust individuality calls out to shamed humanity. It is a reminder of him in whose image we were formed. His Word reframes our understanding. Sin is bracketed. Original dignity precedes original sin. The incarnation and the grace of the cross define the end of sin.

If the words of the Bible were only marks on a page they would bring no help for shame. Indeed, where they are treated as such they are often shame generating. But God's Word is a living word and so is redemptive. A theology of shame calls for a ministry of the Word that so brings the Word to life that the hearer feels the sweet breath of God himself across his or her face. What a relief to recover human finitude in the unmistakable presence of God Almighty. To experience the Word alive is to encounter this living God.

Shame and last things

The Gospel of Jesus Christ transforms our future as well as our present. Because of this, the concept of hope is transformed from the breezy, reality-shy optimism of the secular world, to the reality-anchored, anticipatory hope of the followers of Christ. Whereas in Greco-Roman culture hope was a coward's refuge for those without the teeth to bite fate's bullet, in Christ hope is elevated to that trinity of supreme virtues alongside faith and love.

The very brightness of our future in Christ is healing for shame. We have confidence (no shame) as we approach the day of judgment (1 John 4:17) because the blood of Christ has washed away our sins. Neither are we ashamed of death (Philippians 1:20). Living or dead our lives are hidden in Christ. Our firm belief in the life to come bequeaths us a quiet dignity in the midst of the indignities of this life. This glorious future calls us out and beyond our shameful past. And above all the imminent return of our Lord Jesus Christ, our redeemer, healer, and friend, confirms our sense of self and worth and ensures that shame is always in retreat.

The question theologically at this point is just how much this glorious future impacts the present. And specifically here, how does shame play out in the tension of the "already/not yet"? We look forward to life in heaven totally free from the consequences of sin, including the shame consequence of sin. When the Kingdom of God is fully inaugurated, all darkness will be banished. And, without question, we sample these victories even now. But we only sample. A theology of shame is careful to keep future things future. Both global affirmation and global condemnation are best left for later.

Indeed there is a shamelessness about an overrealized eschatology. Triumphalism is an embarrassment in a "not-yet" world! Health and wealth are not to be assumed here and now. The process of sanctification will not be complete in this life; thus neither guilt recovery nor shame recovery will be complete. A theology of shame recognizes the dynamics of this long trajectory and is not perfectionistic. What is sought is shame's rightful place for this present age, neither a destructive presence nor a destructive (premature) absence.

The time has come to develop a full theology of shame, or at least a theology that incorporates a fuller understanding of the role of shame. The liberals, with some justification, accuse the fundamentalists of preaching a shame-*bound* theology. The fundamentalists, with some justification, accuse the liberals of proclaiming a shame-*less* theology. In the global warming of postmodernity, however, both positions are melting icebergs. May both ends of the theological spectrum together rediscover the fullness of the Gospel that ministers grace to both guilt and shame.

Preaching Grace for Shame

We know by now that ministering grace for shame requires more than words. But words are still vital. There is still a Gospel to be proclaimed. Faith comes by hearing, and faith is evoked in shame-bound people through the proclamation of the Gospel. If it is true, however, that shame is a present and growing reality, we must do more in our preaching than simply increase the intensity and frequency of Gospel texts. We will remember that shame includes both a cultural element that needs understanding and a destructive element that needs healing. Preachers are translators of the Gospel. We will remember that we translate between cultures, not just languages. It is not helpful to translate a Gospel that was originally embedded in an honor-shame culture into a fifteenth-century guilt narrative, when honor and shame are once again significant cultural factors among our twenty-first-century hearers!

There is always an offense that comes with faithful preaching. Some might argue that all this "shame talk" is a way of adapting to the world to reduce offense. But in fact the opposite is true. In reducing Gospel preaching to guilt management, the church has avoided confronting the world in significant ways. Preaching grace for shame risks greater offense by proclaiming an alternate reality that challenges society's deepest held criteria of identity and belonging. Such preaching is anti-gossip. Here the verdict of God is proclaimed against the verdict of the village. Against the values of the world are thrown the values of the Kingdom of God. Preaching grace for shame will stir up the opposition, as it did for Jesus.

The content of preaching

Preaching grace for shame will not replace preaching grace for guilt but will supplement it. Shame needs its own brand of salve. It will feel different. If we are ready to take seriously the need to preach grace for shame, where do we start?

It may seem counterintuitive, but the need to present a theocentric view of reality is paramount. Though an emphasis on a Sovereign Creator God would seem to increase shame, in fact it releases people from having to be God. Not everything that happens is the fault of human beings. What a relief! When God is granted *his* place, we created beings can take *our* place. It becomes possible to be more realistic about goals. A Great God is a wonderful antidote to narcissistic and grandiose thinking. Let's preach a larger God!

It is also helpful to defuse unrealistic human models. Simply to point out, for example, that Jacob was a poor father can lift a huge load off people conditioned to regard all fathers as models of perfection. Human fathers may do their best, but they are not God. It is good news for men and women to learn that we are limited, finite beings.

Since shame is reinforced by a perfectionist theology and the resultant inevitable failure to be perfect, healing must involve a recalibration of beliefs and values. At root is sick religion. What is needed is clearer insight into the true nature of God, who alone is perfect, together with clearer insight into the true, limited, nature of humanity.[5] When self is idolized, shame is just around the corner. Part of the healing process will come from preaching and teaching that correct poor theology. This begins with correcting unbiblical notions about God himself.

But when God is God then it is safe to revel in our humanity. Thus shamed people need to hear the message that they have worth. Pattison writes:

Redeeming shame is different from redeeming guilt. For women and other shamed people, redemption from sin might

---

[5] See Wayne Oates, "Idolatry and Sick Religion," in *A Practical Handbook for Ministry*, Thomas Chapman, ed. (Louisville, KY: Westminster John Knox Press, 1992).

mean more positive self-assertion, self-affirmation and action rather than more repentance, passivity, and ceasing to act in a definite harmful way.[6]

"Christ first, others second, self last" is not the most urgent message for men and women already depleted by shame! It will take large doses of grace before the shame-based person gets any nourishment from sermons on self-denial. We need to hear that unconditional, impartial *agape* love applies to ourselves as well as to others. We need encouragement to exercise our undeveloped self-will. We need to be reminded that our initiative does not threaten the Sovereignty of God! We need to hear that we are even free to protest, as Job was, and as the Psalms so often demonstrate. A high view of God allows for a high view of humanity.

There is also a healthy "edge" to this preaching. Difficult truths are named. And not only the difficult truths about society's false goals and warped values. The church itself makes mistakes from time to time. These mistakes also need to be named. People need to know when things are not their fault. This sets shamed people free from their learned responses of denying their own experience or, worse, of blaming themselves for the sins of others. Along with the need to name difficult truths is the need to be explicit about expectations. The shameful sense of never being "good enough" arises not only from *unrealistic* expectations but from *inexplicit* expectations. Proclaiming clear, concrete, attainable steps is healing for shame.

Preaching and teaching that minister grace for shame will also remind people that the Christian God is Trinitarian. The

---

[6] Pattison, *Shame*, 197.

combination of robust individuality and deep communion in the Trinity is both mysterious and engaging. The Gospel is an invitation to be part of this relationship. The Gospel is a gesture of respect and hospitality from the Father, Son, and Spirit. Shamed people need to hear the Gospel in terms of relationship, not principle. The preaching of principles and distilled truths objectifies the hearer and generates shame. "Truth through personality" (to use that old definition of preaching) is not adequate for shamed people. We need to hear God's voice (not "truth") through the person of the preacher. Our task is to help the shamed person hear this voice of God in the text of Scripture. We have the privilege of exposing old and familiar texts in fresh new ways that help the listener hear God's grace for shame. The preacher is the matchmaker between the shame-shy and their waiting Trinitarian God.

Furthermore, the church and its preachers bring healing to shame by reframing what is shameful and what is honorable in the light of Scripture. Thus if pastors can help people hear that the "poor in spirit" are indeed "blessed" (honorable), they have reduced the burden of shame for the poor in spirit. Here is a new "public of reference." Even the role of leaders is rewritten to include foot-washing as honorable behavior. To preach the Kingdom of God is to preach an alternate set of values that is in itself shame reducing. If worth is no longer dependent on wealth, the poor can be honorable. If worth is not dependent on height, short people can be honorable. Ethnic, economic, and gender criteria are moved from center stage. Shame is reduced as pastors redefine boundaries and thus redefine who is "in."

The Christian Gospel proclaims a new honor system that rearranges the social pecking order and actually gives prominence to the weaker parts (1 Corinthians 12:22-23). That great prophecy is fulfilled: "Whoever believes in him [Christ] will not be put to shame" (Isaiah 28:16, Romans 9:33). Outsiders tried to shame the disciples by calling them "Christians," but for the followers of Jesus, this only increased their honor. The most radical reframing of what is shameful centers on the cross. The once shameful cross is now proclaimed as glory. Preaching that connects the cross with the hearer's life, then unveils the glory of the cross, will be healing for shame. If the shame script of a *cross* can be rewritten, any shame script can be rewritten.

Preaching is one way of administering grace in its "varied" forms:

> As each has received a gift, use it to serve one another, as good stewards of God's varied grace: whoever speaks, as one who speaks oracles of God; whoever serves, as one who serves by the strength that God supplies—in order that in everything God may be glorified through Jesus Christ. (1 Peter 4:10-11)

Smedes writes: "Pardoning grace is the answer to guilt. . . . Accepting grace is the answer to shame."[7] What themes will be heard as Good News by shame-oriented people? Roland Muller gives a helpful list: cleansing the defiled, clothing the naked, visiting the outcast, strengthening the weak, healing the sick, and blessing the cursed.[8] What gracious preaching!

The goal of preaching grace for shame is to help the hearer *feel* God's acceptance. This is no easy matter. For shame-bound people, every instinct is to reject this thought. Berating shame-bound people for their lack of belief only

---

[7] Smedes, *Shame and Grace*, 108.
[8] Muller, *Honor and* Shame, 59f.

serves to embed shame more deeply.[9] So, as one might expect, it is not just *what* we say but *how* we say it that matters. Thus some comments now on the *how* of preaching grace for shame.

The style of preaching

Yes, we preach the Word, which is sharp, deeply penetrating, and relentlessly exposing (Hebrews 4:12,13). There is no question that naming the demons is a critical part of their banishment. Yet in preaching grace for shame it is important to balance the specific and the general. We will give people space and not expose their wounds for all the world to see. People need a kind of "gentle naming."[10] Coming across as the expert, professional know-all, will not heal shame. Even to speak the word shame makes people uneasy. What is needed is an indirect approach that operates out of an understanding of shame, but does not trumpet shame.

This preaching is not only *about* relationships, it is *itself* relational. Some attempted religious help for shamed people is at the level of Job's friends who simply shout the old rules louder and louder. God honors Job, however, by speaking *to* him not *at* him. The preacher signals this relationship in various ways. There is a warmth, a sense of engagement, of understanding. There are echoes of private conversations and personal visits. The preacher is not pronouncing from on high, but coming alongside, sharing in the experience of grace. The words feel like the words of a neighbor. There is a movement from monologue to dialogue.

---

[9] Albers, "The Shame Factor," 348.
[10] James R. Nieman and Thomas G. Rogers, *Preaching to Every Pew: Cross-Cultural Strategies* (Minneapolis, MN: Fortress, 2001), 74.

So acceptance will not only be the *topic* of the sermon it will be *modeled* in the sermon. A simple but powerful adjustment is the elimination of sexist language. The number of people who hear patriarchal language as inclusive is diminishing fast! Inclusive language affirms all participants. This, of course, goes beyond using inclusive pronouns. For example we do well to follow Luke's lead in giving equal time to women. Notice how he pairs stories of men and women in his Gospel and highlights the role of women in Acts. If our heart is inclusive, and not just our vocabulary, this will emerge in an attitude of affirmation and respect regardless of gender, culture, ethnic background, educational level, and the like. Such preaching will breathe acceptance.

This understanding that shame impacts the whole person underlines the fact that preaching needs to be more (though not less) than a rational presentation. Retelling the passion narrative may be more helpful for shamed people than teaching a theory of the atonement. Stories introduce us to other possible ways of being. Preaching needs to call up all five senses. It needs imagination, story, metaphor. It needs to slip beyond the thin layer of gray matter and pour balm into the hurting, hidden recesses. Such preaching is creative, surprising, subtle, powerful—parabolic. Furthermore, sermons for shame will include humor. Humor is often about humiliating (shaming) situations; but, paradoxically, appropriate humor defuses shame. Humor lowers the shame level for both speaker and hearer. When we can chuckle at ourselves, shame is in retreat.

The pastor must come to terms with her own shame if she is to be of much help to others (more on this later). This is particularly important in preaching. Many pastors can identify with Burton, who writes: "As with many of my colleagues, shame led to anger which was expressed as prophetic preaching which maintained the shame of still others."[11] The impact of the emotional content of the sermon is at least as powerful as the impact of the cognitive content. Shame is contagious; but fortunately so is boldness! Let us who preach rejoice in this gift of *parresia* not only for our own sake, but for the sake of our hearers.

Preaching that ministers grace for shame requires much more than making shame the topic for a couple of Sundays. This is an ongoing shape or flavor to preaching that is not only rooted in a well-thought-out theology of shame but also is expressed through the person of a preacher who has come to terms with his or her own shame and thus both expresses and embodies God's grace for shame.

Reading Grace for Shame

As we read through Scripture both privately and publicly, we will be amazed at how frequently we discover grace for shame. Now that our eyes and ears are open to the complex reality of shame, we read the Bible in new ways. We discover a wealth of resources for ministering grace for shame. For us in the West this is a new dimension of the "ministry of the Word." What privilege—what responsibility. A good example of this "new" reading of Scripture is found in Alan Wright's book *Shame Off You: Washing Away the Mud That Hides Our True Selves.* Wright offers an accessible, devotional reading of

---

[11]Burton, "Original Sin or Original Shame," 39.

Scripture that is alert to grace for shame. It has obviously transformed his ministry.[12]

Sometimes the biblical text addresses shame very directly. For example, Psalm 25:1-3:

> To you, O Lord, I lift up my soul.
> O my God, in you I trust;
>   let me not be put to shame;
>   let not my enemies exult over me.
> Indeed, none who wait for you shall be put to shame;
>   they shall be ashamed who are wantonly treacherous.

Here shame is seen within the context of the honor-shame culture. The shame referred to here is not necessarily about sinful behavior; it may simply be the shame of failure and thus loss of honor. But the great promise is that ultimately those who trust in this God will not be people of shame. How liberating for people cowed by shame to see and hear this Word of the Lord. Hope breaks through, grace pours down.

Or consider Romans 10:11, where Paul (for the second time in as many chapters) quotes Isaiah 28:16: "Everyone who believes in him will not be put to shame." This follows immediately a very familiar passage arguing that it is confession and belief that leads to salvation. What, then, does it mean to be saved? Here Paul speaks of salvation in terms of *shame* deliverance. In preaching this text faithfully, we will need to incorporate an understanding of the Gospel as Good News for shame as well as for guilt.

The letter to the Laodicean church comes alive in fresh ways as we read it through the lens of shame. Revelation 3:18:

---

[12] Alan D. Wright, *Shame Off You: Washing Away the Mud That Hides Our True Selves* (Sisters, OR: Multnomah Publishers Inc., 2005).

I counsel you to buy from me gold refined by fire, so that you may be rich, and white garments so that you may clothe yourself and the shame of your nakedness may not be seen, and salve to anoint your eyes, so that you may see.

The shame themes of poverty of person, overexposure and loss of face (sight) are clear. Healing comes with the non-aggressive, non-shaming presence of Christ knocking at the door, offering the shamed occupant the dignity of playing host to God, a relational response to a relational problem.

There are longer passages that lend themselves to an extended treatment of shame. Augsburger points out the contrast between Psalm 31 with its focus on shame and Psalm 32 with its focus on guilt.[13] Odell observes: "Psalm 22 is a fine example of the occurrence of shame in the absence of guilt and, furthermore, of the fact that shame is tied to experience of divine abandonment."[14] In addition, as we have already noted, Hebrews and 1 Peter were both written to help Christians deal with the apparent shame of following Christ. Both letters reframe the situation in such a way that shame is overshadowed by glory.

But we remember that to speak directly about shame often increases shame or drives it underground. Shame is best helped *indirectly.* And so as we read Scripture, we often discover help for shame where the vocabulary of shame is not present. Once we are alert to the dynamics of shame, we take note of such themes as clothing, covering, hospitality, inclusion, welcome, affirmation, adoption, all of which are potentially healing for shame. Not surprisingly these themes emerge most strongly in

---

[13] Augsburger, *Conflict Mediation Across Cultures,* 139.

[14] Margaret Odell, "The Inversion of Shame and Forgiveness in Ezekiel 16:59-63," *Journal for the Study of the Old Testament,* 56 (1992): 105.

the life and ministry of Christ. Stockitt observes, "The most striking thing about the earthly ministry of Jesus is that he frequently chose to enter places of shame and associate with shamed people."[15] A moving example of this is Jesus' encounter with Zacchaeus. Let's examine this encounter in some detail, building on insights from Pattison and Pembroke.[16]

The Gospel according to Zacchaeus

The incident occurs in Luke 19:1-10, towards the end of the long "Journey-to-Jerusalem" section (9:51-19:44). Throughout this section Luke frequently reminds the reader that Jerusalem lies ahead. Thus the whole journey takes place in the shadow of the cross. Jesus' ministry is fulfilled at the cross, including his ministry for shame. At the cross Jesus bears shame for the human race. In the journey to the cross Christ is seen taking on himself the shame of others as he sets them free. He is demonstrating what it means to take up the cross daily (Luke 9:23). To take up the cross daily means, in part, to bear daily the shame of others.

Jesus enters Jericho and is passing through. A man is there by the name of Zacchaeus. He is a chief tax collector and is wealthy. He wants to see who Jesus is, but being a short man he cannot because of the crowd. So he runs ahead and climbs a sycamore-fig tree in order to see Jesus coming down the road.

Zacchaeus is a man ensnared in shame. As a Jewish tax collector, working for the Roman occupying forces, he is a

---

[15] Robin Stockitt, "'Love Bade Me Welcome; But My Soul Drew Back'—Towards an Understanding of Shame," *Anvil: An Anglican Evangelical Journal of Theology and Mission*, 15 (2) (1998): 117.

[16] Pattison, *Shame*, 307f.; and Pembroke, "Toward a Shame-Based Theology of Evangelism," 22.

social outcast, a reject. In fact he is a *chief* tax collector, a title that ironically only makes him *less* honorable (thus more shameful). His mother had named him Zacchaeus, a name that means "pure," or "righteous," but he has grown up a "sinner." His very name mocks him. ("There goes Mr. Clean!")

In meeting Zacchaeus, we are meeting a man who has squandered all of the deposit of honor he received at birth. In a world of honor and shame, his credit rating is zero. His short *physical* stature is a metaphor for his diminished personhood. He is one to be overlooked. Alongside other men he is inconsequential. Nevertheless, he has worked his way into the position of chief tax collector. If he has no respect, at least he has power. And he has money. In his accumulation of power and wealth, he is attempting to make up the deficit in his depleted self. But the inner hunger remains.

Not only is Zacchaeus a shamed person, but he is also shameless! He runs ahead. A mature man in a position of authority would not run in that society. It would be undignified and degrading. But Zacchaeus has now no respect worth protecting. Not only does he run, he also climbs a tree. A ridiculous little man perched like a bird on a branch, but who cares!

> And when Jesus came to the place, he looked up and said to him, "Zacchaeus, hurry and come down, for I must stay at your house today." So he hurried and came down and received him joyfully. (Luke 19:5-6)

Here is the shame-healing presence of Jesus. He "overlooks" no one. He could have chuckled at the sight of the little man in the tree, but he shows deep respect. In using Zacchaeus' name, Jesus recognizes his "distinct subjectivity and personhood."[17]   Furthermore, Jesus "looked up" to Zacchaeus. This becomes a metaphor of Jesus' humility. He reveals himself to Zacchaeus as needy. Jesus needs a place to stay. Zacchaeus is given the dignity of helping out the famous Jesus in his time of need. He gets bragging rights. All of this is, of course, done very publicly. Just as shame is *loss* of public place, honor is *gain* of public place.

We sense, too, that Zacchaeus climbed the tree not only to see but to *be seen*. Shame prompts hiding. It is when shamed people have the courage to expose themselves to the gaze of God that they discover the love of God. Then God's love is "poured into our hearts" (Romans 5:5). Zacchaeus exposed himself in the tree, somehow knowing, trusting, that Jesus would not reject him. "He experiences the joy that accompanies every encounter between a depleted self and positive mirroring."[18]

This is all too much for the crowd:

> And when they saw it, they all grumbled, "He has gone in to
> be the guest of a man who is a sinner." (Luke 19:7)

The "muttering" is negative gossip. Here is widespread public disapproval of Jesus' actions. Luke wants the reader to feel the weight of Jesus' countercultural approach. We can almost hear the derision in their voices.

Remember that shame is contagious. The shame of Zacchaeus now attaches to Jesus. In staying in Zacchaeus' home Jesus is squandering his own honor within the honor-shame rules of the community. True, Jesus lives by other rules, he is demonstrating a radically different honor-shame

---

[17] Pattison, *Shame*, 308.
[18] Pembroke, "Toward a Shame-Based Theology of Evangelism," 22.

construct; but he will pay a price in the local context. This is the journey to Jerusalem and the cross. "He who forgives those we denounce must surely die. And Jesus died."[19]

> And Zacchaeus stood and said to the Lord, "Behold, Lord, the half of my goods I give to the poor. And if I have defrauded anyone of anything, I restore it fourfold" (Luke 19:8)

"Zacchaeus stood." There is a sense of solemnity and formality about this construction.[20] It was fascinating for me to hear this passage preached by a Chinese brother. The shame-healing dynamics of this story were much more apparent to him, speaking out of his roots in a shame-oriented culture. He was especially taken by the verb "stood." Perhaps, for the first time, Zacchaeus stands tall. He stands in dignity.

For Zacchaeus, the verdict of his community no longer is intimidating. He senses, in Jesus, a greater verdict that overrides local convention. Jesus welcomes him into a new community and in so doing welcomes Zacchaeus back to himself. Remarkably, his first words are, "Behold, Lord" (possibly the Hebrew *hineni*)—look at me! His shame is lifted. No more need to hide. He can stand before the Lord openly, boldly, in confidence.

And now we see how, for Zacchaeus, and for many like him, healing for guilt *follows* healing for shame. Zacchaeus needed *ontological* restoration before there could be *ethical* restoration. Now that Zacchaeus finds himself honored and respected, he can begin to think about honoring and respecting

---

[19] Margaret G. Alter, "Human Shame and the Hospitality of God," *Dialog,* 36 (4) (1997): 269.
[20] Alfred Plummer, *A Critical and Exegetical Commentary on the Gospel According to St. Luke* (Edinburgh: T. and T. Clarke, 5th edition, 1922), 434.

others. He is now neither shameful nor shameless. He inhabits the place of the honorable. In a moment of time, his value system is radically realigned. No danger now of Zacchaeus seeking worth in wealth. He has found worth in the eyes of God. He immediately gives away half of his considerable possessions. Then, where he has cheated, he returns 400% (far beyond the 120% required in Leviticus 6:5). Jesus has restored personhood to Zacchaeus and, in consequence, Zacchaeus is no longer able to objectify (depersonalize) others. Jesus has returned Zacchaeus to himself *and* to others.

Here, for the sake of Zacchaeus and anyone else who will listen, Jesus pronounces the verdict of the Kingdom of God on this event.

> And Jesus said to him, "Today salvation has come to this house, since he also is a son of Abraham. For the Son of Man came to seek and to save the lost." (Luke 19:9,10)

What they have just witnessed is salvation! A man was lost, lost to himself as well as others. But now he has been restored—he has been saved. For this Jesus came.

Zacchaeus thought he was seeking Jesus, but Jesus was first seeking him. Jesus came into this world looking for hidden, shamed people. He could not do this from heaven. He had to be Emmanuel. He had to be "God with us." He had to humble himself and become the "Son of Man" in order not to frighten away the Zacchaeuses of this world. Zacchaeus, in lifting his face to Jesus, proves himself to be a true son of Abraham, that great man of faith.

Note also the group orientation, salvation "to this house." There is a corporate quality to New Testament salvation that makes independent westerners nervous, but not Jews! Before this encounter with Jesus, the whole household had suffered from Zacchaeus' dishonorable behavior and thus shared in his shame. Likewise now the whole household shares in the considerable cost of restitution. But see how they also share in the salvation of Zacchaeus. They share in the re-honoring of Zacchaeus as his salvation is applied to them all.

We remember that Jesus says he must "stay" with Zacchaeus. This "staying" (abiding) becomes a permanent relationship and has a two-way quality, a mutuality, as the hospitality of Zacchaeus encounters the greater hospitality of the Lord. Zacchaeus will discover, as all believers do, that the shame-healing presence of Jesus is ongoing. Thus not only is Zacchaeus' past and present transformed, his future is transformed also. What a rich and satisfying conversion this is.

Jesus continues his journey to Jerusalem, bearing now the shame of Zacchaeus which has been transferred to him. At the cross he will take to himself the shame of all the Zacchaeuses of the world. But on the third day he will rise again, then ascend to the right hand of the Father, demonstrating eternal victory over shame. Zacchaeus was simply a firstfruit of all who "share in the glory of our Lord Jesus Christ" (2 Thessalonians 2:14 NIV). Glory is the outcome of grace for shame. It is the hope of all who abide in Jesus.

We who grew up in the West will not instinctively recognize shame in the biblical text. Shame has not been on our conscious agenda. But as we grow in our understanding—as shame comes out of hiding—we will begin to read familiar texts with new eyes. We will learn how to help others see Jesus with new eyes. We will get better at tuning our own ministry to the ministry of Jesus, both in word and life. We will experience the joy of ministering a more comprehensive Gospel.

Praying Grace for Shame

Here in part 3 of this study we are looking at practical responses to shame needs. In this chapter we are focusing especially on the role of words. Ministry is certainly not all about words (especially ministry for shame), but words do play a central role in the Christian faith. So we resist those who devalue words, not least because God has revealed himself in words. And though Jesus is the living word, he too is now revealed through the written Word, as we have just seen. But along with words *from* God and *about* God it is important to reflect on words *to* God. Of course, not all prayer has words. There is an attitude of prayer; there is contemplative prayer. But prayer commonly uses words. It is spoken communication. Thus it is helpful to ask the question: What does this new understanding of shame teach us in regard to prayer, both private and public?

The recovery of intimacy

First, there is *effect* of shame on prayer. One of the characteristics of shame is wordlessness. Deeply shamed people have little to say. There is nobody home to say anything either to people or to God—the self has gone underground. It may be even more difficult for shamed people to speak to God than to people, since we know instinctively that he knows all and sees all: the masks do not work with him. Shamed people will be more comfortable with formula prayers, either written or unwritten.

Thoughtful liturgical prayers go a long way towards meeting the need of the human heart for prayer. They provide words and they also protect the privacy of the pray-er. And yet this can only be a beginning in the pilgrimage of prayer. That very need for privacy is part of the problem. We are the daughters and sons of Adam and Eve, who turned privacy into hiding. Just as shame destroys intimacy between human beings, it also destroys intimacy between creature and creator. God longs for close communion, for open communion. This was his original purpose in creation. And he continues to call us out into the open.

What a joy then to discover healing in Christ. Clothed with grace there is no more need to hide. We approach the throne of grace "boldly," "confidently," with our speech returned to us (Hebrews 4:16). As Christians receive grace for shame, we begin to pray with real intimacy. We begin to reveal our hearts to him as he has revealed his heart to us. We may use Bible prayers to teach us how to pray (the Psalms are wonderful here), but these written prayers do not limit our praying. Rather they lead us on to a greater personal freedom and intimacy in prayer. They open doors for those wanting to progress in prayer.

Sharing our freedom

We are concerned here particularly with the pastoral role in the ministry of grace for shame. In thinking about prayer we naturally think of prayer for others, both in ones and twos and in larger groups. But public prayer that is healing for shame must be a reflection of the personal experience of shame-free prayer. We cannot boldly lead others publicly where we have not first ventured in private. Yet even so there will be a difference between public and private prayers. Jesus called for modesty in prayer (Matthew 6:5f.). Only the shameless parade personal prayer.[21] Susanna Wesley, lacking privacy with her large family, at least threw her apron over her head for her daily prayers. Yes, Jesus allowed others to overhear his prayers. His followers did also (Paul often records his prayers in his letters). Nevertheless public prayers must never be for show. The intimacy must never be contrived. Furthermore the sense of awe will remain, even in moments of deepest intimacy.

How then can we pray publicly in ways that are healing for shame? Surely we need humility in our public prayers. Showing off our boldness without showing off our constant need for grace is hypocritical. Furthermore, if we only convey a sense of expertise and perfection in our prayers, we will simply push prayer further out of reach for the shamed, wordless, imperfect listener. We must not pray *down* but pray *alongside*. We take the fellow pilgrim by the hand and together venture into the Holy Place, gently sharing our covering of grace with those who need it. Once again, as shame is contagious, so is boldness. Our boldness before the Lord will model grace-for-shame, and embolden others. Thus in shared prayers others will see the grace of God at work. It is this grace that lies behind our own experience of boldness.

As we think about the content of our shared prayers, it is obvious too that those prayers must be inclusive if they are to minister grace for shame. Prayers should include women, by

---

[21] Schneider, *Shame, Exposure and Privacy*, 37f.

using not only feminine pronouns, but by including women's concerns. In the same way such prayers need to include children, single people, the weak as well as the strong, people of other cultures and ethnic groups. Prayer should be an exercise in hospitality, especially for those at the margins of life.

We will be careful with the use of names. Some people will be shamed by the use of their name in public prayer. Yet done with care this is helpful. Jesus named Zacchaeus in front of the crowd. He publicly recognized the individuality and distinct personhood of Zacchaeus. When we use personal names in public prayers we draw people out of hiding, we affirm individuality and personhood. We point the way to recovery. Nevertheless, it must be an affirming exposure, not a shameful exposure. Shame-prone congregations will be more likely to resist the use of personal names and lean to formal and falsely "reverent" prayers. Pastors will need to gently lead people into greater freedom and real intimacy.

Furthermore, in countering shame-prone family systems it is helpful to pray about *specifics*, particularly in repentance. This requires great sensitivity. Nevertheless, dwelling on global unworthiness tends to intensify shame and reinforce an environment of shame. One of the marks of genuine spiritual revival is the outbreak of public repentance for specific sins. Pastors need the courage and the wisdom to name specific sins. Such particular repentance is healing for shame.

In all these ways, pastoral prayers can be teaching moments as people learn habits of prayer and attitudes of prayer that are healing for shame.

But is also helpful to encourage others to pray publicly, even, perhaps especially, in Sunday worship. To pray in Jesus' name is a high honor given to all believers. It provides a covering of significance—of power, of authority, of effectiveness, of status. The pastor can use all the inclusive language she wants, but if only she can pray, the real message is clear: others are not good enough! As pastors include others to pray publicly, they make prayer friendlier, less professional, less perfectionistic, and thus more healing for shame. Pastors may also discover that some of their so-called lay people are far ahead of them in this matter of prayer and shame.

When one woman prayed publicly during Communion she thanked God both for his unconditional acceptance and for his forgiveness of confessed sin. She had integrated, into her prayer, her theology of restoration for both shame and guilt (in the right order.) Perhaps the fact that she is Filipina (thus rooted in a shame-oriented culture), as well as a woman, helped develop this understanding.

Gentle confession

There are words to people and there are words to God. But that division must not be drawn too sharply. Confession before people is part of our normal Christian life in this fallen world. But we also remember David's insight in Psalm 51:4, "Against you, you only, have I sinned and done what is evil in your sight...." All real confession is, underneath, confession before God. Confession is prayer also.

How then does the healthy church deal with confession? It is not something to be avoided. Confession is an integral part of conversion and has a critical and ongoing place in the private and corporate life of believers. But confession requires a certain ontological robustness—*I* did wrong, *I* am responsible, *I* need mercy, *I* accept your forgiveness, *I* turn from that behavior. This strong sense of self is the very quality that shamed people lack. Penitence demands personhood. But the deeply shamed have only a shadow of a person to offer.

Pastors can help the church understand that confession need not be the first step in the conversion process. The gracious welcome and acceptance of the Father, embodied in the welcome and acceptance of the healthy church, calls the shamed person out of hiding. Gradually the pilgrim "comes to herself"—at last a "confess-able" person. What happened with Zacchaeus in an afternoon may with us take months or years, but the same God is at work.

The presence of shame must not be allowed to exorcise confession from our spiritual life, but alert pastors will follow the Spirit of Jesus in beginning first with the grace of acceptance. Our salvation is not dependent on our ability to confess. Grace embraces without preconditions, though it is also true that grace (in time) makes possible and evokes in us what we are not able to do alone. How gently the great Pastor drew out that positive confession from Peter with his searching question, "Do you love me?" It was enough. Peter was back home.

So confession must not be forced. The ministry of conviction should be left in the hands of the Spirit who knows our human hearts. Just as Jesus did not drive away the shamed with early demands for confession, so the Spirit will not do so. A church that is healing for shame gently invites people to join in corporate confession. Corporate confession allows the shamed to catch the goodness of confession and learn to anticipate the grace of forgiveness. Good liturgical prayers lie dormant until spring comes to the soul, when they burst upwards vital and personal. Those who cannot yet confess sin may be able to confess a creed, a new story, a new community, or a new Lord. Positive confessions may come sooner than negative confessions. What is needed is authentic discourse. The forced confession is no confession.

If we are truly encountering the Lord of heaven and earth, we need have no fear of sin being taken lightly. As we continue to draw nearer to that burning presence, all dross will be consumed. Confession is a response to how we look to God. "Search me, O God, and know my heart . . ." (Ps. 139:23). But first we have to step out into that gaze. This is the challenge for shamed people. The grace of acceptance allows us first to have the courage to "come out"—to say, "Here I am." Only then can we begin to confess our divergence from that Holiness. Healthy churches are patient with slower pilgrims who limp in their confessional prayers.

The cry for blessing

Like confession, blessings and benedictions are moments of multilevel communication. Blessings and benedictions are prayerful pronouncements, at the same time a word *from* the Lord and a cry *to* the Lord. Blessings and benedictions are streams of living waters to thirsty-souled people. In the healthy church the blessing of God himself comes within reach as blessings and benedictions are spoken into the life of the church by ordinary people, perhaps even with the laying on of hands.

Good touch is part of the incarnational response to shame. We see this incarnational response in the father blessing his children. Isaac was no saint himself. But he did have the courage and grace to bless his rascal runaway Jacob (Genesis 28:1-5). That blessing transformed Jacob's journey from flight to pilgrimage—from a journey with only a backwards orientation towards a tragic past, to a journey with a forward orientation into a hope-filled future. In the new community of God, which we sample in the local congregation, we all have the privilege of being bless-ers and bless-ees as we live under the blessing and presence of God week by week. We are invited to be partners with God as he transforms us from wanderers to pilgrims.

Henri Nouwen tells a story from his days as chaplain at the L'Arche Community in Toronto, a home for mentally and physically handicapped adults. Before a prayer service one day, a member of the community, Janet, asked for a blessing. Henri responded rather automatically by making the sign of the cross on her forehead. Janet protested, "But I want a real blessing." Henri realized he had responded inadequately and asked her to wait until the end of the service.

When the time came Henri still wasn't quite sure how to respond. But Janet knew what was needed. She stood up and came forward putting her head against Henri's chest. He continues:

> Without thinking, I covered her with my sleeves so that she almost vanished in the folds of my robe. As we held each other, I said, "Janet, I want you to know that you are God's beloved Daughter. You are precious in God's eyes. Your beautiful smile, your kindness to the people in the house and all the good things you do show us what a beautiful human being you are. I know there is some sadness in your heart, but I want you to remember who you are: a very special person, deeply loved by God and all the people who are here with you." As I said these words, Janet raised her head and looked

at me; and her broad smile showed that she had heard and really received the blessing.

Janet had broken the ice. Many others, including one of the assistants, came forward that day to receive such a blessing.[22]

Blessings not only voice the loving *affirmation* of God, they also announce the loving, affirmative *presence* of God.

> The grace of the Lord Jesus Christ and the love of God and the fellowship of the Holy Spirit be with you all (2 Corinthians 13:14).

Blessings both call down, and call forth, meaning, purpose, and direction for uncertain people.

> Now may the God of peace who brought again from the dead our Lord Jesus, the great shepherd of the sheep, by the blood of the eternal covenant, equip you with everything good that you may do his will, working in us that which is pleasing in his sight, through Jesus Christ, to whom be glory forever and ever. Amen. (Hebrews 13:20, 21)

Blessings welcome a bright and glorious future into the uncertain, shaky present.

> Now to him who is able to keep you from stumbling and to present you blameless before the presence of his glory with great joy, to the only God, our Savior, through Jesus Christ our Lord, be glory, majesty, dominion, and authority, before all time and now and forever. Amen. (Jude 24,25)

Blessings are an antidote for shame.

---

[22] See Henri J. M. Nouwen, *Life of the Beloved: Spiritual Living in a Secular World* (NY: The Crossroad Publishing Co., 1992), 56f.

The archetype of all blessing is the Aaronic blessing:

The Lord spoke to Moses saying, "Speak to Aaron and his sons, saying, 'Thus you shall bless the people of Israel: you shall say to them,

> The Lord bless you and keep you;
>> the Lord make his face shine upon you
>>> and be gracious to you;
>> the Lord lift up his countenance upon you
>>> and give you peace.'"

"So they will put my name on the people of Israel, and I will bless them." (Numbers 6:22-27)

Here is the ultimate "positive mirroring." The face of God himself, turned towards us, shining with love and joy upon us. Here is the final antidote for shame. May God enable us to make real this blessing to those whose lives we touch. And so may we together delight in the shalom of God.

So we return to a familiar theme. Our preaching and our prayers have both been well informed by a theology of guilt. They need also to be informed by a theology of shame. Old habits die hard. Our very language of prayer needs restructuring. This will not happen by accident. Prayers that minister grace for shame will only arise out of intentional effort. Do we care enough? The church needs prayers that celebrate the hospitality and acceptance of God. The church also needs prayers that rejoice in the victory over shame that is found in Christ. The church needs prayers that lift the believers' heads to bask in the smile of God.

6. Relationships That Heal

Good words are vital in responding to shame. But words alone are not enough. Shame is a relational problem that requires a relational answer. A cognitive response alone is inadequate. Healing for shame requires more than grace-full words: healing for shame requires grace-full relationships.

We begin by looking at the pastor's own shame-healing needs. The ministry of grace for shame begins here. Out of a settled identity and a secure relationship with God, pastors mediate grace for shame-troubled people through relationships and presence. As we deepen in our understanding of shame and grace, we will learn to influence churches to become communities that are more healing than harming for shame. We will also minister with greater wisdom in multicultural congregations. But first: Physician, heal thyself!

Grace for Shame in the Pastor's Own Life

Pastors cannot address shame in the life of the church without first addressing their own shame. Must pastors find complete healing for shame before they can be helpful to others? That would be an unrealistic, and indeed a shaming (perfectionist) target; but we must at least begin to appropriate grace for shame for ourselves before we can do so for others.

When pastors embark on their own pilgrimage of healing, the shame burdens of the whole congregation will begin to lift.

Owning the problem

If shame is the hidden emotion, the first place shame needs to come to light is in the pastor himself or herself—no easy task! Why does it take so long to become aware of our own shame burdens? Pastors navigating the so-called midlife crisis may well discover that unresolved shame is at the root.[23] The masks are wearing thin, the depleted self begins to panic. Time is running out.

How then can we learn to know ourselves? The problem is that we have been taught how to *do* but not how to *be*. We who take pride in our listening skills for others often take little time to attend to ourselves. Tara Brach, a Buddhist writing about shame, speaks helpfully of "pausing" as a way of listening to what we are experiencing. Can I listen to my imperfect self with compassion? At this moment: What am I feeling? What are my desires? What are my deep fears? What am I sensing?[24] In this way I begin to coax my hidden self to come out of hiding and reinhabit my body. We cannot accept ourselves without knowing ourselves.

As Christians, however, we believe that knowledge of self and knowledge of God are interdependent. We have learned that introspection is safest under the gaze of God. So Christian spiritual disciplines such as silence and solitude help to peel away the masks. "Search me O God. Search *for* me O God, that I may know both myself and thee."

---

[23] Harper, *Uncovering Shame,* 38.

[24] Tara Brach, *Radical Acceptance: Awakening the Love That Heals Fear and Shame Within Us* (London: Random House, 2003).

But this solitary introspection will only take us so far. Pastors, like everyone else, will also need help from other human beings in dealing with shame, though of course this too is God at work. This is the incarnational response to shame. Pastors must be willing to expose their shame and receive the gracious gift of affirmation and acceptance from other people. Shame is coaxed out into the open by another true self, appropriately exposed, genuinely present, and respectful of the other. Shame cannot be handled academically. It must be entered and engaged relationally.

All of this may seem daunting, but it must be done. Not least because the pastor who is willing to face her own shame demons will not be tempted to toss easy words to others wrapped in shame. But there are deeper reasons why we pastors must address our shame.

Shame limits capacity

Pastors are limited by their shame in a number of ways. At the most basic level it limits capacity. Stockitt comments that the parable of the talents points to one man whose "gifts and creativity remained frozen. It is a story of a man in the grip of shame."[25]

Shame-bound pastors find it almost impossible to believe that God could use them in the work of his Kingdom. They assume God values them in the same way they value themselves. The first task of each day is to rediscover a sense of purpose. This consumes much energy. Tomorrow will be the same. They frequently wonder if it would be better if someone else took over their position. A strong emphasis on

---

[25] Stockitt, "Love Bade Me Welcome; But My Soul Drew Back," 116.

"empowering the laity" may indicate a disempowered pastor. Unfortunately, however, the contagious nature of shame will undermine any efforts to share ministry. In reality, the laity is better empowered by bold pastors, confident of their place in the household of God.

Where shame-troubled pastors are able to minister, they do so with only limited effectiveness. As Pattison observes: "Depleted selves fleeing their own insignificance often make poor, resentful carers who are uninterested in other's real needs."[26] Their self-preoccupation makes them unable to realistically evaluate themselves and their roles. Pattison rightly points out the dangers of "poorly enselfed, shamed people" finding a sense of "identity, power, and grandiose significance" in a pastoral role. Combine this with a community of people with an inadequate sense of their own self-worth and you have a toxic mix.[27] The pastor blind to his own shame is of dubious benefit to the community of faith.

Shame-bound pastors will seek out organizations that "work" better for them. Capps observes that narcissism and bureaucracy have a symbiotic relationship. In bureaucracies, meaningful personal relationships are discouraged and the narcissist finds an environment in which to succeed.[28] Narcissistic or shame-bound pastors may flourish in bureaucratic churches. And this works both ways. Churches led by pastors with unresolved shame will tend to limit meaningful relationships (though they may be friendly in a superficial way). Because shamed people see themselves as less than persons—rather, as commodities—they don't expect to be

---

[26] Pattison, *Shame*, 114.
[27] Ibid. 280f.
[28] Capps, *The Depleted Self*, 9.

valued as persons. They are strangely willing to sell themselves to the most attractive bidder. Thus overcommitment and unreason-able work hours are a respectable form of prostitution for shame-bound pastors.

Because shame is contagious, pastors blind to their own shame will be shame generators, not shame healers. Not only is shame passively contagious, it can be imposed on others. One way to deal with the intolerable weight of shame is to pass it on. Kaufman notes that shame is transferred down the "dominance hierarchy"[29]—the pecking order. Pity that pastor's secretary! Thus shame problems become power problems. People accumulate power and influence to compensate for shame. Leadership that operates by manipulating shame may be effective in the short term, but the price paid is heavy indeed.

Furthermore, pastors inflict shame when they abuse their position of trust. In the case of sexual abuse, shame is just one of a number of debilitating wounds. Sexual abuse is an area of risk for needy, shame-bound pastors and their congregations.

Shame-bound pastors are often busy, activity focused, difficult, and impatient with others. They may hide the deficit through withdrawal, procrastination, and indecisiveness. They may compensate by people pleasing, perfectionism, material-ism, and overconcern for appearance. What you see is not what is really there; the true person is out of sight.

Because shamed people know their own story is a "cover," they assume other people's stories are also—not exactly a recipe for good pastoral care! Green points out the difficulty shame-bound people have with others who are shame bound.

---

[29] Kaufman, *Shame*, 73.

The reaction is ambiguous. There is a need to care and fix. Yet there may be a sense of being attacked. The pastor's own shame is being stirred up. The pastor becomes angry at being unable to help. She becomes defensive about boundaries in an attempt to defend her own fragile, ineffective self.[30] The shame-bound pastor will have to get beyond thinking that every absent look or turned head is a sign of rejection. There is no joy for pastor or congregation if the pastor overreads every response through his own shame lens.

Shame shrinks the emotional field. Shame-full pastors may feel little beyond rage. Rage is our isolation barrier. The undeveloped pastoral self cannot tolerate another self operating at cross-purposes. Rage is the response. This is not to say that anger is bad, but rage and anger must be differentiated. Anger can be healing. It can invite a relational response. We can be angry *for* others. This can be part of our love for others. But the pastor who is habituated to suppressing his own deep feelings will find it difficult to be angry for the sake of someone else. Pastors who are coming to terms with their own shame will discover their rage being replaced by anger as their emotional field broadens and deepens.

Shame limits true spirituality . . . As the heart hardens against itself, it also hardens against God. That primary relationship, that wellspring of life, is quenched.

Shame limits joy . . . No pastoral ministry will be deeply joyful if it is done out of a need to be needed, or to earn favor, or in some other way to compensate for shame. There is a refusal to risk exposure—a refusal to risk being loved.

---

[30] Daniel Green and Mel Lawrenz, *Encountering Shame and Guilt* (Grand Rapids, MI: Baker Books, 1994), 123.

Shame limits preaching . . . Preaching is a particular kind of exposure. Preachers troubled by shame will shrink back and preach more distant, less personal, "safer" sermons.

Shame limits passion . . . It undermines vitality and enthusiasm in all areas. The fear of being shamed reduces risk tolerance. Shame-bound pastors follow the known safe roads with no surprises, no spontaneity, and no "edge."

For some pastors, the motivation to seek healing comes when the weight of boredom becomes greater than the weight of shame.

The way forward

To move forward is to reengage in the task of growing up. For shame, to a great extent, is a sign of arrested growth. The emerging self did not develop a robust independence. The cause is not so important, but the work cannot be put off. The time has come to "throw off everything that hinders" (Hebrews 12:1 NIV). Yes, the journey out of shame requires patience. The answer does not come in a box. We pastors will struggle personally with the messiness of shame just like anyone else. Some years it will feel like two steps backwards and one step forwards. But this patience is as much a gift from God as the healing itself.

Shame-based people need to develop the capacity to affirm themselves and be comfortable with their own worth. The foundation for this is God's own verdict on his creative work—it was *good!* And the creation of humans was *very good!* (Genesis 1:31). Albers suggests that time spent in the natural environment may help reintroduce a deep sense of primary worth.[31] Such times draw us nearer to that moment of creation when God pronounced his verdict of goodness. We can sit on the earth with our back to a tree and relish the memory of Eden. We can also learn to comfortably inhabit our own bodies. My physical body is the temple of the Holy Spirit! (1 Corinthians 3:16f.) This underlines human, earthly value. Just as shame is often generated viscerally (e.g., through sexual abuse), release may be linked with a visceral sense of worth.

But though it is helpful to hear God's affirmation through the physical world (including our own physicality), healing for shame comes as the pastor hears this word of affirmation personally. As we develop real relationships with other people, their acceptance brings to earth God's acceptance. Pastors, too, need grace for shame *incarnate*. This grace will be dispensed by the church itself. The pastor cannot stand above the community. Pastors need to be pastored.

Can we allow pastoring to be a reciprocal relationship? Given half a chance, the church will pastor the pastor in ways that are healing for shame. Most churches have this ministry in their DNA if the pastor is ready to receive it. After all, the pastor is also a member of the *laos* of God.

But this grace will also be dispensed by individuals. And there will be differences for men and women at this point. For male pastors their marriage relationship, where honor-shame values are deeply engrained, is especially important. Wives hold the honor of their husbands in the palm of their hands. Paul has a wise word to wives in Ephesians 5:33: "let the wife see that she *respects* her husband." Men long to be secure in the respect and honor of their wives. If they are not respected at

---

[31] Albers, "Shame and the Conspiracy of Silence," 62f.

home, that honor deficit will haunt all other relationships. Interestingly, Paul's word to husbands (in the same verse) is, "let each one of you *love* his wife as himself." What a wonderful place for her to go out from and return to. Within the marriage relationship each is instructed to provide the right medicine for the other's ills—the wife to respect, the husband to love.

Good mentoring is also helpful. But the challenge here is how to cope with the presence of a mature, capable, perhaps exemplary mentor. The "largeness" of the one emphasizes the "smallness" of the other! Peer mentoring may initially be more helpful for deeply shamed people.

Whatever the nature of the relationship, shame is healed as relationships are restored. What we need are trusting relationships where we can be open and vulnerable and still find genuine affirmation. Those of us who are not good at self-assessment or who tend to a negative self-assessment are helped by allowing others to assess our abilities, giftedness, worth, etc. The goal is neither extreme dependence nor extreme independence. We seek to be robust individuals warmly connected to each other. Good friendships are gold.

The "good-enough" pastor

The church is naturally a place where we hold up high ideals. The challenge for the church is how to hold up these high ideals without generating shame for those who don't achieve the ideal. Pastors are particularly aware of the painful gap between the real and the ideal in their own life. Alan Wright points to one of the lies of shame: "There is something more that you must do in order to be blessed."[32] And for pastors, there is always something more to be done! In discovering healing for shame, the pastor will at last begin to allow God to be God and begin to come to terms with his or her own finitude.

Susan Miller, in speaking about realistic parenting, introduces the concept of the "good-enough mother."[33] Perhaps some relief from the disparity between the real and the ideal may be found in the concept of the "good-enough" pastor. Yes, there are core competencies that need to be established, but few pastors will be "five-star generals."

What does it mean to be good enough? God delights in the pastor who shows up, who loves in practical ways, who prays for the flock, who ministers the Word with care and diligence, who serves with integrity, and who has a life apart from the church. Healthy modesty is realistic evaluation—neither grandiose nor self-obliterating. I am not "perfect"—why should I expect to be! But I am making a unique contribution to the work of the Kingdom that flows out of my own worth as a unique individual. I am adequate and more.

Recovery from shame is helped by a steady, disciplined diet of daily prayer and meditation. But Paul Goodliff invites us to go beyond meditation to contemplation. He argues that "two theological motifs . . . are central to the alleviation of chronic shame, openness to others and contemplation of the face of Christ."[34] In contemplation we expose ourselves to the gracious gaze of Christ and find healing. In these ways our

---

[32] Wright, *Shame Off You,* 216.

[33] Susan Miller, *Shame in Context* (Hillsdale, NJ: Analytic Press, 1996), 124.

[34] Paul Goodliff, *With Unveiled Face: A Pastoral & Theological Exploration of Shame* (London: Darton, Longman & Todd Ltd., 2005), 109.

false view of the world, built up over a lifetime, is gradually deconstructed and replaced by a world where God is God and I am I. Here again is "positive mirroring" in different words.

If pastors can understand that they are deeply valued as persons before God, they can begin to assess their abilities more realistically and at the same time find release from the often unrealistic and shaming assessments of self and of others. We will be less hungry for "recognition." Is this a search for self-esteem? Green comments helpfully that rather than seeing self-esteem as a goal in itself, it is more constructive to see it as a *consequence* of successful shame resolution.[35]

As pastors and leaders recover from shame they will be more their own persons. This does not mean they will be disconnected from others. They will, however, be at peace within the boundaries of their own persons while still present in the ferment of the church community.

But this will take time. It is a learning process. The recovering pastor will have to learn when to be open and when to be closed. She will tend to make mistakes in both directions. A re-socializing is taking place. This is like the victims of cerebral palsy who need lengthy patterning exercises to develop normal control over muscles and movement. The shamed person feels like a bad actor who doesn't know his lines. He has difficulty with easy familiarity. But, as shame is reduced and the self becomes more robust, intimacy and spontaneity are nurtured, and humor is closer to the surface. Paradoxically, as proper boundaries are established, friendships multiply and go deeper.

---

[35] Green, *Encountering Shame and Guilt*, 109.

Christian boldness

As pastors walk out of shame, they are released to speak and preach with deeper authenticity. Such pastors have come to themselves. They inhabit their own emotions (not other people's emotions). They own their preaching in a new way. Their preaching has, at the same time, more of self and more of God.

As pastors recover from shame, they will experience increasing boldness, confidence, and freedom. Indeed pastors need to *appropriate* Christian boldness. This boldness is a gift purchased at great price. It is not to be sold below market value (Hebrews 10:35). In the pilgrimage out of shame, this boldness is to be savored daily. This boldness is not arrogance. It is simply the birthright of the children of God. This boldness is in part the confident assertion of individuality in the presence of other people. But it is also the confident assertion of individuality in the presence of God—an exceedingly strange concept for people habituated to shame!

Boldness is one of the great discoveries of the believer. It is delightfully contagious. We lift our heads and meet eye to eye the gaze of others. We discover a quiet satisfaction in our accomplishments and abilities that brings joy to those around us as well as to ourselves. At the same time, paradoxically, there will be a true sense of modesty, deference, even shyness, as well as deeper awe and reverence for God. Shame is not removed, but restored to its rightful place as the minder of fences and the guardian of personhood.

Sharing the honor of Christ

We pastors discover the ultimate answer to our shame in Christ. Not only because in him we are cleansed but because in him we are also honored. In Christ we are adopted into the family of God. We hear the wonderful words, "You are my daughter; you are my son. I love you. I am delighted in you!" (see Luke 3: 22). This is so helpful for pastors struggling with the ambiguity of their role. Not everyone in the church will regard the pastor as an honorable person. For some church folk, the pastor will be weighed in the world's scales of honor and shame and be found wanting. For others, the pastor will be forever "too young." In fact, if honor comes too freely from the congregation, we may question the underlying value system. Is this the honor of the Kingdom, or is it the honor of this world?

There is a hiddenness about true spiritual honor. It is not readily apparent. It certainly won't be apparent to people outside the church. In a post-Christian world, the pastoral role carries no honor. Out on the street, both pastor and congregation feel the weight of this new honor deficit. Christians, however, are members of an alternate community where honor is granted according to alternate rules. We have no need to hanker after the threadbare honor of this world. The honor from above is more than sufficient.

Christians share in the very glory of Christ. Like Christ, pastors do not need to advertise this honor. They know who their Father is. Their identity is secure, no longer dependent on human affirmation, either religious or secular. Pastors know that God himself is the guardian of honor. This honor is not earned, it is a gift of grace. It needs no human defense, nor can any be given.

How will the church respond to their new pastor? When pastors see themselves as having little value, they collude with others who also see them as having little value. But as pastors begin to find themselves and take ownership of who they are, they lose their comfortable alliance with those who belittle them. Their sick relationship no longer works for either of them. Can a dysfunctional church tolerate a pastor who is coming to himself and is learning to be a healthy presence? The pastor may be learning to be comfortable with his or her own finitude, but the church may not be so comfortable. Such pastors are not as easily managed. They are learning to resist "commodification." The church now has to contend with a real person! The response will be ambiguous.

Nevertheless there is a great hunger for grace for shame. As pastors address their own shame and own God's grace for themselves, they begin at last to minister more effectively to the growing numbers of people who are also troubled with shame. With quiet confidence they lead others into exposing their shame to the eyes of God, that healing may begin. The wounded one is now the healer. We may not recover totally from the deep emotional impact of shame. We may still "walk with a limp." But we have been touched by God. And that old brokenness just may turn out to be a place of strength.

Pastoral Presence and Grace for Shame

It is important for pastors to address their own shame precisely because ministry for shame is not only about words it, is also about relationships. Relationships can be both healing and harmful for shame. Pastors who avoid their own shame will reinforce the shame of others. On the other hand, pastors who are facing their own shame will discover not just that they are a *safer* presence but that, in God's grace, they are also a *healing* presence.

The gift of presence

The healing presence of pastors arises in part from their growing understanding of shame. They bring no shallow optimism but a healthy appreciation of the weight of shame. They will know better when professional treatment from outside the church is needed. But there is more than this. They will also understand the healing potential of a healthy pastoral presence. They know that healing for shame is incarnational. The model is Jesus, Emmanuel, God with us. Pastors model and mediate the presence of Christ.

It is not the *perfection* of Christ that is modeled. Shame healing pastors are at home in their finite, limited presence. In fact, for people who grew up with the fiction of perfect parents, or the fiction of a perfect church, such honesty is a breath of fresh air. Pastors, simply by their authentic presence, re-interpret the world for shame-bound people. Alongside them the world becomes more livable. People sense that close by the finite, imperfect pastor is the quiet presence of Christ.

The pastor who has encountered himself and embraced himself can now accept others without reserve. This unconditional acceptance provides a "floor of grace"[36] on which to reconstruct the self. This acceptance is only partly conveyed in words. It is also powerfully conveyed in body language, particularly facial expression. The root of this acceptance is preverbal. For the pastor plays a kind of re-parenting role. Here is an opportunity for depleted persons to

---

[36] Augsburger, *Conflict Mediation Across Cultures*, 135.

receive the positive mirroring that was previously missing. The shame-healing pastor welcomes hidden souls into the world of real people, with recognition, with respect, with warmth, and with delight. He enlarges their hopes and dreams.

The notion of positive mirroring turns out to be even more powerful than acceptance, helpful though that is. Acceptance is too near "tolerance." Positive mirroring is a more enthusiastic and engaged form of love. Pembroke puts it this way, "In pastoral relationships availability is before skills and techniques and confirmation is beyond empathy and acceptance."[37] The positive mirroring of the pastor opens the possibility for the other's self-mirroring.

Just as good mothering must be incarnational, so good pastoring must be incarnational, that is to say, face-to-face.

Feeling the "Yes" of God

We can all learn to be more fully present with each other. But pastoral presence is more. It is a more intentionally priestly presence. The pastor is, in a special way, set apart, for a time, as a representative of God. Until shamed people feel God's *acceptance*, they will have little appreciation of God's *forgiveness*. The pastor makes *tangible* divine acceptance. The warmth and delight of the pastor makes the warmth and delight of the heavenly Father seem possible to the shame-bound person. It is this heavenly "Yes!" that finally quiets the shamed person's "No!" And to feel the "Yes" of God is to be deeply honored.

People are restored as honor is restored. The honor holder dispenses honor to the honor deficient. This deposit of honor

---

[37] Neil Pembroke, *The Art of Listening: Dialogue, Shame and Pastoral Care* (Grand Rapids, MI: Eerdmans, 2002), 215.

must, however, be *felt* as honoring by the person. This is one place where cultural sensitivity is so important. Not everyone feels honored when singled out in a large group. At the same time, this deposit of honor must be *seen* as such by the community in order to be effective. Honor is always in the eyes of others.

The presence of the pastor makes tangible the heavenly deposit of honor. This is especially so in pronouncing the blessing of God. How wonderful to hear spoken the Aaronic blessing. Here it is once again:

> The Lord bless you and keep you;
>> the Lord make his face shine upon you
>>> and be gracious to you;
>> the Lord lift up his countenance upon you
>>> and give you peace.
>>>> (Numbers 6:24-26)

Shamed people need blessing. They need to hear the words. But canned blessings don't cut it! Those words are delivered through the living, present, known voice of the pastor.

Showing up

So shame-healing pastors show up. They show up at house-warmings, in hospital rooms, at workplaces, weddings and funerals, at kids' birthday parties and golden anniversaries. They show up not begrudgingly but respectfully, expectantly, delighting in the other. They share "Wisdom's" heart:

> I was filled with delight day after day,
>> rejoicing always in [the Lord's] presence,
> rejoicing in his whole world
>> and delighting in mankind. (Proverbs 8:30,31 NIV)

The shame-bound person loses hope of finding a way back into normal human relationships and community. Shame healing pastors are not afraid to show up in the hidden places. They have a "go to" ministry as well as a "come to" ministry. They have discovered that grace is portable! They are at home in the wide world because it is their Father's world and their people's world. They are learning to follow in the footsteps of Jesus, even inviting themselves into the home of Zacchaeus to break bread with the dishonored.

Eating together in group cultures is highly significant. It is a bonding experience. The visitor identifies with the host. While eating together in the West does not carry the same weight as it does in the East, it is, nevertheless, a powerful way of being present. In multicultural communities pastors may discover that in some homes the significance of sharing a meal together is very similar to biblical days. Eating is intimate, it is earthy. Eating emphasizes the physical, fleshly presence that is the very essence of incarnation. A ghost does not eat with people! Eating is an invitation to openness. Eating together emphasizes the vulnerability of presence. It is a kind of risk—an exposure. We cannot eat with a veil in front of our face. When the pastor joins in the laughter and talk around the kitchen table shame melts away. If the pastor can come for lunch perhaps God has not abandoned us after all.

The place of touch

Careful, appropriate touch can be healing for shame-bound people. Touch emphasizes presence. We can only touch if we are physically present. Human touch is a way of making real and present the love of God. Kaufman points out that physical touch, from a handshake to an arm around the shoulder to a hug, can help restore a deep sense of security. Touching helps dissolve the paralyzing effects of deeply rooted shame. Shamed people may have been deprived of touching and holding. Even later in life, touch may play a significant role in recovery.[38] Rick Warren's instruction to church greeters—"a smile, a word, and a touch"—is healing for shame.[39]

The key is that the touch be appropriate. It is the pastor's responsibility to monitor the boundaries of healthy relationships. There will be times when it is not the pastor's job to hug but to see that a person gets hugged. After an emotional session the pastor's wife may hug the troubled woman. Blessed is the congregation that has a smiling, loving, ninety-year-old couple at the door who warmly embrace all comers!

The grace of respect

At the root of the shame-healing presence is a deep sense of respect. Burton writes: "Respect is essential to the healing of shame, and can be defined as the honoring of the 'otherness' of the other without denying the 'selfness' of one's own being." Here Burton quotes James Children: respect can be understood as "answering that of God in every person."[40] So the pastor lives as though Genesis chapter 1 were true! She greets expectantly each child, each businessman, each immigrant, each senior, knowing that here is one made in the image of God.

Respect for others parallels respect for self. The pastor who cannot yet say "yes" on behalf of self cannot yet say "yes"

---

[38] Kaufman, *Shame*, 48, 50, 122.

[39] Rick Warren, *The Purpose-Driven Church: Growth Without Compromising Your Message and Mission* (Grand Rapids, MI: 1995), 214.

[40] Burton, "Respect," 146.

on behalf of others. The pastor who has not yet come to terms with his own depleted, nonrespected self cannot respect others authentically. But the pastor respectful of his own company will be respectful of other people's company.

Respectful relationships avoid the language of "should" and "ought." This is the language of control. "Should" statements *dictate* what we do, know, or feel. They imply an anonymous source—there is no accountability—no one to complain to, They describe ideals that may or may not be attainable. They hint at a threat: "You should do or be such and such if you expect to be valued, accepted, etc." All of this is potentially shame generating. Better to use: "It might be more helpful if . . . ."

Yes, it is possible and desirable to influence people for good. This is part of the pastor's work of love. The question is how. Gregory the Great, in his sixth century classic on pastoral care, has good, practical advice for dealing with the "timid." First look for things to praise.

> [This] fosters their sensitive feelings . . . . Usually we make better progress with these people if we recall their good deeds, and, if they have done something out of order, we do not reprimand them as if for a fault they have already committed, but we prohibit it as something they are not to do in the future. Thus our appreciation will encourage what we approve of, and a modest exhortation will count more with them against what we censure.[41]

Note his emphasis on "deeds." Exuberant global praise can lead to an unhealthy global self-focus (especially in children).

---

[41] Gregory the Great, *Pastoral Practice,* Translated by John Leinenweber (Harrisburg, PA: Trinity Press International, 1998), 18.

This, in turn, may make us vulnerable to a global negative self-assessment (shame).[42] If I am a Somebody because I do something well, then I am a Nobody if I do something badly. Better to praise specific actions or attributes.

Many people have been shamed through loss of power, especially through loss of power over their own persons. Respect means allowing and encouraging people to declare their own "Yes" and "No," even (perhaps especially!) in opposition to the pastor. Shame is reduced as people are encouraged to form boundaries. In this way power is shared. Jesus paid special attention to the powerless. He loved them in practical ways. He sat with them and transformed their place of non-power to one of power. He identified himself with them so that they could identify themselves with him. This was a mark of deep respect. They too could act, teach, heal, forgive, in Jesus' name. Shame-healing pastors risk empowering people.

And somehow pastors need to remember people's names! The Good Shepherd knows the name of each sheep and each lamb. Jesus recognized children, thus rewriting their "non-person" script. Children *mattered* to him. Surely he knew their names. Shame is concerned with the fear of insignificance as well as abandonment. Naming highlights uniqueness. Naming calls forth the individual from the shadows onto the stage of life. To name is to acknowledge, to welcome, and to affirm. Name is close to honor. To be named is to be honored and respected for who we are. We will remember people's names when they matter to us.

When people know they matter to the pastor, their shame scripts also begin to be rewritten. But if shame-prone people

---

[42] M. Lewis, *Shame*, 168.

are only seen as "objects of compassion," they will not be helped. We must approach people as equals. Paternalism (and maternalism!) engender shame because they do not receive the other as an adult. They reduce the other to the incompleteness of childhood.[43] Even empathy, as Hultberg observes, when it is "active, penetrating, intrusive," can be an act of violation that generates shame. Empathy is helpful if it is "passive, nourishing, receptive."[44] So if someone insists he is a failure, it might be helpful to accept his assessment! This is a way of respecting another person's opinion of himself. Such unexpected deference may open the door to real engagement.

Getting to know someone involves carefully stepped exposure (lowering the guard). Too much too fast, and the other runs. Too little too slowly, and the other senses indifference. Relationships involve risk. The rules for appropriate risk are subtle and culturally shaped. Good pastoring is tactful where "tact is the ability to understand the other person's nearness to shame."[45] From within the respectful, Spirit-led heart of the pastor, deep calls to deep, and the shamed person takes courage and says, "Here am I. *Hineni!* Behold—Me!"

Holding the honor of the community
We need to take this further. The importance of the pastoral presence is not limited to private or informal encounters, vital though they are. Pastors mediate grace for shame for the church as a community, not only by what they say and do, but by their presence, their way of being. Like it or not, the culture of the

---

[43] Burton, "Respect," 146.
[44] Hultberg, "Shame—A Hidden Emotion," 121.
[45] Leon Wurmser, quoted by Nathanson in *Shame and Pride,* 391.

church is shaped by the ontological robustness of the pastor, or lack thereof. If the church indeed functions as a village or kinship group (a small face-to-face community), then the pastor needs to acknowledge his or her role as chief.

Studies of honor-shame cultures have alerted us to the powerful role the leader plays in the *tribal economy* of shame. The honor (or lack of honor) of the pastor will signal the honor (or lack of honor) of the whole group. As the chief of the tribe, the pastor holds the honor of the tribe. The church that is led by an uncertain, insecure pastor will feel unsettled and vulnerable. Pastors who behave in ways judged dishonorable by the community will bring dishonor on that community. Some pastors may even, though perhaps subconsciously, behave badly to "get even," knowing instinctively that shame is the greatest of pains one can inflict. But even the "squeaky clean" (guilt-free) pastor must still take stock of his or her ability to retain the honor of the community or his or her "leadership" will be called into question.

People long for heroic leaders. Heroic qualities are evaluated instinctively and quickly—an important factor in a mobile, drop-in society. For better or worse, heroic pastors retain more visitors.

So in the life of the church community the influence of the pastor may well lie in his ability to sustain or build the honor of that community. This is surely a factor in the continuing prevalence of congregations in the 80-120 range. It will need a leader of unusual charisma and heroic qualities to maintain the cohesion of larger groups. If "ordinary" ("good-enough") pastors can satisfy the honor of 80-120 people, what does this say about church growth? Here is a new aspect of the "Peter principle" that needs to be explored. Is it possible to grow the church beyond our capacity to sustain the honor of the church? It may be more helpful and healthier for churches to multiply rather than grow. Or is this simply a concession to the honor-shame paradigms of this world?

Then again, if it is true that the influence of the pastor may well lie in his ability to sustain the honor of that community, what happens when that "he" is a "she"? For women in leadership, the persistence of traditional (unconverted) honor-shame dynamics offers additional challenges. If the church community still operates, at the emotional level, out of cultural values that differentiate male-female roles along traditional hierarchical lines it will resist the woman pastor. "How can a female leader bring honor to the tribe?" will be the unstated question.

The only way forward is to lie close to the Gospel of Jesus that continually challenges all cultures, including traditional honor-shame cultures. Though Paul may at times appear to make concessions to the demands of particular, local situations, his bottom line is clear: "For as many of you as were baptized into Christ have put on Christ. There is neither Jew nor Greek, there is neither slave nor free, there is neither male nor female, for you are all one in Christ Jesus" (Galatians 3:27-28). Where the Gospel of Jesus is front and center, women will be set free for ministry.

Pastors receive a free deposit of honor when they join a new church. In this new setting they are no longer the home-town prophet without honor! But how long will this last? In honor-shame communities, honor is always challenged. How will the pastor handle himself? Peristiany observed this behavior in his studies of Mediterranean culture. "The entire society watches for the young shepherd's first quarrel, that is, for his first chance to prove himself."[46] Having passed this first test, the ongoing challenge for the pastor will be to sustain honor even though this new church quickly becomes the new "hometown." Familiarity does not necessarily breed honor! How important it is at this point not to pursue honor through improper means. I wonder if some of the acerbic denunciation of the "world," or particular groups within that world, may be the depleted pastor's desperate attempt to restock his honor account on the home front.

Hidden in Christ

So pastors wrestle with the paradox that the deepest honor is hidden in Christ in weakness and cruciform life. This will not always mesh with the longings of the congregation (nor with the longings of the pastor's own heart). The church tries to invest the pastor with honor by fitting out a grand office. But the pastor finds herself working off a different honor-shame script than the honor-shame script (job description?) of the congregation. To complicate matters more, the congregation will have a collection of diverse honor-shame scripts. In the same pew, on the same Sunday, will sit postmoderns, moderns, and premoderns, each with their own prescriptions for honor. Thus the pastor, in faithfulness to his Lord, may at times seem to have more of the *shame* of Christ than the *glory* of Christ. We will cycle between death and resurrection. We will only *taste* Easter Sunday victory. As A. J. Dewey correctly notes, "One's honor is essentially eschatological."[47] It cannot be fully realized in this life. We receive it now by faith not sight.

---

[46] Peristiany, *Honor and Shame*, 15.
[47] A. J. Dewey, "A Matter of Honor: A Socio-Historical Analysis of 2 Corinthians 10," *Harvard Theological Review*, 78 (1985): 216.

Thus the astute pastor may find it helpful to have in pocket a supply of "small change" honor to quiet the immediate needs of a pilgrim people. It doesn't hurt the cause of Christ to be dressed appropriately, to be well groomed, to hit the odd home run or win the bowling prize from time to time! But such honor is at best fleeting, and the wise pastor never forgets that. Though this world's categories of honor and shame may be the default setting of small face-to-face communities, including churches, Christ has radically re-written the rules. And the wise pastor remembers that the Gospel stands over all cultures to revise and correct all cultural honor-shame scripts.

But this is not an easy road to walk. The ministry of grace for shame will always be a cross-bearing ministry. As we offer grace for shame there will, at times, be those who want to crucify us as they did Christ.

Thus pastors must flee the temptation to acquire honor by illegitimate means. Power games, displays of wealth, denunciation of outsiders, even sexual prowess, may build honor in communities with unconverted honor-shame scripts. But the faithful pastor cares only for heaven's verdict. The extent of Paul's divergence from the heroic leader of honor-shame culture can be seen, for example, in the Corinthian letters (e.g., 1 Corinthians 2:1-5, 2 Corinthians 1:8-10, 4:7, 12:9, 13:3-4).[48] Paul emphasizes his shamefulness (lack of honor). Yet he also argues that it is through his honor deficit that God's honor credit is emphasized.

So while pastors need to be present as people who are no longer under shame, they have not bought cheap honor in the

---

[48] Peter Marshall, "A Metaphor of Social Shame: *Thriambeuein* in 2 Corinthians 2:14," *Novum Testamentum,* 25 (4) (1983): 302-317.

world's marketplace, but have been graced with the deep honor of Christ in the heavenlies. Behind the shame-healing pastoral presence is the shame-healing reality of God's presence, "Fear not, I am with you." Pastors are present, but they are present in Jesus' name.

Is it easy to be present in Jesus' name? Jesus paid a price for his presence. Pastors will also pay a price as they walk in his footsteps. We may even get nostalgic for the days when pastoral ministry focused on guilt management. How much simpler and easier it was! But we realize now it was a constricted ministry. Ministering grace for shame is much messier, it bares one's soul, it demands one's very being. But ah the joy of a community that basks in the delight of the Lord and of each other. This is a foretaste of heaven!

Nurturing a Healing Community

Because shame is rooted in relational fracture, healing comes as broken relationships are restored. But we need to push this further. Shame is also a dynamic of unhealthy relational *systems*. And so we discover that healing for shame must move beyond not only the healing word but also beyond the healing pastoral presence, to the healing congregation. Healing comes with addressing broken relational systems.

Life together
Astute pastors are well aware that churches function as large family systems. The critical question is: How healthy is the system? This is difficult for the pastor to assess, not least because he or she is part of the system. Furthermore, as we

have seen, unhealthy pastors may survive reasonably well in partnership with unhealthy systems. Do pastors have the courage to allow the light to shine in? Pattison is just one voice calling for a reexamination of problematic ideologies and institutions that generate and exploit shame. Somewhat pessimistically he writes: "Where two or three people are gathered together in a group, there is always the possibility of shame and exclusion arising as norms, roles and practices are defined in the interests of personal and group identity."[49] To state this more positively, one of the most powerful ways a pastor can minister grace for shame is by nurturing a shame-healing community.

Community is not an optional extra for the human race, it is an inescapable part of who we are. God said it was not good for man to be alone. Surely God was speaking out of his own Trinitarian experience. Human beings image God most faithfully in community. The Apostle Paul is clear that Christ's costly ministry was intended to restore community savaged by sin. At times Paul even appears to give priority to what may be called the horizontal reconciliation (or community recon-ciliation) over the vertical reconciliation (reconciliation with God) though he does not separate them (see, for example, Ephesians 2:14-18).

A guilt-oriented theology finds it difficult to give community the weight it deserves. A shame-oriented theology will be much more aware of the place and value of community since honor and shame are group-culture values. Here we see the genius of the Christian Gospel expressed as the New Community and practiced corporately in the life of the church.

---

[49] Pattison, *Shame*, 276f.

The individualist, guilt-only emphasis that has marked so much of Western Christianity is hardly up to the ministration of the whole Gospel. Thankfully the current awakening to a more relational, guilt *and* shame understanding of the Gospel opens the door to a fuller expression of that Gospel. This will be manifest in the corporate life of the congregation.

Unhealthy systems

What are the marks of an unhealthy community? Insights from studies of shame-prone family systems are helpful here.

We can begin with communication. In unhealthy churches there is a lack of good communication. There is a high level of secrecy (often expressed in terms of "confidentiality"). Much of the communication happens behind the scenes, either in formal closed-door meetings or in less formal, gossipy ways. In particular, the congregation does not talk openly about shameful or abusive behavior. When there is a forum for discussion, people have difficulty moving beyond surface issues. It is not safe to bring deeply held feelings to the table.

Shame-bound congregations are also very concerned about rules. The rules attempt to guard against shame but in fact become shame generating. For example, there are rules about behavior: dress codes, clapping, language used, and levels of exuberance. The rules themselves are not necessarily unhealthy, but the way they are made and applied is unhealthy. In unhealthy systems the rules are not applied evenly—we discover that some people are more equal than others. Furthermore part of the problem in unhealthy systems is that some rules are not put into words. For example, there are rules about people: who is important, who needs to know, and who is welcome, but they are not written in the by-laws. We discover we have broken the rules by the shame we receive.

Like rules, power is an unavoidable dynamic of community life. Again it is not power itself that is unhealthy but the way it plays out. When churches authorize or legitimize power games (either consciously or unconsciously), one fallout is shame. Power is being used in unhealthy ways when decisions are made and implemented without due process. For example, some people may be excluded from the process. This can happen intentionally as decisions are made in backrooms rather than open meetings, or when consultation is deliberately limited. Or people may be excluded unintentionally by the use of processes they don't understand or that are culturally foreign to them. Sometimes the very appeal for due process is simply a cover for bullying.

Shame is reinforced not just by the experience of powerlessness but by the experience of being manipulated. Manipulation is deeply disrespectful and potentially shaming. Related to this is a climate of control. The few at the controlling center consume much attention. Often the real power structure does not appear on the organizational flow chart (the organist is married to the chairman of the board!). Control is sustained by manipulation, by withholding finances, permission, or presence, or by a martyr complex.

In unhealthy church systems there is an atmosphere of perfectionism. God is demanding. Spiritual transformation must take place quickly and thoroughly. There is an emphasis on performance. Perfectionism generates a pervasive sense of unworthiness. Judgmentalism and denial are defense mechanisms. Where communication does happen the focus is on failures. A lot of effort is put into determining who to blame. To the outsider it is apparent that this is often scape-goating.

There is a constricted quality to life in a shame-bound congregation. There are few common goals and purposes, and there is little vision. There is a feeling of stuckness. Change feels threatening, especially to leaders. The public face may look good, but behind the scene there is much chaos. Individuals within the system find little real intimacy. It is a lonely place. Yet small groups that might nourish intimacy are considered dangerous, cliquish. There is a reduced sense of security and protection from abuse. Personal boundaries are fragile. It is difficult to say yes or no freely. Anger, and especially rage, is a sign of boundary violation ("Those are *my* marbles!"), and this atmosphere of ongoing boundary violation may result in an emotional response out of proportion to the immediate context. Thus people walk on tiptoes, watch their backs, and limit exposure. The church may look good; but as new members move beyond the warm honeymoon period, they gradually discover the less appealing hidden life of the church.

Such congregations do not consciously choose to generate shame. This is the only system they know. It feels better than no system. Pattison, always incisive, writes: "A congregation of conforming, hungry, expectant, unresolved dependent 'children' may not represent a vision of human wholesomeness or maturity. However, it does comprise a church that has members who will continue to support its work"[!][50]

---

[50] Pattison, *Shame*, 280.

To harm or to heal?

The goal here is not to focus on the problem but to seek answers. Yet it is important to spend time thinking about unhealthy systems in order to highlight the importance of healthy systems. It is because the church has the potential for so much *healing* for shame that it also has the potential for so much *harm* when things go wrong. Furthermore, we need to think intentionally about unhealthy systems because, once again, shame, and shaming systems, remain stubbornly hidden. It is so difficult to see what lies in front of our face. In fact pastors are often co-conspirators in shaming systems. True, it is not helpful to talk about unhealthy and healthy churches in black and white terms (that itself is shaming), but pastors must consciously seek to move congregations towards greater health. It is a move into a culture of grace.

The danger is not that the church becomes an honor-shame culture community: that is a given. Honor and shame will always be prominent in close, face-to-face communities. The danger is that the honor-shame script will not align with the values of the Kingdom of God. The church in Corinth was a deeply troubled community, obsessed with hierarchy and status. Paul's pastoral response was to hold up Christ crucified, the new epicenter of the revised honor-shame system.

This concern for re-visioning honor and shame can be seen throughout Paul's letters. So, for example, Paul's instruction to husbands to "love your wives, just as Christ loved the church and gave himself up for her" (Ephesians 5:25) is a "genuine reversal of ancient heroic models of male authority families."[51] Moxnes argues, I believe correctly, that

---

[51] Don S. Browning, Bonnie J. Miller McLemore, Pamela D. Couture, and K. Brynolf Lyon, *From Culture Wars to Common Ground: Religion and*

Christian communities did not replace honor and shame values with, say, humility and love (less competitive values), but they did revise the value system, "especially the emphasis on ambition that led to strife and conflict in the community."[52]

It is a feature of honor-shame societies that honor does not have a fixed meaning and finds particularity only in the context of particular communities. In other words, the precise definition of what is honorable varies from group to group. Because of this it is even more important that honor be carefully defined within Christian groups. Unexamined honor values are a church health hazard! As pastors look for ways to bring change to their communities, they will be helped by insights from both psychological and cultural studies, as well by returning again and again to the living Word of Scripture for recalibration.

Healthy systems

So what do we look for in churches that are healing for shame? What are some of the characteristics of a healthy ecclesiastical ecology? Here are ten places to begin.

1. Genuine respect

Healthy systems are respectful systems. Respect is at the heart of the acceptance that shamed people long for. Respect means recognizing others for who they are (not for what they have to offer or for who they might become). If disrespect generates

---

the *American Family Debate* (Louisville, KY: Westminster John Knox Press, 2000), 141.

[52] Halvor Moxnes, "Honor, Shame and the Outside World in Paul's Letter to the Romans," in *The Social World of Formative Christianity and Judaism,* Jacob Neusner and Peder Borgen, eds. (Philadelphia: Fortress, 1988), 175.

shame, genuine respect nurtures a robust sense of self. People are even allowed to solve their own problems! (Respectful pastors don't overfix!)

Healthy churches have a high level of affirmation and encouragement because they consciously model God's affirmation. In experiencing the affirmation of the Christian community, the door is opened to experiencing God's affirmation. Pastors could take a handful of church leaders to an Alcoholics Anonymous meeting to see and feel heartfelt acceptance of broken people. For those worried about accepting the sin with the sinner, AA models the clear distinction. As people discover a community where they are loved and valued they begin to recover and value their own self. Now they are ready to address behavioral problems.

Healthy churches model the gracious acceptance of Christ that opens the door to the experience of forgiveness. The church is one place where even sinners are respectable! And if sinners are respectable, certainly everyone else is! Pastors, in both teaching and behavior, can lead congregations to be communities of equal respect where children, women, foreigners, marginal and low functioning people are genuinely valued and enjoyed. The newcomer says, "I feel, at last, I have come home."

2. Warm hospitality

Respect is the chief ingredient of warm hospitality. Healthy churches accept people as they are and thus make them more acceptable (hospitable) to themselves. This begins with the initial hospitality of the warmth, welcome, openness, and humor of greeters. Walking through that door is a great risk. It is an exposure. The visitor walks along the cliff edge of shame.

Acceptance at that moment is critical or the adventure will be stillborn.

But hospitality in the church must be deeper than friendliness. It must reflect the hospitality of Christ, who rewrites the rules of who is in and who is out. Healthy churches are not only non-elitist (that goes little beyond mere tolerance), they are places where the little people of the world are actively loved and specifically honored. Can we recognize the face of Christ in the one before us? Can we offer them not just tea, but the things that are really precious to us—like power? Pastors who empower readily nurture shame-healthy communities. When we can share power, we are getting serious about hospitality. When the church council has the same diversity as the church pew, we are getting serious about hospitality. Pastors cultivate this healthy environment by modeling the hospitality of Christ. At the very least they will be referees who call for equal time!

The table is the most visible sign of hospitality. Pastors can maximize opportunities for the church to eat together. Eating together nurtures an atmosphere of acceptance and safe intimacy. People relax around an informal meal and begin to reveal their true selves. Communion is the liturgical eating together. But the church needs to make communion less somber and sterile, and more celebratory, joyful, and welcoming, so that real sinners are not ashamed to participate.[53] Emphasizing only guilt and forgiveness at communion will tend to exclude those who are dealing with shame and loss of identity. We need to remind each other that when we eat and drink this meal together we proclaim the

---

[53] Jewett, "Honor and Shame in the Argument of Romans," 27f.

shame of the Lord's death till he comes. Communion is a reminder that Christ bore our shame. It is a messianic banquet where we celebrate our deliverance from shame.

Though it is God's court of reputation that ultimately determines who is honorable, the church here and now needs to find ways to express this. The reality of God's gracious acceptance, "Just as I am without one plea," must be felt as well as "telt." If baptism is silent, dutiful, and "reverent," it will not do much for shame. Let it be a welcome home party, complete with cameras flashing, noisy applause, and why not balloons and a cake? The ongoing celebration of communion builds on the joyful momentum initiated at baptism.

Many churches feel a duty to exclude certain people from the communion table. The question cannot be dealt with in depth here. But if Jesus allowed Judas to partake, and Peter, might we not safely enlarge the circle? Wesley called the Lord's table a "saving ordinance." Might not the Lord's Table be a place where those on the edge are drawn in closer as the atoning work and person of Christ are brought within tasting distance again and again? Rites and rituals go where words may not, even to the hidden recesses of the shamed person.

3. Delightful diversity

In healthy congregations it is OK to be different. Unhealthy church systems encourage the fiction of homogeneity. Shame-bound people seek out such systems because they feel shame when they don't conform to the norm. In the desire to belong, they bury part of themselves, to their own destruction. But healthy systems actually encourage differentiation. They welcome people as they really are. Thus healthy churches have a high level of commitment. Individuals are comfortable adhering to this diverse group and don't fear loss of personal identity. Members revel precisely in their differences, which become even more evident as they commune with different others. Together they rejoice in a wholly other God. Shaming systems not only promote a thin, surface sameness, but create God in their own image. In contrast, people in awe of each other's uniqueness together bow in awe before the utterly different, the Holy Other God.

Edwin Friedman has helpful insight for pastors at this point. He argues that healthy change in the church comes best not from charismatic leaders nor consensus builders but from leaders with a clearly developed sense of self who differentiate but do not withdraw.[54] We pastors need to be careful about "fitting in." We serve best when we are fully present in all our one-of-a-kind created selves.

And surely God is encouraging people to differentiate from himself also. Does every detail of our lives have to be brought up for approval before "God's will"? Is this the kind of child our Heavenly Father wants to raise? When do the obedient become the pliant? Will our initiative really undermine the sovereignty of God? Has our Creator not given us our own hearts and minds? God seeks persons, not robots, to love. He even loves his faithful rebels. So should we!

This rejoicing in difference echoes the Creator's delight as he called for increasing diversity and differentiation on each succeeding creation day. But this diversification did not tear the universe apart. All was knit together into an incredible

---

[54] Edwin H. Friedman, *Generation to Generation: Family Process in Church and Synagogue* (New York: The Guilford Press, 1985). See, for example, 240.

ecology of interdependence. Even the vastly different worlds of the masculine and the feminine were not designed for separation! Meaningful unity is built on difference, not sameness. Only truly diverse congregations know what it means to experience true unity.

4. Attainable goals

Healthy churches are led by pastors who are human! They model finitude and refuse to be worshiped. By God's grace they are "good enough" even in their brokenness. Such pastors affirm the congregation as a home for finite people. Fossum and Mason note, "We found a high correlation between shame and dependency in families bound by and entangled in rigid, perfectionist rule systems."[55] Pastors counteract this by setting attainable goals, upholding realistic models, and celebrating victories. In contrast, for example, "health and wealth" teaching engenders shame because of the way it links "strong faith" with prosperity and a trouble-free life. Those who don't prosper are, at best, mere survivors under such a system. In healthy churches Jesus is an *inspiration* not a *blueprint*.

True, there is still a need in the shame-healthy church for discipline. Here shame takes its proper role as guardian of good behavior. In fact a church that allows anything and everything, without limit, is shameless! Discipline sometimes means exclusion. But the rules for excluding someone from fellowship must be clear, public, and equally applied. The New Testament provides examples. Paul writes: "If anyone does not obey what we say in this letter, take note of that person, and have nothing to do with him, that he may be ashamed" (2 Thessalonians

---

[55] Fossum, *Facing Shame*, x.

3:14). But this has rightly been recognized as an extraordinary measure. For example, the Rule of Benedict does provide for exclusion from the monastic family, but this is regarded as severe punishment and a last resort.[56] Though Paul made this provision for exclusion, his hope was that the pain of exclusion would lead to repentance. His pattern was to leave the door open (2 Corinthians 2:5f). In the healthy church, "love covers a multitude of sins" (1 Peter 4:8).

The problem with perfectionism in any form is that there is no room for error. In such an environment mistakes are "forever" and are nonrepairable: mistakes are a global failure. When pastors acknowledge their own finitude they give permission to the system, and to individuals in the system, to be finite. They give permission for limitations, shortfalls, rough edges, weak moments, irritants, and inconsistencies. This is partly about general ability and fitness. For example, in healthy churches parents don't have to have perfect children. But this is also about spirituality. Healthy churches acknowledge that sanctification is a process that extends beyond this world. In healthy churches it is possible to fail and not have to leave.

5. Good communication

There are two sides to good communication, quantity and quality. Good communication first means much communication. Everyone knows. No one is out of the loop. The minutes of the council meeting are posted next to the coffee urn. Redundancy is built in. We always underestimate how much communication we need. When it *feels* like "much communication" to the people on the edge, then there is enough

---

[56] Benedict, *The Rule of St. Benedict,* chapters 24, 25, 44.

communication. Furthermore there is enough communication when everyone has a voice. Not only is no one silenced, but space is made for those with little voices. The shy are actually asked. Opportunities are created for real sharing. Translation is readily available where needed. Good communication is a function of good listening.

But good communication also refers to the quality of communication. It is real and honest. It represents what is really happening. It is free of propaganda, and motivations are transparent. All letters are signed. Job descriptions more closely resemble actual expectations. Rules and boundaries are clearly outlined and made public. Good communication is not manipulative.

Good communication is also affirming. For people whose grip on hope is often weak, it opens doors by naming strengths, opportunities, and possibilities. Whatever is true, whatever is noble, whatever is right, whatever is pure, whatever is lovely, whatever is admirable—if anything is excellent or praiseworthy—communicate these things within the church!

Pastors can subvert unhealthy systems by refusing to play by the old communication rules. They can speak openly about hidden issues. This eases the way for "unspeakable" topics to be spoken about. Church family secrets can be discussed openly. That which people hide from themselves, they hide from God, who is the source of healing. In the healthy church, feelings are expressed appropriately to the appropriate person. Pastors model good communication when they refuse to keep quiet what needs to be public, and refuse to make public what needs to be private.

6. Healthy sexuality

If there is one place where shame has remained on the radar of the church it is in the area of sex. Responses vary. One way to attempt to reduce shame is to change the rules. For example, if adulterous or homosexual behaviors are no longer on the list of sins, perhaps these behaviors will no longer cause shame. But rule changing turns out to be not so simple. The village knows better. Rules for sexual conduct are rooted in our very identity. Common (corporate) sense rebels. An alternate attempt to reduce shame is to strike at the offender. The stoning response (and its modern equivalents) is the small, face-to-face group preserving its honor in the face of deep violation.

But pastors are called to declare the culture of the Kingdom. Pastors challenge both the rule changers and the stoners. They call on the village to pause and reflect—not an easy call when passions are running high. Pastors are wary of simply reacting to the presenting issues. Pastors follow in the footsteps of Jesus and break open the nest, exposing the deeper roots. When Jesus pulled back the curtain on the hypocrisy and opportunism of the group condemning the woman caught in adultery, they all left, one by one. Their opportunism and hypocrisy were a more urgent though less visible problem than the woman's adultery. Pastors conspire with the Holy Spirit to expose unhealthy, single-issue righteousness. At the same time, they do not pretend that the old rules for behavior will melt away. Jesus told her clearly: "Go and sin no more."

But Jesus' admonition to that woman was remarkably subdued. Healthy systems do not insist on having sexual sins at the top of the transgression pyramid. Thoughtful pastors help the church put sex in context. Sexuality is affirmed as normal, healthy, and good. Sex is, in fact, healing for shame when there is trust, openness, and affirming love in a heterosexual marriage. The church is helped when pastors teach and preach about sex in healthy ways, when they point out both the male and female attributes of God, and when they recall that Song of Songs is, after all, canonical. The church is also helped when pastors point out the sexual failings of the "saints"—Abraham, David, and others. Often the road to recovery begins when the sins of the fathers are named. The church is helped when the rules of appropriate sexual conduct are applied *evenly*, to rich and poor, deacons and backbenchers, ordained and lay, males and females, old and young, East and West.

7. Fewer secrets

But this move to more openness will not be easy. Individuals with sexual secrets will feel threatened. Those committed to the "no-talk" rule will feel threatened. Some may even seek to harm the pastor or church leader, though they may not understand why. As there was with Jesus, there is a risk of retaliation. One of the difficulties of expressing judgments about sexual behavior is that sexuality is tied so closely to identity. Thus any judgment about sexual behavior feels like a judgment about self—it feels like a global condemnation. But the truth needs to be told. Sexual sins have consequences that persist over generations. The journey of recovery for victims of sexual abuse is long and tortuous. In the case of sexual abuse by clergy, there are additional severe consequences including the loss of a spiritual home. Despite the awkwardness, healthy churches deal more openly with sexuality and are safer places because of it.

One of the deep secrets of the church is abortion. Mary Comm, in her book *Secret Sin: When God's People Choose*

Abortion, argues that the secrecy in the church surrounding abortion closes the door to healing. In the U.S. one in three women will have had at least one abortion by the age of forty-five. It is those with the most deeply held religious views, i.e., those in our churches, who are most likely to have post-abortion trauma. Where will these women and their men find help for their shame?

Comm lists ways in which the church can become a safer place. Break the silence with compassion and mercy. Shut down condemnation and soften the hearts of those have not experienced abortion. Share the hope of the Gospel. Tell the stories and testimonies of healing. Provide trained counselors. Be alert to the bitter wounds in those near to the abortion (husband, relative, etc.) She writes: "So what is the key to turning the tide? Very simply it is telling the truth within the church, loving and accepting this wounded population as Christ does, and helping them find healing through Christ so that they can join the chorus of truth tellers."[57] Healthy churches refuse to maintain the secret of abortion in the church.

8. Fun and games

Healthy churches play together! Think of the shame-healing environment of an informal volleyball game. It is a group activity. It gets people out of themselves. At the same time, relationships are rearranged as overtight clusters are broken up and teams rotate players. People are laughing at themselves and others. The bodily exercise restores the soul. There is energetic effort towards a common goal with clear rules. Games teach

---

[57] Mary Comm, *Secret Sin: When God's People Choose Abortion* (Garden City, NY: Morgan James Publishing, 2007), 63f, 76.

people to take on healthy roles in healthy ways. Games build immunity to shaming roles.

Pastors can tell jokes! Nathanson observes, "If love is the balm that heals the pain of individuals, comedy is the solace, consolation and relief for entire tribes."[58] In healthy congregations, humor abounds. Humor breaks negative emotional feedback cycles. Humor is a reset button to release hot air and return perspective. Humor dispels the grandiose. People are secure enough in their own eyes and in the eyes of others that they do not have to take themselves seriously. Of course, the laughter must be respectful. It must be funny for everyone, to be healing for shame. Nathanson again, "We all live on some line between shame and pride. The mark of comedy is to make this border a bit safer."[59] So laughter increases the sense of being in control—we remember what is important and what is not.

9. Small groups

Healthy churches gather in small as well as large groups. The goal is an atmosphere of face-to-faceness, an openness to self, others and God. Small groups are effective because they nurture these kinds of authentic relationships. It is difficult to hide in small groups. The informal setting encourages people to let their guard down. Ongoing small groups provide opportunities for meaningful relationships to develop. They make possible an atmosphere of warmth, understanding, and safe exposure. Honor and shame dynamics are a fact of life in small groups; but when the groups are led well, there is the constant input of heavenly perspective that infuses health.

---

[58] Quoted by Pattison, *Shame*, 161.
[59] Nathanson, *Shame and Pride*, 17.

Small groups coax the shamed out of hiding and prepare them for a more normal life in the real world.

Surely the success of the Alpha program is due in part to its shame-healing formula. The atmosphere is welcoming and non-judgmental. Participants are listened to and respected. People eat together and share small talk in their small groups. The leader is warm, smiling, humorous. Time is allowed for shame to lift before guilt is addressed. Conversion is viewed as process not event. People first commit to the community, then later to the Lord of the community.

10. Healthy good-byes

Just as toxic shame is fostered in significant relationships, so healing for shame demands significant, committed, meaningful, long-term relationships. Because caregivers, particularly pastors, are seen to be representing God, they need to counter the shamed person's experience of abandonment with faithful presence that mirrors God's faithful presence. Thus pastors who move every couple of years will not be the most helpful in ministering grace for shame.

But what happens when the time does come for the pastor to move on? Even Jesus said, "It is better that I go"! The problem is that the withdrawal of love and the consequent sense of abandonment may amplify shame. In fact, the threat of desertion or abandonment is a method of control in unhealthy systems.

How can pastors leave the church in a way that does the least shame-harm? In healthy churches everyone knows that the Lord is the chief shepherd of the church. His shepherding never ends, his love never fails, he will never leave nor forsake.

True, Jesus' physical presence is no longer with us. But his comforting Spirit presence is always nearby. If the pastor has, all along, refused to take too much to himself or herself, the congregation will be used to walking with the Lord. Pastors need to be present, in significant and meaningful ways, but always present *in the Lord's name*. It is a *representational* presence intended to help people discover the ever-presence of God himself.

The shame effect of leaving is also reduced if the pastor is moving on to an honorable role (as judged by the community). If the pastor simply drops out of church life, the people will be troubled. If the pastor is seen to be continuing strong in the larger work of the Kingdom of God, this will help to settle troubled hearts. We cannot avoid partings, and leaving always involves grief; but leaving does not need to amplify shame. May we be more aware of the various ways leaving plays out in the emotional life of the church. If we minister well in our presence, we will minister well in our absence.

Grace for Shame in the Multicultural Congregation

Jesus said: "I tell you, many will come from east and west and recline at table with Abraham, Isaac and Jacob, in the kingdom of heaven" (Matthew 8:11). What a remarkable, shame-healed, celebratory, inclusive future! John the apostle records another vision of that future: "After this I looked, and behold, a great multitude that no one could number, from every nation, from all tribes and peoples and languages, standing before the throne and before the Lamb" (Revelation 7:9). All churches, ready or not, are on a trajectory that ends with this incredible unity-in-diversity, which will be our life together in eternity future. It is no surprise that increasing numbers of churches today are intentional about growing in cultural and ethnic diversity as they anticipate that great day.

If we do not yet hear the eschatological call of the future on our churches, we should at least allow the changing demographics of our cities to push us forward. Mass communication and reduced travel costs have shrunk the world and fueled mobility. For example, Statistics Canada reports that as of 2001 only fifty percent of people in Vancouver, Canada claimed English as their mother tongue. Vancouver is just one of numerous cities around the world that can be described as international. Faithful churches are adjusting to the dynamics of this new multicultural world. If we are serious about reaching modern cities our churches will have a membership that reflects the diversity of our surrounding communities.

Thus the question for pastors now is not only: How do we minister grace for shame? It is also: How do we do so in a plurality of cultures? How do we do so when Estonian, Ethiopian, Filipino, German, Scottish, and Taiwanese sisters and brothers sit together in the same pew? Once again, the challenge here is to put our own culture in perspective. Can we overcome our prejudice against other cultures? Are we ready to acknowledge that other cultures even exist? Cross-cultural training and adaptability will go a long way towards helping church leaders minister effectively in regard to shame. But what a blessing it is when the cultural diversity of the pastoral team reflects the cultural diversity of the congregation. It is a sign that the church is beginning to take the mission seriously.

Seeing beyond ourselves

The reality is that other groups experience life very differently. We cannot underestimate how deeply embedded these cultural differences are. Once we learn to see beyond ourselves, the evidence of other worlds is everywhere. Francis Hsu contrasts the design of U.S. and Chinese homes as a way of illustrating differences in culture. The traditional low picket fence symbolizes the open stance of the U.S. family to the outside world. Within the home, individuality is highlighted by assigned private space (rooms with doors). In contrast, Chinese homes are hidden behind high fences; yet within the home there is little privacy. The family is one unit.[60] So the Chinese child grows up seeing the world as a network of relationships, rather than a collection of individuals. Perhaps the cell phone is ubiquitous in Asian cultures because it facilitates and maintains relationships in a fragmenting world. It keeps people connected when connectedness is highly valued.

We think also of the concept of "saving face" which is widespread in group cultures. Where the wishes and integrity of the group are of high importance face is "saved" before the group. The goal is maintaining harmony, even at a cost to the individual that would be unacceptable to Westerners. This cannot be ignored in the local multicultural congregation. Think again of Robert's Rules of Order from the perspective of a group-oriented culture. To stand alone and make a motion is a very dangerous thing. If the group does not agree there is great loss of face. Pastors wonder why people from some cultures "don't participate"! Even the seating arrangements of Western meetings, where people sit as individuals in rows,

---

[60] Francis Hsu, *American and Chinese: Passage to Differences* (Honolulu, HA: University of Hawaii Press, 1991), 78f.

limits input from people of cultures that require the face-to-face interaction of circular arrangements, where all of the nonverbal as well as verbal signals can be read. Can we run meetings that are truly affirming and nonshaming for all participants?[61]

Consider child care. If one group of parents values independence in child raising and another group values dependence, it will be difficult to maintain consistent policies in the church nursery! An Asian mother would be ashamed to abandon her child to strangers. A Western mother is ashamed when the child is "clinging."

Then again, when definitions of punctuality vary widely, how does one affirm the arrival of each person? Or personal space? . . . A comfortable amount of personal space for me as a northern European feels like cold standoffishness for my Mediterranean brother! On the other hand, where we might assume that the person avoiding eye contact is unfriendly or even unreliable, people in other cultures may consider sustained eye contact shameful behavior. Also, the public use of first names may be either a sign of friendliness or rudeness, depending on one's culture of origin.

We remember too that male-female roles are clearly differentiated in many cultures. Thus male-female distinctions (e.g., appropriate clothing and hair length) are very important for honor maintenance in some cultures.

And how is it possible to live with the widely divergent perceptions of power, and specifically pastoral power and authority, that come with divergent cultures? The list can go on. Questions of honor and shame intersect all of these issues.

---

[61] See Eric H. F. Law, *The Wolf Shall Dwell with the Lamb: A Spirituality for Leadership in a Multicultural Community* (St. Louis, MO: Chalice Press, 1993).

Navigating cultural cross-currents

Thus nurturing a congregation that is nonshaming is even more complex when a number of cultures are worshiping together. But this is the new reality. Willingly or unwillingly, pastors must stretch in these areas.

Pastoral anger and frustration may be an indication of cultural dissonance. We are like the Japanese woman (described by Ruth Benedict) going to the United States to study, feeling as though she had dropped from another planet. For two or three years she simply felt bewildered and angry, totally unprepared for social interaction in this new culture.[62] Pastors will have to overcome their sense of cultural lostness and locate new points of reference that allow them to navigate in new, intercultural waters.

This journey into greater cultural awareness and sensitivity may well be frustrating and painful. There must first be an unlearning, an awareness that "it's not working." Then gradually comes reflection, relearning, and reorganization.[63] At last comes acceptance, then affirmation. Given the Western shift towards shame orientation, plus the immigration of people rooted in group-oriented cultures, pastors have no choice but to learn new cultural languages if they are to remain effective.

Shame, for shame-oriented groups, is not necessarily a negative factor. It simply means that shame is nearer the surface and plays a larger policing role in personal behavior. Shame results when an individual moves beyond the accepted behavior of the group. The shamed person fears separation or abandonment.

---

[62] Benedict, *The Chrysanthemum and the Sword*, 226.
[63] Nieman, *Preaching to Every Pew*, 143.

One of the challenges, however, for pastors of multi-cultural congregations is to deal with differences between the honor-shame values of the group and the honor-shame values of the Kingdom of God. For example, Asian people highly value reciprocity in relationships. Favor needs to be repaid. If favor cannot be repaid, the result is shame. The inability to pay back grace is a major source of shame in Asian cultures.[64] Pitt-Rivers illustrates this from his experience of Mediterranean culture: "A nobleman . . . ran his friend through with his sword at the end of a drinking bout, because the latter insisted on footing the bill!"[65] Thus the very notion of grace can be shaming for group-oriented cultures.

Pastors need to be alert to this prejudice against grace itself. How can we minister grace, in ways that will be received, without adulterating the message? For group-oriented people, grace must not be in-your-face, but gentle, unobtrusive, respectful, indirect, and creative. We can gently remind people to consider how God feels when we are slow to receive his grace. When a gift is given in group-oriented cultures, there is a risk of shame if the gift is not warmly received. We risk shaming the Lord of the universe if we refuse his grace. Here again, incarnational grace is powerful. Jesus allowed Zacchaeus the dignity of "paying the bill" by eating the meal that Zacchaeus provided. Yet at a deeper level, Jesus was paying the bill by being willing to be seen dining with such a "sinner." In multicultural contexts it is even more important that pastors enjoy being with people.

---

[64] You, "Shame and Guilt Mechanisms in East Asian Culture," 63.
[65] Pitt-Rivers, "Honour and Social Status," 59.

Gracious confrontation

The Gospel confronts all cultures. This may be less dramatic in the West because of the long Christian influence, but it is still essential. When welcoming new immigrants, we should allow the weight of the cultural challenge of the Gospel to be fully felt. But this is a gracious confrontation. It takes time. Our experience in the multicultural church is that many people, especially Asian immigrants, are involved in the life of the church for two years or more before they are ready to be baptized. In part this reflects the extensive rewriting of world-view that must take place. But it also suggests that when conversion is more shame oriented than guilt oriented it will be more of a process than an event. People are drawn in by the love of the community. They find acceptance. They find a home. They sense they are loved and appreciated. All of which paves the way for the appropriation of forgiveness.

Even in majority Western culture churches, it is a kind of fiction to assume that each person lives as a completely independent human being. This is not really what is going on. Churches are like little villages with long memories and multiple layers and relationships. Touch one part and the whole community has to readjust to find the new equilibrium, like the mobile hanging over the baby's crib. We need a theology of the *community* that counterbalances our theology of the *person*. This will allow pastors to loosen up a little and not feel we must be always resolving the guilt of individuals.

As we welcome and embrace whole groups, we can allow nonbelievers to be swept in with the tide. We can relax and give them time to absorb the values and beliefs of this new kinship, time to be re-embedded into this new community. Their dependency formation may be so thorough that they may never really respond as individualist-culture people expect. However we try to shut out the social context ("every head bowed, every eye closed") these men and women are social people, shaped by how they are seen by those around them. Perhaps the Lord has plans for them *as a family*, as he did for the household of the Philippian jailer (Acts 16:31-34). And we remember again God's promise to Abraham: "In you all the *families* of the earth will be blessed" (Genesis 12:3).

Pastors must not underestimate the drive-to-belong in group-oriented cultures. This has been shaped from birth. Standing alone is not an option. When fractures occur in relationships, new alliances immediately form. Disputes between individuals send ripples through the whole community. But in the same way, when two people are reconciled, healing comes to the whole group. So ministry within group cultures is never about just one or two people; indirectly, the whole community is just out of sight in the background. Just as the shame of one affects the whole group, so the honor of one affects the whole group. Ministry in group-oriented cultures is always a group process, even when only one member of the group is present.

Group cultures expect from the pastor not just "presence" but "*heroic* presence." The pastor is the adopted chief who upholds the honor of the community. And the community wants "strong" leadership. If the pastor is seen as too soft on the aberrant behavior of one member (especially concerning sexual sins), the pastor will be felt to be dishonoring the whole group. If one member sins in a way that is considered particularly shameful, the group may press for public confession, even if the sin is a private matter. Because the group has a deep desire to restore its honor, the pastor may have to restrain the group on behalf of the sinning individual. The group expects more law than grace from its chief. It is true that the Gospel is no stranger to honor-shame cultures; indeed it was birthed in an honor-shame context. Nevertheless, pastors need to be able to reframe these honor concerns in the light of the honor-shame rules of the Kingdom of God. Pastors are called to help the group move beyond the default honor-shame settings of this world, particularly in regard to honorable leadership. The model for heroic presence is our nail-scarred Savior.

Cross-cultural sanctification

Original sin skews both group-oriented and individualistic cultures. The downside of high-context (group) cultures is the tendency to develop criteria for behavior that are internally consistent, but divergent from Kingdom values. For example, lying is acceptable if it protects relationships. From outside, individuals in high-context groups may appear to "have no principles" (at least they are not *our* principles).

In contrast, the downside of low-context (individualistic) cultures is the tendency to focus on principle to the exclusion of relationship. For example, precious relationships are broken because of rigid adherence to abstract principles. From outside, individuals in such low-context groups appear shameless—they don't care what others think!

The wise pastor in a multicultural congregation will be alert to both movements. A healthy congregation benefits from this tension between high- and low-context cultures, welcome-ing both and excluding neither. Simply by dwelling together, each exposes the other's blind spots. For example, we

Westerners know that our beloved principles need interpretation. But we discover that the group provides a safer interpretation than the individual. Together we can travel further down the road of sanctification.

The reality of shame in Christian congregations requires preaching and teaching that encompasses a broader range of redemption themes. The presence of high-context cultures simply underlines this. For people culturally shaped to be more sensitive to shame than to guilt, the Gospel needs to be presented differently or it will not be *heard* as Good News. So along with atonement and justification, pastors need to preach reconciliation, adoption, and inclusion. As Kraus points out, emphasizing "relationships and ideals will be more important and persuasive than law and punitive threats."[66] Yes, hell is a stark reality that needs to be taught. But for high-context people the experience of letting go of their *old* community will feel like hell already unless they understand, see, and feel that they are entering a *new* community.

There are other aspects of the Gospel that are especially helpful to high-context groups. Pastors can emphasize the victory of Jesus. Let's recover the old Latin slogan, *Christus Victor*. Jesus is an honorable leader! Yes, we need to encourage people to pause and meditate on Good Friday; but then we must lead them on to Resurrection Sunday and the reality of our victorious Lord. Notice how important the resurrection is in the Acts speeches.

Furthermore, high-context groups will resonate with teaching on the Trinity, as long as the Trinity is portrayed relationally not mechanically. For example we could make use

---

[66] Norman C. Kraus, *Jesus Christ Our Lord: Christology from a Disciple's Perspective* (Scottdale, PA: Herald Press, 1987), 224.

of J. Y. Lee's suggestion that because the "yin-yang" principle emphasizes relationship more than substance, it is more helpful for understanding the Trinity than some Western approaches.[67]

All cultures struggle with the balance between interdependence and independence. What can pastors offer to individuals enmeshed in strong group-oriented cultures? Such people may need special permission to differentiate, especially from parents and family. The reaction from the home group may be harsh. It will feel like betrayal. Individuals who differentiate will be vulnerable to shame. Nevertheless, pastors can teach that God's acceptance is of greater worth than the acceptance of any group. God's acceptance is focused in Jesus who takes human shame on himself. Thus human shame is objectively removed, and Christians are adopted into a new community that supersedes the old community, with new allegiances that supersede the old allegiances. Pastors, however, must accept that this conversion is a process that may not be completed in one or two generations!

Learning to embrace

A common way to relieve the stress of shame is to shame others. Thus shame may be a subtle but powerful force in inter-racial and intercultural discord. Racial prejudice provides a ready and seemingly respectable outlet for the shame-bound person. In multicultural contexts we quickly discover that prejudice moves in multiple directions! It takes time to exorcise the demons. The Gospel contrast is the truly affirming community. But it is not enough to *feel* love for someone; that love needs to be *expressed* in ways that communicate. Cultural

---

[67] Lee, J. Y., *The Trinity in Asian Perspective*, 60f.

expectations complicate this greatly. Pastors need to learn the language of love for people of other cultures. Love and acceptance must be *heard*.[68]

Charles Foster speaks of the "practices of embrace," by which he means "the movement of different peoples in community that seek to be close to others without losing the integrity of their own identities."[69] The "practices of embrace" infuse health and life into shame-bound communities. One way to include is through embracing the music of another's culture. Music touches the depths of human otherness. Musical hospitality provides deep welcome and affirmation.[70] Another way is through sharing and appreciating each other's food. Our different foods also express deeply our different cultures. And where one culture is dominant, is that culture willing to allow the other to play the role of host? This is a way of learning respect. The guest respects the "etiquette, rituals, secrets, and privacy" of the host. "The guest does not claim ownership of the other's story. . . . The guest does not overstay his or her welcome; the privilege of being in another person's world is not taken lightly."[71] The long-term goal is "mutual invitation."[72]

In the multicultural church, we may ask why some groups cluster together during group events. In part it may be so they

---

[68] Tom Lin, *Losing Face and Finding Grace* (Downers Grove, IL: InterVarsity Press, 1996), 29f.

[69] Charles Foster, *Embracing Diversity: Leadership in Multicultural Congregations* (Bethesda, MD: Alban Institute, 1997), 2.

[70] Martin Tel, "Music: The Universal Language," in *Making Room at the Table: An Invitation to Multicultural Worship,* Brian Blount and Leonora Tubbs Tisdale, eds. (Louisville, KY: Westminster John Knox Press, 2000), 166f.

[71] Augsburger, *Conflict Mediation Across Cultures,* 367.

[72] Law, *The Wolf Shall Dwell with the Lamb,* 79.

can relax and speak in their heart language. But beyond language is the deep group orientation instilled from birth. These are "my people." I am who I am only in the context of these people. I can only stand back temporarily. For community-oriented people, being together is critical for forming understanding, for clarifying issues, and for establishing identity.

A truly welcoming and affirming congregation gives people space to be with their own kind—a kind of nesting place within the larger community. It respects the significance not only of shared language, but of a different way of being that is inseparable from the group. At the same time the multicultural church welcomes each group and each individual to the *one* table of Christ, where together we discover ever greater riches to the mystery of unity-in-diversity, which is the glory of life together in Christ.

A place to call home

Healthy, shame-healing multicultural congregations feel good and look good, to use the language of family therapists. All members (not only the majority-group members) are proud of their church. They feel valued, secure, and safe, and they experience loving, close relationships. There is a sense of unity, and common purpose and values. There is good, open communication and interaction. Members feel they have some control over what happens. They adapt to changes and deal well with crisis. There is surplus capacity. Visitors may not understand what they are encountering, but it feels alive and good. People from minorities, new immigrants, and mixed-culture couples and families, as well as singles, all have a sense of homecoming.

In fact, a reasonably healthy, shame-healing congregation is very attractive to people from group-oriented cultures. We may struggle to know how to move independent Westerners beyond a superficial encounter with the church, but group-culture people jump in with both feet! They understand the dynamics of small face-to-face communities very well. This is home. They like the new tribe. Their honor rating has gone up because they have joined this respectable community.

But caution is necessary at this point. Though they may be the most committed of church members, they may still know little of the Gospel! It will take time and conscientious Gospel ministry to help these good folk to feel the call of Christ as he challenges their culturally shaped hearts. So we must not forget to preach to the choir. The church community cannot be allowed to become one more nice tribe. We are called to be a radically new court of reputation, and to testify to an alternate reality grounded in the resurrected Jesus Christ.

Leading beyond our culture

So we who lead need to be 150 percent culture people. We must grow beyond our own culture. True, we will never do other cultures without an "accent." And we will often be surprised to discover new layers in our own cultural captivity. We must be realistic about the depths of our own cultural shaping. But we can at least begin to be alert to how we are seen and heard, and how the Gospel is seen and heard, and so learn better what it means to share in God's ministry of grace in this world.

We never forget who is the first Pastor of the church. Who but God could provide cohesion for people shaped differently to the very core of their being? If the existence (and especially the persistence) of the church is one of the greatest evidences of the existence of God, then the existence of the multicultural church is even stronger evidence!

Effective pastoral ministry requires cultural astuteness. This is hard work, but the benefits are far-reaching. A ministry that deliberately engages the needs of shame sensitive people opens great doors of hope for large and growing constituencies. Nevertheless, it is important to keep cultural concerns in perspective. In the end we are more like than different. While we do well to explore the complex dynamics of shame in various cultural contexts, in order to better understand and serve different people and communities, it is important to remember that the key shame problem, from a biblical perspective, is the shame of Adam and Eve, the shame of sinners in the presence of a Holy God. What we have to offer is the Gospel of reconciliation with God through Christ. This is grace for shame.

Postscript

Thank you for spending time with this book. It takes courage to stare shame in the face. No wonder this subject has been left on the shelf for so long. Guilt was much easier to define and resolve. Shame is messier, harder to put into words, more difficult to resolve, less manageable, and generally more uncomfortable for all concerned. But there has been a breakthrough. At last shame is off the shelf and on the table.

What is the urgency? It is simply that shame is so devastating. Shame consumes life. Shame eclipses the soul. Shame sucks the life out of the church. Shamed people, without help, are survivors at best. The sparkle, the vibrancy, the élan, the creative, adventurous, risk-taking spirit, are absent. The self has gone underground. What remains is an artificial self, a safe mask. Surely this is not the crown of creation over which the Lord of the universe pronounced, "It is very good!" If Satan wanted to ruin God's party, what better way than to sow shame among the beloved?

But God is not God for nothing! He left his glory and depleted himself of honor, taking human shame on himself. For one terrible moment even the sun hid its face as God himself experienced the very depths of shame. But neither death nor shame could hold him. The captive was released; the darkness was broken; shame itself was shamed. Satan's worst displayed God's best. Yes, the Christian Grand Narrative *is* Good News! And it is good news for shame, as well as guilt. Let's get out and minister grace for shame as competent coworkers with God in this world.

BIBLIOGRAPHY

Albers, Robert H. "Shame: A Dynamic In the Etiology of Violence." *Dialog,* 36 (4) (1997): 254-265.

_____. *Shame: A Faith Perspective.* New York: Haworth Press, 1995.

_____. "Shame and the Conspiracy of Silence." *Journal of Ministry in Addiction & Recovery,* 7 (1) (2000): 51-68.

_____. "The Shame Factor: Theological and Pastoral Reflections Relating to Forgiveness." *Word and World,* 16 (3) (1996): 347-353.

Alter, Margaret G. "Human Shame and the Hospitality of God." *Dialog,* 36 (4) (1997): 266-269.

Anderson, Ray S. "Shame: Letting Go of Emotional Self-Abuse." In *Self Care: A Theology of Personal Empowerment and Spiritual Healing.* Wheaton, IL: Bridgepoint Books, 1995.

_____. *The Gospel According to Judas.* Colorado Springs, CO: Helmers and Howard, 1991.

Aron, Elaine N. *The Highly Sensitive Person: How to Thrive When the World Overwhelms You.* New York: Broadway Books, 1996.

Athanasius. *The Incarnation of the Word.* Crestwood, NY: St. Vladimir's Seminary Press, 1975.

Augsburger, David W. *Conflict Mediation Across Cultures: Pathways and Patterns.* Louisville, KY: Westminster John Knox Press, 1992.

_____. *Pastoral Counseling Across Cultures.* Philadelphia, PA: Westminster Press, 1986.

Ausubel, David P. "Relationships Between Shame and Guilt in the Socializing Process." *Psychological Review,* 62 (1955): 378-390.

Avery, Brice. *The Pastoral Encounter: Hidden Depths in Human Contact.* London: Marshall Pickering, 1996.

Bailey, Kenneth E. *Finding the Lost: Cultural Keys to Luke 15.* St. Louis, MO: Concordia Publishing House, 1992.

Baker, Susan S. "Lessons Learned in Multiethnic Ministry." *Urban Mission,* 13 (1996): 57-58.

Batten, Alicia. "Dishonor, Gender and the Parable of the Prodigal Son." *Toronto Journal of Theology,* 13 (2) (1997): 187-200.

Baumli, Francis. "On Men, Guilt, and Shame." In *Men Healing Shame: An Anthology.* Roy U. Schenk and John Everingham, eds. New York: Springer Pub. Co., 1995.

Bechtel, Lyn M. "The Perception of Shame Within the Divine-Human Relationship in Biblical Israel." In *Uncovering Ancient Stones: Essays in Memory of H. Neil Richardson.* L. Hopfe, ed. Wonona Lake, IN: Eisenbrauns, 1994.

Benedict. *The Rule of St. Benedict.* Mineola, NY: Dover Publications, 2007.

Benedict, Ruth. *The Chrysanthemum and the Sword.* New York: Meridian Books, 1946.

Berecz, John M., and Herbert W. Helm. "Shame: The Underside of Christianity." *Journal of Psychology and Christianity,* 17 (1998): 5-14.

Bergant, Dianne. "'My Beloved is Mine and I am His" (Songs 2:16): The Song of Songs and Honor and Shame." *Semeia,* 68 (1996): 23-40.

Bibby, Reginald W. *Mosaic Madness: The Poverty and Potential of Life in Canada.* Toronto: Stoddart, 1990.

Black, Kathy. *Culturally-Conscious Worship.* St. Louis, MO: Chalice Press, 2000.

Blount, Brian K., and Leonora Tubbs Tisdale, eds. *Making Room at the Table: An Invitation to Multicultural Worship.* Louisville, KY: Westminster John Knox Press, 2000.

Bondi, Richard A. "Become Such as I Am: St. Paul in the Acts of the Apostles." *Biblical Theology Bulletin,* 27 (1997): 164-176.

Bondi, Roberta C. "Out of the Green-Tiled Bathroom: Crucifixion." *Weavings,* 9(1994): 6-27.

Bonhoeffer, D. *Ethics.* New York: The Macmillan Company, 1965.

Bourdieu, Pierre. "The Sentiment of Honour in Kaybele Society." In *Honor and Shame: The Values of Mediterranean Society.* J. G. Peristiany, ed. Chicago, IL: University of Chicago Press, 1966.

Boyle, Timothy D. "Communicating the Gospel in Terms of Shame." *Japanese Christian Quarterly,* 50 (1984): 41-46.

Brach, Tara. *Radical Acceptance: Awakening The Love That Heals Fear and Shame Within Us.* London: Random House, 2003

Bradshaw, John. *Healing the Shame That Binds You.* Deerfield Beach, FL: Health Communications, 1988.

Browne, R., ed. *Forbidden Fruits: Taboos and Tabooism in Culture.* Bowling Green, OH: Bowling Green University Popular Press, 1984.

Browning, Don S., Bonnie J. Miller-McLemore, Pamela D. Couture, and K. Brynolf Lyon. *From Culture Wars to Common Ground: Religion and the American Family Debate.* Louisville KY: Westminster John Knox Press, 2000.

Bultmann, Rudolf. "*Aischuno.*" In *Theological Dictionary of the New Testament.* G. Kittle and G. Friedrich, eds. B. W. Bromley, translator. Grand Rapids, MI: Eerdmans, 1964.

Burton, Laurel Arthur. "Original Sin or Original Shame?" *Quarterly Review,* 8 (1998): 31-41.

_____. "Respect: Response to Shame in Health Care." *Journal of Religion and Health,* 30 (1991): 139-148.

Cairns, Douglas L. Aidos*: The Psychology and Ethics of Honor and Shame in Ancient Greek Literature.* Oxford: Clarendon Press, 1993.

Capps, Donald. *The Depleted Self: Sin in a Narcissistic Age.* Minneapolis, MI: Fortress Press, 1992.

Chance, John K. "The Anthropology of Honor and Shame: Culture, Values, and Practice." *Semeia,* 68 (1996): 139-151.

Chapman, Thomas W., ed. *A Practical Handbook for Ministry, from the Writings of Wayne Oates.* Louisville, KY: Westminster John Knox Press, 1992.

Clapp, Rodney. "Shame Crucified." *Christianity Today,* March 11 (1991): 26-28.

Cohen, D., J. Vandello, and A. Rantilla. "The Sacred and the Social: Cultures of Honor and Violence." In *Shame: Interpersonal Behavior, Psychopathology, and Culture.* Paul Gilbert and Bernice Andrews, eds. New York: Oxford University Press, 1998.

Comm, Mary. *Secret Sin: When God's People Choose Abortion.* Garden City, NY: Morgan James Publishing, 2007.

Corrigan, Gregory. "Paul's Shame for the Gospel." *Biblical Theology Bulletin,* 16 (1986): 23-27.

Creighton, Millie R. "Revisiting Shame and Guilt Cultures: A Forty-Year Pilgrimage." *Ethos,* 18 (1990): 279-307.

Crook, Zeba Antonin. "Paul's Riposte and Praise of the Thessalonians." *Biblical Theology Bulletin,* 27 (1997): 153-163.

Daube, David. "Shame Culture in Luke." In *Paul and Paulinism: Essays in Honor of C. K. Barrett.* M. Hooker and S. Wilson eds. London: SPCK, 1982.

_____. *The New Testament and Rabbinic Judaism.* Peabody, MA: Hendrickson Publishers, 1956.

Delli-Carpini, John. "Preaching and Feelings of Shame: "The Minister's Black Veil.'" *Preaching,* 16 (3) (2000): 47-48, 50.

Desilva, David A. "Despising Shame: A Cultural-Anthropological Investigation of the Epistle to the Hebrews." *Journal of Biblical Literature,* 113 (3) (1994): 439-461.

_____. *Honor, Patronage, Kinship and Purity: Unlocking New Testament Culture.* Downers Grove, IL: InterVarsity Press, 2000.

_____. "The Wisdom of Ben Sira: Honor, Shame, and the Maintenance of the Values of a Minority Culture." *The Catholic Biblical Quarterly,* 58 (3) (1996): 433-455.

Dewey, A. J. "A Matter of Honor: A Socio-Historical Analysis of 2 Corinthians 10." *Harvard Theological Review,* 78 (1985): 209-217.

Elliott, John H. "Disgraced Yet Graced. The Gospel According to 1 Peter in the Key of Honor and Shame." *Biblical Theology Bulletin,* 25 (4) (1995): 166-178.

Euripides, *The Phoenician Maiden*. Translated by Arthur Sanders Way. Cambridge, MA: Harvard University Press, 1962.

Everingham, John. "Some Basics About Shame." In *Men Healing Shame: An Anthology*. Roy U. Schenk and John Everingham, eds. New York: Springer Pub. Co., 1995.

Fajans, Jane. "Shame, Social Action and the Person Among the Baining." *Ethos,* 11 (1983): 166-184.

Ferguson, Sinclair B., D. G. Wright, and J. I. Packer, eds. *New Testament Dictionary of Theology*. Downers Grove, IL: InterVarsity Press, 1988.

Ford, Josephine M. *Redeemer: Friend and Mother*. Minneapolis, MN: Fortress Press, 1997.

Forrester, John A. "*Parresia* in the New Testament: Openness and Confidence in Christian Communication." ThM Thesis, Regent College, 1995.

Fossum, Merle A., and Marilyn J. Mason. *Facing Shame: Families in Recovery*. New York: W. W. Norton and Co., 1986.

Foster, Charles R. *Embracing Diversity: Leadership in Multicultural Congregations*. Bethesda, MD: Alban Institute, 1997.

Foster, Charles R., and Theodore Brelsford. *We Are the Church Together: Cultural Diversity in Congregational Life*. Valley Forge, PA: Trinity Press International, 1996.

Fowler, James W. *Faithful Change: The Personal and Public Challenges of Postmodern Life*. Nashville, TN: Abingdon Press, 1996.

_____. "Shame: Towards a Practical Theological Understanding." *Christian Century,* 110 (1993): 816-819.

Frame, Tom. "Original Shame and the Christian Gospel: A Theological Response to Shameful Autobiographies." *St. Mark's Review,* 179 (1999): 32-34.

Friedman, Edwin H. *Generation to Generation: Family Process in Church and Synagogue*. New York: The Guilford Press, 1985.

Garriott, Craig W. "Leadership Development in the Multiethnic Church." *Urban Mission,* 13 (1996): 24-37.

Gilbert, Paul, and Bernice Andrews, eds. *Shame: Interpersonal Behaviour, Psychopathology, and Culture.* New York: Oxford University Press, 1998.

Glaz, Maxine, and Jeanne Stevenson Moessner, eds. *Women in Travail and Transition.* Minneapolis, MN: Fortress Press, 1991.

Goodhue, Tom. "Shame." *Quarterly Review,* 4 (2) (1984): 57-65.

Goodliff, Paul. *With Unveiled Face: A Pastoral & Theological Exploration of Shame.* London: Darton, Longman & Todd Ltd., 2005.

Green, Daniel, and Mel Lawrenz. *Encountering Shame and Guilt.* Grand Rapids, MI: Baker Books, 1994.

Gregory the Great, *Pastoral Practice.* Translated by John Leinenweber. Harrisburg, PA: Trinity Press International, 1998.

Hanson, K. C. "How Honorable! How Shameful! A Cultural Analysis of Matthew's Makarisms and Reproaches." *Semeia,* 68 (1996): 81-111.

Harper, James M., and Margaret H. Hoopes. *Uncovering Shame: Integrating Individuals and Their Family Systems.* New York: Norton, 1990.

Hellerman, Joseph H. "Challenging the Authority of Jesus: Mark 11:27-33 and Mediterranean Notions of Honor and Shame." *Journal of the Evangelical Theological Society,* 43 (2) (2000): 213-228.

_____. "The Humiliation of Christ in the Social World of Roman Philippi, Parts I & II." *Bibliotheca Sacra,* 160 (2003): 321-336, 421-433.

Hengel, Martin. *Crucifixion in the Ancient World and the Folly of the Message of the Cross.* Philadelphia: Fortress, 1977.

Hess, Margaret B. "A Portrait of Shame." *Christian Century,* 114 (1997): 509.

Hesselgrave, David J. "Missionary Elenctics and Guilt and Shame." *Missiology,* 11 (4) (1983): 461- 483.

Hopfe, L., ed. *Uncovering Ancient Stones: Essays in Memory of H. Neil Richardson.* Wonona Lake, IN: Eisenbrauns, 1994.

Horst, Elizabeth A. *Questions and Answers About Clergy Sexual Misconduct.* Collegeville, MN: Liturgical Press, 2000.

_____. *Recovering the Lost Self: Shame Healing for Victims of Clergy Sexual Abuse.* Collegeville, MN: Liturgical Press, 1998.

Hsu, Francis L. K. *Americans and Chinese: Passage to Differences.* Honolulu: University of Hawaii Press, 1981.

Hugen, Melvin D., and Cornelius Plantinga Jr. "Naked and Exposed: The Resurrection of the Shamed." *Books and Culture,* 2 (1996): 3, 27-29.

Hultberg, P. "Shame—A Hidden Emotion." *Journal of Analytical Psychology,* 33 (1988): 109-126.

Hunsinger, Deborah van Deusen. *Theology and Pastoral Counseling: A New Interdisciplinary Approach.* Grand Rapids, MI: Eerdmans, 1995.

Hunter, George. *The Celtic Way of Evangelism: How Christianity Can Reach the West . . . Again.* Nashville, TN: Abingdon, 2001.

Hutch, Richard A. "Confessing Dying Within." *Journal of Pastoral Care,* 48 (4) (1994): 341-352.

Jewett, Robert. "Babette's Feast and the Shaming of the Poor in Corinth." *Dialog,* 36 (4) (1997): 270-276.

_____. "Honor and Shame in the Argument of Romans." In *Putting Body & Soul Together: Essays in Honor of Robin Scroggs.* Virginia Wiles, Alexandra Brown and Graydon F. Snyder, eds. Valley Forge, PA: Trinity Press International, 1997.

_____. *St. Paul Returns to the Movies: Triumph Over Shame.* Grand Rapids, MI: Eerdmans, 1999.

Junker, Beth C. "Where the Sidewalk Ends." *Mars Hill Review,* 9 (1997): 116-118.

Karen, Robert. "Shame." *Atlantic Monthly,* Feb. 1992: 40-70.

Kaufman, Gershen. "The Meaning of Shame." *Journal of Counseling Psychology* 21 (6) (1974): 568-574.

_____. *The Psychology of Shame: Theory and Treatment of Shame-Based Syndromes.* New York: Springer Pub. Co., 1989.

_____. *Shame: The Power of Caring.* Cambridge, MA: Shenkman, 1980.

Kaufman, G., and Lev Raphael. "Shame as Taboo in American Culture." In *Forbidden Fruits: Taboos and Tabooism in Culture.* R. Browne, ed. Bowling Green, OH: Bowling Green University Popular Press, 1984.

Kee, Howard Clark. "The Linguistic Background of "Shame" in the New Testament." In *On Language, Culture, and Religion.* M. Black and W. A. Smalley, eds. The Hague: Mouton, 1974.

Khayyat, Sana. *Honour and Shame: Women in Modern Iraq.* London: Saqi Books, 1990.

Kittle, G., and G. Friedrich, eds. *Theological Dictionary of the New Testament.* Translated by B. W. Bromley. Grand Rapids, MI: Eerdmans, 1964-76, 10 volumes.

Knight, Henry F. "From Shame to Responsibility and Christian Identity: The Dynamics of Shame and Confession Regarding the Shoah." *Journal of Ecumenical Studies,* 35 (1998): 41-62.

Kraus, C. Norman. *Jesus Christ Our Lord: Christology from a Disciple's Perspective.* Scottdale, PA: Herald Press, 1987.

_____. "The Cross of Christ—Dealing with Shame and Guilt." *Japan Christian Quarterly,* 53 (1987): 221-227.

Kressel, Gideon M. "An Anthropologist's Response to the Use of Social Science Models in Biblical Studies." *Semeia,* 68 (1996): 153-161.

Lake, Frank. *Clinical Theology: A Theological and Psychiatric Basis to Clinical Pastoral Care.* London: Darton, Longman and Todd, 1966.

Laniak, Timothy S. *Shame and Honor in the Book of Esther.* Atlanta, GA: Scholars Press, 1998.

Lasch, Christopher. *The Culture of Narcissism: American Life in an Age of Diminishing Expectations.* New York: Routledge, 1979.

Law, Eric H. F. *The Wolf Shall Dwell with the Lamb: A Spirituality for Leadership in a Multicultural Community.* St. Louis, MO: Chalice Press, 1993.

Lebra, Takie Sugiyama. "Shame and Guilt: A Psychological View of the Japanese Self." *Ethos,* 11 (1983): 192-209.

_____. "The Social Mechanism of Guilt and Shame: The Japanese Case." *Anthropological Quarterly,* 44 (1971): 244-255.

Lee, Jung Young. *The Trinity in Asian Perspective.* Nashville, TN: Abingdon Press, 1996.

Lewis, C. S. *A Grief Observed.* London: Faber and Faber, 1961.

Lewis, Helen Block. *Shame and Guilt in Neurosis.* New York: International Universities Press, 1971.

Lewis, Michael. *Shame: The Exposed Self.* New York: Free Press; 1992.

Lin, Tom. *Losing Face and Finding Grace.* Downers Grove, IL: InterVarsity Press, 1996.

Lindsay-Harty, J. "Contrasting Experience of Shame and Guilt." *American Behavioral Scientist,* 27 (6) (1984): 689-704.

Lingenfelter, Judith E., and Sherwood G. Lingenfelter. *Teaching Cross-Culturally: An Incarnational Model for Learning and Teaching.* Grand Rapids, MI: Baker, 2003.

Lingenfelter, Sherwood G., and Marvin K. Mayers. *Ministering Cross-Culturally: An Incarnational Model for Personal Relationships.* Grand Rapids, MI: Baker, 1986.

Louw, J. P., and E. A. Nida, eds. *Greek-English Lexicon of the New Testament Based on Semantic Domains.* New York: United Bible Societies, 1988.

Lynd, Helen Merrell. *On Shame and the Search for Identity.* New York: Harcourt Brace, 1958.

Maggay, Melba P. "Towards Sensitive Engagement with Filipino Indigenous Conscience." *International Review of Mission,* 87 (344) (1988): 361-373.

Malina, Bruce J. *The New Testament World: Insights from Cultural Anthropology.* Atlanta, GA: John Knox, 1993.

Malina, Bruce J., and Jerome H. Neyrey. "Honor and Shame in Luke-Acts: Pivotal Values of the Mediterranean World." In *The Social World of Luke-Acts: Models for Interpretation.* Jerome H. Neyrey, ed. Peabody, MA: Hendrickson Publishers, 1991.

Mann, Alan. *Atonement for a "Sinless" Society: Engaging with an Emerging Culture.* Milton Keynes, U.K.: Paternoster Press, 2005

Marsella, A. J., M. D. Murray, and C. Golden. "Ethnic Variations in the Phenomenology of Emotions: Shame." *Journal of Cross-Cultural Psychology,* 5 (3) (1974): 312-328.

Marshall, Peter. "A Metaphor of Social Shame: *Thriambeuein* in 2 Corinthians 2:14." *Novum Testamentum,* 25 (4) (1983): 302-317.

Martin, Sara Hines. "Shame-Based Families." *Review and Expositor,* 91 (1994): 19-30.

Matthews, Victor H., and Don C. Benjamin. "Social Sciences and Biblical Studies." *Semeia,* 68 (1996): 7-21.

May, David M. "Mark 3:20-35 from the Perspective of Shame/Honor." *Biblical Theology Bulletin,* 17 (1987): 83-87.

McClintock, Karen A. *Sexual Shame: An Urgent Call to Healing.* Minneapolis, MN: Fortress Press, 2001.

McGrath, Joanna, and Alister McGrath. *The Dilemma of Self-Esteem.* Cambridge: Crossway Books, 1992.

McNish, Jill L. *Transforming Shame: A Pastoral Response.* Binghamton, NY: The Haworth Press, 2004.

McVann, Mark. "Reading Mark Ritually: Honor-Shame and the Ritual of Baptism." *Semeia,* 67 (1994): 179-198.

Miller, Susan. *Shame in Context.* Hillsdale, NJ: Analytic Press, 1996.

Morrow, William S. "Toxic Religion and the Daughters of Job." *Studies in Religion,* 27 (3) (1998): 263-276.

Moxnes, Halvor. "BTB Readers Guide: Honor and Shame." *Biblical Theology Bulletin,* 23 (1993): 167-176.

_____. "Honor and Righteousness in Romans." *Journal for the Study of the New Testament,* 32 (1988): 61-77.

_____. "Honor, Shame and the Outside World in Paul's Letter to the Romans." In *The Social World of Formative Christianity and Judaism.* Jacob Neusner, and Peder Borgen, eds. Philadelphia: Fortress, 1988.

Muller, Rolland. *Honor and Shame: Unlocking the Door.* Bloomington, IN: XLibris Corporation, 2000

Musk, Bill A. "Honour and Shame." *Evangelical Review of Theology,* 20 (1996): 156-167.

Nathanson, Donald L. *Shame and Pride: Affect, Sex, and the Birth of the Self.* New York: Norton, 1992.

Newbigin, Leslie. "The Trinity as Public Truth." In *The Trinity in a Pluralistic Age.* Kevin J. Vanhoozer, ed. Grand Rapids, MI: Eerdmans, 1997.

Neyrey, J. H. "Despising the Shame of the Cross: Honor and Shame in the Johannine Passion Narrative." *Semeia,* 68 (1996): 113-137.

_____. *Honor and Shame in the Gospel of Matthew.* Louisville, KY: Westminster John Knox Press, 1998.

_____. "The Trials [Forensic] and Tribulations [Honor Challenges] of Jesus: John 7 in Social Science Perspective." *Biblical Theology Bulletin,* 26 (1996): 107-124.

Nieman, James R., and Thomas G. Rogers. *Preaching to Every Pew: Cross Cultural Strategies.* Minneapolis, MN: Fortress, 2001.

Noble, Lowell Lappin. *Naked and Not Ashamed: An Anthropological, Biblical and Psychological Study of Shame.* Jackson, MI: The author, 1975.

Nouwen, Henry J. M. *Life of the Beloved: Spiritual Living in a Secular World.* New York: Crossroad Publishing Co., 1992.

Oates, Wayne. "Idolatry and Sick Religion." In *A Practical Handbook for Ministry.* Thomas Chapman, ed. Louisville, KY: Westminster John Knox Press, 1992.

Odell, Margaret S. "The Inversion of Shame and Forgiveness in Ezekiel 16.59-63." *Journal for the Study of the Old Testament,* 56 (1992): 101-112.

Oden, Thomas C. *Pastoral Theology.* San Francisco, CA: Harper Collins, 1983.

Pattison, Stephen. *A Vision of Pastoral Theology: In Search of Words That Resurrect the Dead.* Edinburgh: Contact Pastoral Limited Trust, 1994.

_____. *Shame: Theory, Therapy, Theology.* New York: Cambridge University Press, 2000.

Patton, John. *Is Human Forgivness Possible?* Nashville, TN: Abingdon Press, 1985.

Peace, Richard V. *Conversion in the New Testament: Paul and the Twelve.* Grand Rapids, MI: Eerdmans, 1999.

Pederson, Johannes. *Israel, Its Life and Culture I – II.* Copenhagen: Dyva and Jeppesen, 1926.

Pembroke, Neil F. *The Art of Listening: Dialogue, Shame and Pastoral Care.* Grand Rapids, MI: Eerdmans, 2002.

_____. "Toward a Shame-Based Theology of Evangelism." *Journal of Psychology and Christianity,* 17 (1) (1998): 15-24.

Peristiany, Jean G., ed. *Honor and Shame: The Values of Mediterranean Society.* Chicago, IL: University of Chicago Press, 1966.

Piers, Gerhart and Milton B. Singer. *Shame and Guilt: A Psychoanalytic and a Cultural Study.* Springfield, IL: Charles C. Thomas, 1953.

Pitt-Rivers, Julian. "Honour and Social Status." In *Honour and Shame: The Values of Mediterranean Society.* J. G. Peristiany, ed. Chicago, IL: University of Chicago Press, 1966.

Plummer, Alfred. *A Critical and Exegetical Commentary on the Gospel According to St. Luke.* Edinburgh: T. and T. Clarke, 1922,

Powers, Marie. *Shame: Thief of Intimacy.* Ventura, CA: Gospel Light, 1998.

Pruyser, Paul W. "Anxiety, Guilt, and Shame in the Atonement." In *Religion in Psychodynamic Perspective: The Contributions of Paul W. Pruyser.* H. Newton Malony and Bernard Spilka, eds. Oxford: Oxford University Press, 1991.

Ramsey, Nancy. "Sexual Abuse and Shame." In *Women in Travail and Transition.* Maxine Glaz and Jeanne Stevenson, eds. Minneapolis, MN: Fortress Press, 1991.

Robert, Henry M. III, William J. Evans, Daniel H. Honemann, and Thomas J. Balch. *Robert's Rules of Order (Newly Revised).* Cambridge, MA: Perseus Publishing, 2000.

Rosser, Russell C. "A Multiethnic Model of the Church." *Direction,* 27 (1998): 189-192.

Schenk, Roy U., and John Everingham, eds. *Men Healing Shame: An Anthology.* New York: Springer Pub. Co., 1995

Schore, Allan. "Early Shame Experiences and Infant Brain Development." In *Shame: Interpersonal Behavior, Psychopathology, and Culture.* Paul Gilbert and Bernice Andrews, eds. New York: Oxford University Press, 1988.

Schneider, Carl D. *Shame, Exposure and Privacy.* Boston, MA: Beacon, 1977.

Simkins, Ronald A. "'Return to Yahweh': Honor and Shame in Joel." *Semeia,* 68 (1996): 41-54.

Singgih, E. G. "Let Me Not Be Put to Shame: Towards an Indonesian Hermeneutics." *Asia Journal of Theology,* 9 (1) (1995): 71-85.

Smedes, Lewis B. *Shame and Grace: Healing the Shame We Don't Deserve.* San Francisco: HarperSanFrancisco, 1993.

Smith, Gordon T. *Beginning Well: Christian Conversion & Authentic Transformation.* Downers Grove, IL: InterVarsity Press, 2001.

Spencer, F. Scott. "Paul's Odyssey in Acts: Status Struggles and Island Adventures." *Biblical Theology Bulletin,* 28 (1999): 150-159.

Sphar, Asa. "A Theology of Shame as Revealed in the Creation Story." *Theological Educator: A Journal of Theology and Ministry,* 55 (1997): 64-74.

Spicq, Ceslas. *Theological Lexicon of the New Testament.* James D. Earnest, translator. Peabody, MA: Hendrickson, 1994.

Stansell, Gary. "Honor and Shame in the David Narratives." *Semeia,* 68 (1996): 55-79.

Stendahl, Krister. *Paul Among Jews and Gentiles.* Philadelphia, PA: Fortress Press, 1976.

Stiebert, Johanna. *The Construction of Shame in the Hebrew Bible: The Prophetic Contribution.* New York: Sheffield Academic Press, 2002.

_____. "Shame and Prophecy: Approaches Past and Present" *Biblical Interpretation,* 8 (3) (2000): 255-275.

Stockitt, Robin. "'Love Bade Me Welcome; But My Soul Drew Back'—Towards an Understanding of Shame." *Anvil: An Anglican Evangelical Journal of Theology and Mission,* 15 (2) (1998): 111-119.

Tangney, June Price, and Kurt W. Fischer, eds. *Self-Conscious Emotions: The Psychology of Shame, Guilt, Embarrassment, and Pride.* New York: Guilford Press, 1995.

Tel, Martin. "Music: The Universal Language." In *Making Room at the Table: An Invitation to Multicultural Worship.* Brian Blount and Leonora Tubbs Tisdale, eds. Louisville, KY: Westminster John Knox Press, 2000.

Thomas, Bruce (pseudonym). "The Gospel for Shame Cultures: Have We Failed to Reach Muslims at Their Point of Deepest Insecurity?" *Evangelical Missions Quarterly,* 30 (1) (1994): 284-290.

Thompson, J. Earl. "Shame in Pastoral Psychotherapy." *Pastoral Psychology,* 44 (1996): 311-320.

Thurston, Nancy Stiehler. "When 'Perfect Fear Casts Out All Love': Christian Perspectives on the Assessment and Treatment of Shame." *Journal of Psychology and Christianity,* 13 (1994): 69-75.

Twitchell, James B. *For Shame: The Loss of Common Decency in American Culture.* New York: St. Martin's Press, 1997.

Underland-Rosow, Vicki. *Shame: Spiritual Suicide.* Shorewood, MN: Waterford Publications, 1995.

Unnik, W. C. Van. "The Semitic Background of *Parresia* in the NT." In *Sparsa Collecta.* Volume II. Leiden: E. J. Brill, 1980.

Vaage, Leif E. "Like Dogs Barking: Cynic *Parresia* and Shameless Asceticism." *Semeia,* 57 (1992): 25-39.

Wallbott, Harald G., and Klaus R. Scherer. "Cultural Determinates in Experiencing Shame and Guilt." In *Self-Conscious Emotions: The Psychology of Shame, Guilt, Embarrassment, and Pride.* June Price Tangney and Kurt W. Fischer, eds. New York: Guilford Press, 1995.

Warren, Rick. *The Purpose-Driven Church: Growth Without Compromising Your Message and Mission.* Grand Rapids, MI: 1995.

Whitehead, James D., and Evelyn Eaton Whitehead. *Shadows of the Heart: A Spirituality of the Negative Emotions.* New York: Crossroad, 1994.

Willard, Dallas. *The Divine Conspiracy: Rediscovering Our Hidden Life in God.* San Francisco, CA: HarperSanFrancisco, 1998.

Wilson, Sandra D. *Released from Shame.* Downers Grove, IL: InterVarsity Press, 1990.

Wright, Alan D. *Shame Off You: Washing Away the Mud That Hides Our True Selves.* Sisters, OR: Multnomah Publishers, Inc., 2005.

Wright, N. T. *Jesus and the Victory of God.* Minneapolis, MN: Fortress Press, 1996.

Wurmser, Leon. *The Mask of Shame.* Northvale, NJ: J. Aronson, 1981.

Yancey, Philip. "A Tale of Two Sisters: Can We Find a Place for Both Shame and Grace?" *Christianity Today,* 39 (1995): 80.

You, Young Gweon. "Shame and Guilt Mechanisms in East Asian Culture." *The Journal of Pastoral Care,* 51 (1) (1997): 57-64.